Emotional Vampires

Dealing with People Who Drain You Dry

Albert J. Bernstein, Ph.D.

McGRAW-HILL

NEW YORK   CHICAGO   SAN FRANCISCO
LISBON   LONDON   MADRID   MEXICO CITY
MILAN   NEW DELHI   SAN JUAN   SEOUL
SINGAPORE   SYDNEY   TORONTO

McGraw-Hill

A Division of The McGraw·Hill Companies

2 3 4 5 6 7 8 9 0   DSH/DSH   0 1 0 9 8 7 6 5 4 3 (PBK)

1 2 3 4 5 6 7 8 9 0 DOC/DOC 0 9 8 7 6 5 4 3 2 1 0 (HC)

ISBN 0-07-138167-8 (PBK)
ISBN 0-07-135259-7 (HC)

This book was set in Times Ten Roman by North Market Street Graphics.

Printed and bound by R. R. Donnelley & Sons Company.

McGraw-Hill books are available at special quantity discounts to use as premiums and sales promotions, or for use in corporate training programs. For more information, please write to the Director of Special Sales, Professional Publishing, McGraw-Hill, Two Penn Plaza, New York, NY 10121-2298. Or contact your local bookstore.

TO LUAHNA

Contents

Acknowledgments   xi

1. Children of the Night   1
Who are these Emotional Vampires?

Are They Really Vampires? 3
Antisocial Vampires   4
Histrionic Vampires   5
Narcissistic Vampires   6
Obsessive-Compulsive Vampires   7
Paranoid Vampires   8

2. Maturity and Mental Health   11
If Emotional Vampires are children, what does it take to be a grown-up?

What Causes People to Become Emotional Vampires?   13
Immaturity versus Evil   13
The Everybody and Nobody Rule   14
What If You See Yourself?   14

3. The Way of Vampires   17
How Emotional Vampires are different, and more dangerous than other annoying people.

Vampires Are Different   17
Vampires Prey on Humans   19
Vampires Can Change Their Shapes   19

Vampires Can't See Themselves in a Mirror   20

Vampires Are More Powerful in the Dark   20

A Vampire's Bite Can Turn You into a Vampire   20

Protecting Yourself from Vampires   20

4. Dark Powers   23
Emotional Vampires use hypnosis. Here's how to keep them from making you think you're a chicken.

The Structure of Magic   24

Recognizing Hypnosis When You See It   26

The Danger Signs of Hypnosis   27

Hypnosis and Seduction   29

What to Do If You Discover You've Been Hypnotized   30

Part 1   The Antisocial Types: Lovable Rogues   33

The Ferrari-Toyota Dilemma   35

How to Recognize an Antisocial Vampire   36

The Antisocial Emotional Vampire Checklist: Listening to the Call of the Wild   37

5. Vampire Daredevils   41
Sexy, thrilling, and definitely bad for your health.

The Physiology of Excitement   41

Daredevil Hypnosis   42

How Vampires Keep You Coming Back for More   44

The 10 Elements of Vampire Fighting Strategy: Resisting the Forbidden Fruit   47

6. Vampire Used Car Salesmen   53
Slicker than cheap polyester, so always remember to read the fine print.

Used Car Hypnosis   55

Is Honesty Really the Best Policy?   62

How Do You Tell If Somebody Is Lying?   62

The 10 Elements of Vampire Fighting Strategy: Protect Yourself from Predators in Polyester 63

7. Vampire Bullies 69
Big, scary, powerful, and stupid as the guys who used to take lunch money.

The Instinct for Aggression 69
Vampire Bully Hypnosis 71
What to Do About Bullies 71
How to Do the Unexpected 73

The 10 Elements of Vampire Fighting Strategy: Don't Let Vampires Kick Sand in Your Face 77

Therapy for Antisocial Vampires 84

Part 2   The Histrionic Types: Show Business, Vampire Style 87

What's It Like to Be Histrionic 89
The Histrionic Dilemma 90
The Histrionic Vampire Checklist: Living a Soap Opera 90

8. Vampires Who Ham It Up 95
Whether it's sex, sickness, or secrets of success, there's only one show business.

Ham-it-up Hypnosis 97
Writing a Safe Role for Yourself 99
Illness as Theater 100
Histrionic Vampires and Motivation 100

The 10 Elements of Vampire Fighting Strategy: How to Keep from Joining the Cast 103

9. Passive-Aggressive Vampires 109
Deliver us from ghoulies and ghosties and people who are only trying to help.

Giving Until It Hurts 113
Illness as Metaphor 114

Passive-Aggressive Hypnosis   115
Passive-Aggressive Behavior in Relationships   115
The High Self-Esteem Syndrome   116

The 10 Elements of Vampire Fighting Strategy: Enduring the Terrible Meek   117

Therapy for Histrionic Vampires   126

Part 3   The Narcissistic Types: Big Egos, Small Everywhere Else   129

What It's Like to Be Narcissistic   131
The Narcissistic Dilemma   131
Narcissism and Self-Esteem   132
The Narcissistic Vampire Checklist: Identifying the Smartest, Most Talented, All-Around Best Person in the World   133

10. Vampires Who Are Legends in Their Own Minds   139
With talent like theirs, who needs performance?

How Narcissistic Legends Prevent Themselves from Succeeding   142
Narcissistic Legend Hypnosis   143
Another Narcissistic Dilemma   146
How to Socialize Narcissistic Legends   147

The 10 Elements of Vampire Fighting Strategy: Getting Geniuses to Do Something Useful for a Change   148

11. Vampire Superstars   155
You've got to love these guys! Worship them, actually.

Dealing with Superstars' Insatiable Needs   156
Special People Expect Special Treatment   159
Who Cares What the Little People Think!   160
Superstar Hypnosis   161

Superstar Sex   162

The Plot to Change Superstars' Style   164

Superstar Depression and Anger   165

The 10 Elements of Vampire Fighting Strategy: How to Stop Being Treated Like a Groupie   168

Therapy for Narcissistic Vampires   176

Part 4   The Obsessive-Compulsive Types: Too Much of a Good Thing   179

What It's Like to Be Obsessive-Compulsive   181

How Much Is Too Much?   181

Punishment, Where Good and Evil Meet   182

The Obsessive-Compulsive Vampire Checklist: Vice Masquerading as Virtue   183

12. Vampire Perfectionists and Puritans   187
Can the undead be anal-retentive?

Why Do They Always Seem Angry?   188

Obsessive-Compulsive Hypnosis   188

Product versus Process   189

Demanding Priorities   190

Perfectionists   191

How the Imperfect Can Deal with Perfectionists   193

Puritans   194

Why Are Puritans So Mean?   195

Dealing with Puritans without Getting Burned   196

The 10 Elements of Vampire Fighting Strategy: What to Do When the Good Guys Are After You   199

Therapy for Obsessive-Compulsive Vampires   204

CONTENTS

Part 5   The Paranoid Types: Seeing Things That Others Can't   207

Paranoid Purity   209

What It's Like to Be Paranoid   210

The Narcissist-Paranoid Dilemma   211

The Paranoid Emotional Vampire Checklist: Next Stop, the Twilight Zone   211

13. Vampire Visionaries and Green-Eyed Monsters   215
Inspiration always involves blowing things out of proportion.

The Paranoid Quest   215

Paranoid Hypnosis   216

Visionaries   217

How to Recognize Crazy Ideas   218

Paranoids and Religion   221

Green-Eyed Monsters   221

The 10 Elements of Vampire Fighting Strategy: How to Give Paranoids a Glimpse of Reality   225

Therapy for Paranoid Vampires   230

Sunrise at Carfax Abbey   233

Index   235

Acknowledgments

Without the following people's help and support, this book could never have materialized:

Mindy Ranik came up with the title, and about 10,000 miles worth of support during the writing.

My esteemed colleagues, Luahna Ude and Bob Poole, clinicians of rare wisdom and rarer wit, shared countless insights into the minds of vampires.

Sydney Craft Rozen taught me how to write.

My agent, Sherry Bykovsky, and my editor, Betsy Brown, helped me turn a scattered pile of ideas into something resembling a book.

Most of all, I want to thank my family—Luahna, Jessica, and Josh—for putting up with me while writing, a feat requiring as much courage and forbearance as visiting Carfax Abbey at midnight.

1 Children of the Night

Who are these Emotional Vampires?

There are lights again in Carfax Abbey. Rumor has it that the ruin has been purchased by an eccentric Eastern European nobleman. Strange creatures have been seen at night, moving silently through the fog. People find it hard to sleep for the howling of dogs and noises that sound like fluttering of bats' wings against window panes. In the city's finest homes, young women have been awakening from feverish dreams feeling drained and listless. Some have not awakened at all.

Something is dreadfully wrong, but the only explanation that fits the facts sounds like superstitious prattle in daylight. Vampires are a myth, aren't they? What place is there in the modern world for undead souls who walk at night to prey on the living?

The tall, dark man in evening clothes laughs. "Vampires? They are a fairy tale that old women tell to frighten the children." His eyes glow with inner light that draws you into their depths. "Allow me to introduce myself," he says. "I am Count Dracula."

Vampires stalk you, even as we speak. On broad daylit streets, under the blue pulsations of your office fluorescents, and maybe even in the warm lights of home. They're out there, masquerading as regular people until their internal needs change them into predatory beasts.

It's not your blood they drain; it's your emotional energy.

Make no mistake, we aren't talking about everyday annoyances that swarm around you like bugs in a porch light, easily whisked away with affirmations and assertive *I*-statements. These are authentic creatures of darkness. They have the power not only to aggravate you, but to hypnotize you, to cloud your mind with false promises until you are tangled in their spell. *Emotional Vampires draw you in, then drain you.*

At first, Emotional Vampires look better than regular people. They're as bright, talented, and charming as a Romanian count. You like them, you trust them, you expect more from them than you do from other people. You expect more; you get less, and in the end you get taken. You invite them into your life, and seldom realize your mistake until they've disappeared into the night, leaving you drained dry with a pain in the neck, an empty wallet, or perhaps a broken heart. Even then, you wonder—is it them or is it me?

It's them. *Emotional Vampires.*

Do you know them? Have you experienced their dark power in your life?

Have you met people who seemed so perfect at first, but later turned out to be a perfect mess? Have you been blinded by brilliant bursts of charm that switched on and off like a cheap neon sign? Have you heard promises whispered in the night that were forgotten before dawn?

Have you been drained dry?

Emotional Vampires don't rise from coffins at night. They live down the street. They're the neighbors who are so warm and cordial to your face, but spread stories behind your back. Emotional Vampires are on your softball team; they're star players until a call goes against them. Then, they throw tantrums that would embarrass a three-year-old. Emotional Vampires work at your office; they're highly paid managerial types so involved in politics and petty intrigues that they don't have time to do their jobs. Emotional Vampires may even run your company; they're bosses who give lectures about empowerment and positive reinforcement, then threaten to fire people for the tiniest mistakes.

Emotional Vampires could be lurking within your family. Consider your brother-in-law, the genius who can't hold down a job. What about that vague, almost invisible aunt who takes care of everybody else until her strange and debilitating illnesses force you to take care of her? Do we even need to mention those loving, infuriating parents who are always telling you to please yourself, then expecting you to please them?

A vampire may even share your bed, a loving partner one minute and in the next, a cold, distant stranger.

ARE THEY *REALLY* VAMPIRES?

Though they act like creatures of darkness, there's nothing supernatural about Emotional Vampires. The melodramatic metaphor is nothing more than clinical psychology dressed up in a Halloween costume. Emotional Vampires are people who have characteristics of what psychologists call *personality disorders*.

In graduate school, I learned this simple distinction: When people are driving themselves crazy, they have neuroses or psychoses. When they drive other people crazy, they have personality disorders. According to the diagnostic manual of the American Psychiatric Association, a personality disorder is:

An enduring pattern of inner experience and behavior that deviates markedly from the expectations of the individual's culture. The pattern is manifested in two (or more) of the following areas:

1. Ways of perceiving and interpreting self, other people, and events.
2. Range, intensity, lability, and appropriateness of emotional response.
3. Interpersonal functioning.
4. Impulse control.*

The manual describes diagnostic patterns of thoughts and behavior for 11 different personality disorders, of which we will consider the 5 most likely to cause you trouble in your daily life: *Antisocial, Histrionic, Narcissistic, Obsessive-Compulsive,* and *Paranoid.*

Each of these types, though pathological and draining, also has characteristics that people find very attractive. Over the course of almost 30 years as a psychologist and business consultant I have seen, time and time again, that these disorders consistently cause the most trouble for the most people, at home, at work, and everywhere in between.

The bulk of the Emotional Vampires discussed in this book are not severely disturbed enough to qualify for an official diagnosis of personality disorder, but the ways they think and act still correspond to the patterns described in the diagnostic manual. Think of the patterns as a catalog of the

---

*American Psychiatric Association: *Diagnostic and Statistical Manual of Mental Disorders,* 4th ed. Washington, DC: American Psychiatric Association, 1994.

ways that difficult people can be difficult, ranging from severe enough to be hospitalized, to mild enough to behave normally until subjected to significant stress. In the world of psychology, everything is on a continuum.

All the patterns derive from the fact that Emotional Vampires see the world differently than other people do. Their perceptions are distorted by their cravings for immature and unattainable goals. They want everybody's complete and exclusive attention. They expect perfect love that gives but never demands anything in return. They want lives filled with fun and excitement, and to have someone else take care of anything that's boring or difficult. Vampires look like adults on the outside, but inside, they're still babies.

Just as movie vampires cringe in the presence of crosses, garlic, or holy water, Emotional Vampires are inordinately threatened by common adult experiences, including boredom, uncertainty, accountability, and having to give as well as receive.

The easiest way to classify Emotional Vampires is according to the personality disorders to which their thoughts and actions are most similar. Each vampire type is driven by a particular immature and impossible need that, to the vampire, is the most important thing in the world. Vampires themselves are usually not aware of the childish needs that drive them. That's all the more reason you should be.

ANTISOCIAL VAMPIRES

Antisocial vampires are addicted to excitement. They're called antisocial, not because they don't like parties, but because they're heedless of social rules. These vampires *love* parties. They also love sex, drugs, rock 'n' roll, and anything else stimulating. They hate boredom worse than a stake through the heart. All they want out of life is a good time, a little action, and immediate gratification of their every desire.

Of all the vampires, Antisocials are the sexiest, the most exciting, and the most fun to be around. People take to them easily and quickly, and just as quickly get taken. Aside from momentary fun, these vampires don't have much to give back. Ah, but those moments! Like all the vampire types, Antisocials present you with a dilemma: They're Ferraris in a world of Toyotas, built for speed and thrills. You're apt to be very disappointed if you expect them to be reliable.

"What's wrong, honey?" Vampire Adam asks.

Elise's jaw swings open on its own. "Adam, I cannot believe you'd ask me that. You think it's okay with me that you go around kissing other women right in front of my face?"

Adam puts an arm around Elise's shoulder and she knocks it off.

"Honey," Adam says, "it was a party and I was drunk. Anyway, it was just a little peck."

"A little peck that lasted five minutes?"

"Sweetheart, you know that didn't mean anything. You're the one I really love. The only one. Come on, darlin', trust me."

Without Antisocial vampires there would be no country and western music. If you think the only people susceptible to their charms are dewy-eyed romantics, you haven't seen them do a job interview or a sales pitch. Your best protection against these vampires is to recognize them before they turn on the charm. When you see them coming, hold on to your heart and hide your wallet until you've checked their references. What Antisocial vampires have done in the past is the best predictor of what they'll do in the future.

HISTRIONIC VAMPIRES

Histrionic vampires live for attention and approval. Looking good is their specialty. Everything else is an unimportant detail. Histrionics have what it takes to get hired into your business or your life, but be careful. Histrionic means dramatic. What you see is all a show, and definitely not what you get.

Vampires can't see their reflections in a mirror. Histrionics can't even see the mirror. They're experts at hiding their own motivations from themselves. They believe that they never do anything unacceptable, like making mistakes or having bad thoughts about anyone. They're just nice people who only want to help. If you question that, you're likely to suffer. It's amazing how much damage nice people can do.

Liz hurries to catch up with Vampire Gail in the hallway. "Gail, wait a minute. Do you have those projections I asked you to work up?"

"What projections?"

"On the Lawton deal. You remember, we talked about them at the meeting last week, and I sent you an e-mail on Tuesday."

"I didn't get any e-mail."

Liz feels a cold prickle at the back of her neck. "Does that mean you don't have any projections on Lawton?"

"I thought Jeff was supposed to get me a breakdown on those changes in production costs. I was waiting to hear from him."

"Gail!" Liz hears panicky shrillness in her own voice. "I needed those projections yesterday. Go back to your office and get to work on them now."

"Okay," Gail says. "No problem."

Two hours later, Liz is at her desk, feverishly trying to put together a credible proposal with no hard numbers in it, when she gets a call from her boss. "Liz," he says, "I need to see you right away. One of your people just filed a verbal abuse complaint with HR."

In the world of Histrionic vampires nothing is ever quite as it seems. The important thing to understand is that their behavior is directed more toward fooling themselves than toward fooling you. If you try to get them to admit what they're *really* doing, you'll always end up looking far worse than they do. Instead, you can protect yourself by taking advantage of their acting ability and devising a less destructive role for them to play. The chapters on Histrionic vampires will show you how. With a little creativity, you may be able to avoid being helped to death.

NARCISSISTIC VAMPIRES

Have you ever noticed that people with big egos tend to be small everywhere else? What Narcissistic vampires want is to live out their grandiose fantasies of being the smartest, most talented, and all-around best people in the world. It's not so much that they think of themselves as better than other people as they don't think of other people at all.

Narcissistic vampires are legends in their own minds. Surely, you don't expect them to live by the rules of mere mortals.

*Vampire Lewis Hunter III, the CEO, speaking to his management team: "I don't like to call it downsizing," he says. "It's more like **right** sizing. There can be no question in anybody's mind that our overhead is simply unacceptable for these market conditions." He pauses to let the implications of his words sink in. "It is with heavy heart, then, that I'm forced to announce that each of you will have to submit a budget* *that reflects a 25 percent reduction from present spending levels. There is no other viable choice. In the spirit of teamwork, I think it's only fair that the adjustments be spread evenly, throughout all the departments."*

What Vampire Lew's managers don't know is that earlier in the day, Lew asked the board for a raise for his efforts in leading the company through what he called "the times that try men's souls." Lew got the raise. His salary increase will cancel out about 10 percent of the reductions.

Narcissistic vampires present a difficult dilemma. Though there is plenty of narcissism without greatness, there is no greatness without narcissism. Without these vampires there wouldn't be anyone with the chutzpah to lead.

Regardless of what they say, Narcissistic vampires seldom do anything that isn't self-serving. As long as you can tie your interests in with theirs, they'll think you're almost as great as they are.

OBSESSIVE-COMPULSIVE VAMPIRES

Obsessive-Compulsives are addicted to safety, which they believe they can achieve through scrupulous attention to detail and complete control over *everything.* You know who they are: anal-retentive people who can't see the forest because of the excessive number of superfluous, overabundant, and redundant trees. What you may not know is that all that attention to detail is designed to keep the Antisocial vampire inside safely contained.

Without Obsessive-Compulsives none of the world's difficult and thankless tasks would ever get done, nothing would ever work the way it should, and none of us would do our homework, ever. For good or ill, Obsessive-Compulsives are the only people watching to see that the rest of us don't go too far astray. We may not always like them, but we need them.

For Obsessive-Compulsive vampires, the most important conflicts are internal. They take no joy in hurting others, but they will hurt you if your actions threaten their sense of control. To Obsessive-Compulsives, surprises—even pleasant ones—feel like an ice cold spray of holy water. They don't mean to retaliate, but they do feel compelled to state their opinion.

"Tah dah!" Kevin says, as Vampire Sarah walks through the front door. "After all these months, I finally painted the living room!"

> *He waits a minute for Sarah to react, but she says nothing.*
> *"Well, what do you think?"*
> *"It's wonderful. But . . ."*
> *"But what?"*
> *"It's just that, well, I didn't think we had decided on a color yet."*

The second-longest wait in the world is for Obsessive-Compulsives to make a decision. The longest wait is for them to speak even a single word of praise.

PARANOID VAMPIRES

In common parlance, *paranoid* means thinking people are after you. On the face of it, it's hard to imagine that there could be anything attractive about delusions of persecution. The lure of Paranoids is not their fears, but what lies behind them. Paranoia is really a supernatural simplicity of thought that enables these vampires to see things that others can't. Their goal is to know the Truth and banish all ambiguity from their lives.

Paranoid vampires live by concrete rules that they believe are carved in stone. They expect everybody else to live by these rules as well. They're always on the lookout for evidence of deviation, and they usually find it. Think of them as the police officers of the vampire world. You feel safe and secure in their certainty. Until you become a suspect.

> *Vampire Jamal strolls into the kitchen wiping his hands on a paper towel. "I just changed your oil and I noticed that your gas tank was almost empty."*
> *Theresa shrugs. "So?"*
> *"I just filled it up on Saturday."*
> *"Well, duh. I've been driving the car all week."*
> *Jamal throws away the paper towel. "You know," he says, "it's kind of funny. I don't ever remember you using a whole tank of gas in a week. Your car gets, what, 35 miles to the gallon? So that's about 450 miles."*
> *Theresa smiles and shrugs. "Busy week, I guess."*
> *Jamal looks directly into Theresa's eyes. "Where did you go?"*

The only thing Paranoid vampires can't see is that it's their own behavior that makes other people go after them.

Paranoid vampires see below the surface of things to hidden meanings and deeper realities. Most great moralists, visionaries, and theorists (and any therapists worth their salt) have a touch of the paranoid, or else they would merely accept everything at face value. Unfortunately, paranoia makes no distinction between theories of unseen forces in physics and those of unrecognized aliens trying to take over the world. The same motivation that led to the great religious truths of the ages leads also to burning heretics at the stake.

If you have anything to hide, a Paranoid vampire will find it. Your only protection is the plain, unvarnished truth. Tell it once, and never submit to cross-examination. Easy to say, hard to do. The chapters on Paranoid vampires will show you how.

2 Maturity and Mental Health

**If Emotional Vampires are children, what does it take
to be a grown-up?**

So far as I'm concerned, maturity and mental health are the same thing.
Both are made of three essential attitudes.

The Perception of Control

To be psychologically healthy, we have to believe that what we do has some
effect on what happens to us. Even if the perception of control is delusional,
it usually leads to more productive action than believing that what we do
makes no difference.

Over time and with reflection, our choices get better, and we perceive
even more control over our fate. This is the main benefit of growing up.

Emotional Vampires never grow up. Throughout their lives, they see
themselves as victims of fate and the unpredictability of others. Stuff happens, and they just respond to it. As a result, they have no opportunity to
learn from their mistakes, and they just keep on making the same ones over
and over.

The Feeling of Connection

Human beings are social creatures. We can experience our full humanity
only in the context of connection to something larger than ourselves. It is
our connections and commitments that give meaning to our lives.

Becoming an adult human being means learning to live by social rules
that become such a part of our reality that most of us follow them without
even thinking.

Other People Are the Same as I Am.   As normal people grow, they come to appreciate more and more their similarity to others. Empathy is what maturity is all about.

Vampires just don't get this concept. To them, other people are there to supply their needs.

What's Fair Is Fair.   Social systems are based on reciprocity in everything from back scratching to telling the truth. Adults develop a sense of fairness and use it as a yardstick for measuring their behavior. Vampires don't; their idea of fair is that they get what they want when they want it.

What You Get Is Equal to What You Put In.   Adults understand that the more you give, the more you get. Vampires take.

Other People Have the Right to Deny Me.   Human relationships depend on a clear perception of the psychological line between what's mine and what's yours. Robert Frost said it well: "Good fences make good neighbors."

Vampires have a hard time seeing this all-important boundary. They believe that whatever they want should be given to them immediately, regardless of how anyone else might feel about it.

Social creatures trust each other to follow these basic rules, and Emotional Vampires betray that trust.

The lack of connection to something larger than themselves is also the reason for vampires' internal pain. The universe is a cold and empty place when there is nothing in it bigger than your own need.

The Pursuit of Challenge

To grow is to do things that are difficult. Without challenge, our lives shrink to safe but unsatisfying routines. Challenges come in all shapes and sizes. The ones that help most force us to face our fears, back them down, and widen the scope of our existence. Vampires are sometimes better at this than we are. In addition to being pains in the neck, Emotional Vampires are artists, heroes, and leaders. Because of their immaturity, they can do things we can't. The forces of darkness always swirl at the edges of creativity and great deeds. A world without vampires would be less stressful, but deadly dull.

To deal effectively with vampires, we have to think new thoughts and take unaccustomed actions. At times that may be scary, but facing fear is the kind of challenge that makes us grow.

WHAT CAUSES PEOPLE TO BECOME EMOTIONAL VAMPIRES?

Just as some of the newer stories about real vampires ascribe their delicate condition to a blood-borne virus, so there are many theories about the personality disorders that afflict their emotional cousins. Presently, some of the most fashionable involve unbalanced brain chemistry, early trauma, or the long-term deleterious effects of growing up in a dysfunctional family.

Forget the theories; they will hurt you more than help you in your quest to understand vampires. There are two reasons for this. First, understanding where a problem comes from is not the same as solving it. Second, Emotional Vampires already see themselves as the innocent victims of forces beyond their control. If that's how you see them, their past can distract you from paying attention to the choices that you and the vampires are making in the present.

Many self-help books have long sections about how difficult people got to be that way. This one doesn't. After years in the therapy business, I have come to believe that it is far more important to understand the mechanics of human problems, how they operate and what to do about them, than it is to speculate about what causes them.

IMMATURITY VERSUS EVIL

Emotional Vampires are not intrinsically evil, but their immaturity allows them to operate without thinking about whether their actions are good or bad. Vampires see other people as potential sources for whatever they happen to need at the moment, not as separate human beings with needs and feelings of their own. Rather than evil itself, vampires' perceptual distortion is a doorway through which evil may easily enter.

The purpose of this book is not to consider the morality of Emotional Vampires, but to teach you how to spot them in your life, and give you some ideas about what to do when you find yourself under attack by the forces of darkness.

Understanding Emotional Vampires' immaturity is your ultimate weapon. Many of their most outrageous actions would make perfect sense if they were done by a two-year-old. Don't let vampires' chronological age or positions of responsibility fool you. They *are* two-year-olds, at least when they're acting up. *The most successful strategies for dealing with Emotional Vampires are precisely the same ones you'd use on young children—setting limits, arranging contingencies, being consistent, keeping lectures to a bare minimum, rewarding good behavior and ignoring bad, and occasionally putting them in time-out.*

You probably know these techniques already, but you may not have known they were applicable to adults. Or perhaps you thought you shouldn't *have* to use them on grown-ups. You do, at least if you want to keep from being drained dry. Vampires are difficult enough to handle already; there's no point in ignoring effective strategies just because you think they're only for kids.

THE EVERYBODY AND NOBODY RULE

Human beings don't fit neatly into diagnostic categories, no matter how elegant or well conceived. As you read further, you'll probably discover that everybody you know, including yourself, has some characteristics of each of the vampire types. Everybody has some, nobody has all. *Most difficult people are a blend of two or more vampire types.* The chances are good that you will find your bullying boss or your supercilious former spouse scattered all over the pages of this book. Feel free to use the techniques that seem most appropriate, regardless of which chapter they appear in. Many of the techniques are introduced in the earlier chapters and refined later in the book. You'll probably find it most helpful to read straight through so that by the time you reach the later, more complex types of vampires, you'll have a whole arsenal of techniques from which to choose.

WHAT IF YOU SEE YOURSELF?

If you see yourself among the vampires, take heart; it is a very good sign. We all have some tendencies in the direction of personality disorders. If you recognize your own, they are apt to be less of a problem than if you have no insight.

Each section ends with a description of treatment approaches for the various vampire types. These should help you in working on your vampire issues yourself, or in selecting an appropriate therapist or therapy technique for you or for the vampires in your life.

Emotional Vampires have a tendency to prefer therapy approaches that make them worse rather than better. People who throw tantrums like two-year-olds hardly need to be encouraged to get their feelings out into the open, or, God forbid, get in touch with their inner child.

The opinions about therapy are, of course, my own, and certainly not shared by all psychologists. No opinions are shared by all psychologists. I believe that Emotional Vampires can grow up and become healthy human beings, but it takes a real effort on their part. And yours.

I hope you'll find this book useful, both at home and at work. Beyond that, I wouldn't be in the least upset if it gave you a chuckle here and there—and, if it would not be too much to wish for, the occasional glimmer of hope for the human condition that comes with understanding.

3 The Way of Vampires

How Emotional Vampires are different, and more dangerous than other annoying people.

Professor Van Helsing, eminent expert on the occult, has been summoned. He steps off the train into the swirling mists on the platform. He's wearing thick tweeds and carrying a battered leather valise that rattles when he walks, as if it were filled with wooden stakes. Van Helsing shakes his head. "You do not know with whom you are dealing."

Muttering under his breath, he sets his valise down and fumbles around inside it. He takes out an ancient book with a large crucifix embossed on its cover. "You must learn the way of vampires. Read this before sunset!"

In many ways, people with even small traces of personality disorders really are like the vampires we read about in books and see in movies. Consider this chapter to be the dusty volume that Professor Van Helsing thrusts into your hands, saying, "Read this before sunset!" To protect yourself, you must know with whom you are dealing.

Here, then, is the way of vampires.

VAMPIRES ARE DIFFERENT

This is the crux of the matter. In the movies and horror stories, or in your everyday life, the most dangerous mistake you can make is believing that underneath it all, vampires are really regular people, just like you. If you interpret what they say and do according to what *you* would feel if you said or did the same thing, you'll be wrong most every time. And you'll end up drained dry.

In the last chapter, I listed the social rules that most of us have been following since childhood without so much as a thought. Vampires play by different rules entirely. They're not fair, but they're fairly consistent. Here are the social rules that vampires follow. Study them well so you won't be blindsided.

My Needs Are More Important Than Yours.   Vampires operate with the selfishness of predators and young children. Regardless of what they say, most of what they do is guided by their desires of the moment rather than by any moral or philosophical principles. As we'll see in later chapters, if you understand the momentary need, you understand the vampire.

If your needs coincide with theirs, Emotional Vampires can be hard workers, caring companions, and all-around good company. That's why most of the annoying people in this book seem relatively normal most of the time. Everything changes when your needs come in conflict with theirs. That's when the fangs come out.

The Rules Apply to Other People, Not Me.   The technical term for this belief is *entitlement,* and it is one of the most exasperating characteristics of Emotional Vampires. At work, on the road, in relationships, or wherever, people follow the basic rules of fairness they learned in kindergarten. They take turns, wait in line, clean up after themselves, and listen while other people talk. In kindergarten, Emotional Vampires learned how easy it is to take advantage when you're not bound by the rules that other people follow.

It's Not My Fault, Ever.   Vampires never make mistakes, they're never wrong, and their motives are always pure. Other people always pick on them unfairly. Vampires take no responsibility for their own behavior, especially when it leads to negative consequences.

I Want It Now.   Vampires don't wait. They want what they want when they want it. If you get in their way, or try to delay their gratification, they'll come at you snapping and snarling.

If I Don't Get My Way, I Throw a Tantrum.   Emotional Vampires have elevated the tantrum to an art form. When they don't get their way, they can create a sumptuous array of miseries for the people who tell them no. As we'll see in later chapters, each vampire type specializes in a particular kind of manipulative emotional explosion. Many of the annoying and draining things that vampires do make complete sense when you see them as tantrums.

Emotional Vampires may look like ordinary people. They may even look better than ordinary people, but don't be fooled. Vampires are, first and foremost, different. To keep from being drained, you must always be aware of what those differences are.

VAMPIRES PREY ON HUMANS

Night-stalking vampires will drain your blood. Emotional Vampires will use you to meet whatever needs they happen to be experiencing at the moment. They have no qualms about taking your effort, your money, your love, your attention, your admiration, your body, or your soul to meet their insatiable cravings. They want what they want, and they don't much care how *you* feel about it.

When Emotional Vampires offer to help you or give you something, they usually have a hidden agenda. The creatures of darkness are most dangerous when you need something and your guard is down. What other people might see as a friend in need, vampires see as a golden opportunity. They *always* get back more than they give. If they've taken advantage of you before, be careful about giving them a second chance.

VAMPIRES CAN CHANGE THEIR SHAPES

Storybook vampires can change themselves into bats, wolves, or a cold, formless mist that seeps through unguarded windows. Emotional Vampires can turn themselves into whatever you want to see, but only long enough to lure you in. To say that they are consummate actors doesn't do them justice. Often, they play their roles so well that they fool themselves into believing that they are who they pretend to be.

Emotional Vampires lack integrity. This is not a moral judgment; rather, it's a comment on the structure of their personalities. Vampires are hollow inside. They have very little idea of who or what they really are; they only know what they want.

Not only are vampires confused about their own identities, they can confuse you about yours as well. If you get too closely involved with them, you'll hardly know yourself.

VAMPIRES CAN'T SEE THEMSELVES IN A MIRROR

If you want to know if someone is a vampire, hold up a mirror and see if there's a reflection. If you want to know if someone is an Emotional Vampire, hold up a self-help book that describes his personality perfectly and see if there's a spark of recognition. With both kinds of vampires there will be nothing there. Night-stalking vampires have no reflections; Emotional Vampires have no insight.

Vampires can learn about themselves and make real changes, but it takes years of hard work. It absolutely never happens in a single moment of blinding realization. If you believe you see a sudden blaze of self-understanding in a vampire's eyes, you're likely to be the one who gets burned.

VAMPIRES ARE MORE POWERFUL IN THE DARK

Both kinds of vampires thrive on darkness. Blood-hungry vampires stalk the night. Emotional Vampires lurk in the darker side of human nature. They take power from secrets. Your dealings with them will usually involve a few little details that you'd rather not share, because other people wouldn't understand.

A VAMPIRE'S BITE CAN TURN YOU INTO A VAMPIRE

Throughout the ages, vampirism has been contagious. A few bites and vampires can have you acting just as immaturely as they do.

PROTECTING YOURSELF FROM VAMPIRES

The most effective strategy is to know vampires for who and what they are. Pay attention to the words and actions of difficult people in your life and see how closely that behavior corresponds to the patterns described in this book. The vampire identification checklists in each section will help you. The higher the score, the more dangerous the vampire. The vampire therapy sections at the end of each part offer self-help and professional therapeutic approaches that may be beneficial.

The checklists and therapies may be useful, but your own intuition is essential. *Emotional Vampires often provoke strong and immediate reactions, both positive and negative. They're the best or the worst, seldom any-*

thing in between. As you come to know them better, your own responses will be the most reliable cues for identifying vampires.

When you deal with annoying people, pay attention to what's going on in your mind and body. If you have a headache, the person you're dealing with is probably a vampire. If the hairs at the back of your neck are prickling, you can just about be sure.

Dealing with Emotional Vampires requires a lot of effort. They may be worth it, they may not. Only you can decide. Sometimes it's better to run away, or not get involved in the first place. I hope this book will help you choose the best approach with the vampires you face in your day-to-day life. Each chapter offers both tactics for fighting and suggestions about how to retreat.

4 Dark Powers

**Emotional Vampires use hypnosis. Here's how to
keep them from making you think you're a chicken.**

*"Hypnosis? Yeah right." The vampire shakes his head in disgust. "Are you
going to let some idiot in a turban make you think you're a chicken? Give
me a break! Nobody **intelligent** believes in that nonsense."*

*"Forget about that hypnosis stuff," he says. "Let's talk about something
important." He pops open his attaché case. "Have you thought about what
goals you have for your financial future?"*

Vampires can't hurt you unless you invite them in; any 10-year-old knows
that. But why in the world would anyone say to a vampire, "Sure, come on
in and give me a pain in the neck"?

If you have to ask, you don't know vampires.

In the movies, they float at your windows, and stare at you with those
glowing, you-are-in-my-power eyes. In real life, they're a bit more subtle.
They start with a killer first impression. Somehow, they look a little better
than other people—more talented, more interesting, more competent, more
caring, more glamorous, or just more fun. Then, they're easy to talk to. They
seem to understand you right away, to know what you want. Even when you
suspect smoke and mirrors, you almost believe that what you think you see
is what you'll actually get.

In the movies and reality it's the same; the dark power that Emotional
Vampires hold over normal people is hypnosis.

THE STRUCTURE OF MAGIC

There's nothing magical about hypnosis. It's definitely not supernatural, and, when you pay close attention to what's going on, it isn't even mysterious. The techniques are simple and straightforward; they work because they're presented in a way that makes it hard to pay attention to what's really going on.

Emotional Vampires use many of the same techniques as stage hypnotists. Vampires have no formal training in hypnosis; they operate by instinct, often without a clear understanding of what they're doing and why. They do what they do because it works.

To protect yourself, you need to recognize hypnotists when you see them, hopefully *before* you go into a trance. The strategies they use are the same whether they want to make you think you're a chicken, buy a used car, or get into bed with them. Here's how they do it.

Misdirection

Hypnotists invite people to focus attention on them, not on what they're doing. Misdirection is the number one secret of hypnosis, whether it's practiced on a nightclub stage or in your office.

Hypnotic communication is purposely distracting and confusing. You're expected to give up trying to understand, turn off your critical thinking, and just go along.

Critical thinking is the most important tool you have for protecting yourself from Emotional Vampires. *If you feel confused, don't do anything until you've figured out what's going on.* In later chapters we'll see how this simple tactic can be a lifesaver with each of the vampire types. For now, just remember to keep your eyes open and your automatic pilot switched off.

Identification

Hypnotists identify people who are likely to give them what they want. The trick to making hypnotic subjects act like chickens is not saying magic incantations; it's finding people who'll do what's expected of them even if they think it's foolish. The best subjects are always the ones who have hypnotized themselves into believing they can't be hypnotized.

Isolation

Hypnotists isolate their subjects. Nightclub hypnotists invite the most suggestible people in the audience up to the stage. Once they're up there, blinded by the lights and hearing only the hypnotist's voice, subjects are much less likely to think critically. They're happy to believe they've been called to the stage because the hypnotist has recognized their hidden talents rather than their gullibility.

Emotional Vampires also like to keep their subjects close to them, and far from people who might ask too many embarrassing questions. A relationship with a vampire is always somehow special, and often involves a few little secrets shared only with each other. Hypnosis can make you believe that these little secrets are treasures rather than traps.

Control

Hypnotists use people's desires to control them. Hypnotists and vampires usually know what people want better than they do themselves. The interpersonal world they see is a webwork of unacknowledged desires, as easy to read as a subway map. When normal people recognize these vulnerabilities in others, it usually elicits empathy and understanding. What Emotional Vampires see is a ticket to ride.

Alternate Reality

Hypnotists create an alternate reality. Hypnosis, like any art, makes people believe in something that isn't there. The most effective artists always use the stuff of secret dreams to construct their fantasies.

Emotional Vampires, with their instinctive awareness of what people want, are adept at creating alternate realities. As we'll see in later chapters, each type of vampire appeals to different needs, and specializes in creating particular kinds of illusion.

Another reason vampires are good at creating fantasy worlds is that they live in them.

False Choices

Hypnotists put subjects in a bind. A bind looks like a choice between two alternatives but really isn't, because one of the options is almost unthinkable. Stage hypnotists offer their subjects a choice between clucking and squawking like a chicken or showing the world that they don't have what it takes to be a star.

Emotional Vampires can put their victims into similar binds. In the chapters on each of the vampire types we'll examine the mechanics of these false choices in great detail. For now, remember that binds work because one of the possible choices *seems* unthinkable. Vampires exploit the fact that fear of negative consequences is usually greater than the consequences themselves. Thinking about that at the right time may save you from a tremendous pain in the neck.

RECOGNIZING HYPNOSIS WHEN YOU SEE IT

If hypnotists invite you on stage, you can be pretty sure they're going to try to trick you into doing their will. In the real world, when an Emotional Vampire walks into your office and starts using hypnotic techniques on you, the tricks may be a little harder to spot. A good place to start our examination of how Emotional Vampires use hypnosis is by looking at a job interview.

> As Bill, the VP for operations, ushers Vampire Jason into his office for a job interview, Jason instinctively begins searching for cues about who Bill is and what he needs.
>
> Books, pictures of Bill shaking hands with various dignitaries. One looks like Stephen Covey. Behind the credenza, in a place of honor, hangs a row of plaques: Continuous Quality Improvement awards from 1992 to the present.
>
> "Quite a collection," Jason says. "It looks like you're the man to beat when it comes to quality."
>
> Bill shakes his head. "Not me. As far as I'm concerned, these plaques belong to the team." He gestures at the busy workers outside his door. "Those are the folks with the guts; they deserve all the glory. I'm just the guy who keeps things organized."
>
> Jason recognizes the rhetoric of management by humility. He figures the guy in the picture really **is** Stephen Covey.
>
> "You know," Jason says, "that reminds me of something I read in **First Things First.** Uh, what was it exactly—?"
>
> "Oh, you're a Covey fan," Bill says. "You'll love this." He swivels around, and points to his bookshelf. "Every word Stephen Covey ever wrote." Bill pulls out **Seven Habits** and reverently turns to the title page. "This one's autographed."
>
> "You actually know him?" Jason gasps, creating an alternate reality in which anyone who associates with Stephen Covey sits at the right hand of God.

> *Bill beams. "I wouldn't say I know him, but I've talked to him a couple of times."*
>
> *"That must have been great," Jason says. "I'd really love to talk to that guy. What he must be able to teach!" This opens the door for Bill to tell about his dialogues with Covey.*
>
> *After a couple of hours of stimulating conversation Bill feels that he can develop a real win-win working relationship with Jason. Bill offers the job on the spot; he doesn't even check references. He should have.*

Of course Emotional Vampires are good at job interviews! For a vampire, almost every conversation is an interview for something. Jason has developed instinctive skills born of long experience. Whether you call it hypnosis or sucking up, it still works.

Does Jason really think about what he's doing in the way I've described? Probably not. He does know that interviewers usually believe that the candidate they like best is the one who'll do the best job. Really, that's all he needs to know.

Jason's secret for making people like him is to get them to talk about themselves. This is a good plan, based on years of psychological research about which Jason is completely unaware. He just knows what works.

In his quest to be likable, Jason stumbles over the fact that Bill has a hard time acknowledging his own ego, at least directly. Jason uses this information to create an instinctive, but nonetheless elegant bind. How can Bill turn away somebody who sees him as a superior human being because of his association with a disciple of humility?

THE DANGER SIGNS OF HYPNOSIS

How do you recognize hypnosis when it's being done to you? How can a person like Bill tell when a vampire is casting a predatory spell?

The important thing to realize is that the signs of hypnosis are easier to spot in the responses of the subject than in the actions of the hypnotist. Here's what to look for.

Deviating from Standard Procedure

Bill's first clue that something was amiss should have been the fact that he wasn't following his typical job interview pattern. In other interviews Bill would have been trying to elicit information; in this one he seems to be doing most of the talking.

If you ever find yourself veering sharply from your usual way of doing things, especially in response to a person you don't know very well, stop right then and ask yourself why. Listen very closely to your answer.

Thinking in Superlatives

If Bill had asked himself why he was doing things differently in response to Jason, the answer would probably have contained some sort of superlative. Jason was the *best,* or *most promising* candidate Bill had seen in 20 years. Bill should have asked himself how he came to such a far-reaching conclusion so quickly. If he had, Bill might have realized that Jason was the best, not because of his own qualifications, but because he saw Bill in precisely the way Bill wanted to be seen.

Distorted perceptions usually involve superlatives. If you find yourself thinking that someone is radically different from other people, quickly ask yourself why. Remember, *worst* and *most annoying* are superlatives also.

Instant Rapport

Bill felt that Jason understood him immediately, but the feeling wasn't exactly accurate. What Jason understood was that Bill wanted someone to see him in the same way Bill saw Stephen Covey. Jason was just giving Bill what he wanted, in the hope that Bill would reciprocate. He did.

Getting to know and appreciate another person usually involves time and effort. Be careful when rapport seems to be developing too quickly, no matter how good the process feels. Instant understanding is usually the result of someone recognizing how you would really like to be seen and pretending to see you that way.

Seeing the Person or Situation as Special

Not only did Jason charm Bill into giving him the job. Jason also set the stage for a working relationship with Bill that would be different than the relationship Bill has with other people. Jason presented himself to Bill as a prospective disciple, someone who would stop in for advice and guidance from Bill's vast store of business knowledge. Jason not only won himself the job, but a special place in Bill's heart.

Defining an interaction as a special case that doesn't follow the normal rules is a clear sign that an Emotional Vampire is turning on the predatory charm. We will examine this process in detail in the chapters on specific vampire types. For now, remember that vampires excel at getting you to notice them, not what they're doing. Pay attention!

Lack of Concern with Objective Information

Somehow, Bill decided that he didn't need to know much about Jason's history. Maybe he didn't want to know. If Bill looked too closely at the facts, he might discover something that would break the pleasant spell.

Your two most important sources of objective information about another person are the details of that person's history and the opinions of other people. If for some reason you find yourself avoiding those sources, or thinking that they don't apply, watch out.

Confusion

If you asked Bill how he drew so many unusual conclusions from a single interview, his answer would probably be rather vague. Bill's haziness about the details of the conversation, and how they led him to make the decisions he did, would probably not affect his certainty that his decisions were correct. That last part is the dead giveaway.

Hazy understanding of the reasons for your own reactions, coupled with unusual certainty, is a pretty clear sign that somebody has been messing with your mind. The main purpose of this book is to help you discover who it was, and how they did it.

HYPNOSIS AND SEDUCTION

What is seduction but another kind of job interview? As always, hypnosis works here too.

> *Leeanne is late to the meeting. In front of everyone, she has to wend her way around tables, flipcharts, and various kinds of projectors. Back in the corner of the room, she can see Alec, that cute guy from the computer department. He's looking at her! She wonders what he's thinking, and tries hard not to trip over her own feet.*

> *As Leeanne gets to the back of the room, Alec smiles and pats the seat next to him. "I was watching as you came in," he says. "You have such a distinctive way of walking. It's—I don't know . . ."*
>
> *Leeanne looks down at her traitorous feet. "You think there's something wrong with the way I walk?"*
>
> *Alec thumps his forehead with the heel of his hand. "There I go again," he says. "Open mouth and insert foot. What I meant was, you walk like a dancer. I think it's the way you hold your head up and kind of sway around the tables. You have had some dance training, haven't you?"*
>
> *Leeanne feels blood rushing to her face. "I did take a few dance classes back in the dark ages."*
>
> *"I could tell," Alec says as he pulls out her chair. "So, do you know how to tango?"*

Alec is so good he could make a living wearing a turban and swinging a watch. He probably saw Leeanne alternating between stiffness and grace, and from that small piece of information he learned everything he needed to know. By admiring a part of Leeanne about which she's self-conscious, Alec sets up an alternate reality in which the two of them are already dancing together. Antisocials, lovable rogues that they are, are masters at weaving an erotic spell. In Chapter 5, on vampire Daredevils, we'll continue the story of the ill-fated office romance between Leeanne and Alec.

WHAT TO DO IF YOU DISCOVER YOU'VE BEEN HYPNOTIZED

When you find yourself in a hole, the first thing you should do is stop digging. If you discover that you've been hypnotized, first you have to admit it to yourself—bring it out into the daylight. Don't try to hide the fact that you've gone along with the charade.

Forget about trying to convince Emotional Vampires that they weren't playing straight with you. They'll laugh and recite back your conversations chapter and verse to show that they made no promises or, if they did, how it was somebody else's fault that they broke them. Even with a good lawyer, it's usually not possible to get back what vampires have taken from you. Don't even try. Just don't let them take any more.

"Jason, why don't you have a seat?" Bill says, drawing a chair close to his desk and turning his monitor so both of them can see it.

"Is there something wrong?" Jason asks.

"You could say that," Bill says as he moves his mouse to bring up the spreadsheet for Jason's department. "You've seen these figures, haven't you?"

Jason lets out a sigh of relief. "Oh, those. Remember, I told you last week that this data is incomplete. The software's been down and we've still got a stack of production reports to input. That's why this figure is so low." He points to the bottom line.

"Jason, you've been here seven months, and you still haven't been able to give me an accurate picture of what's going on in your department."

Jason laughs. "Bill, I don't like to point the finger, but the way Tim Norton set things up when he was managing makes it almost impossible to tell what's going on. I've been trying to do a little reengineering. You know, like Hammer and Champy said. Having the team question every single process to see what we're trying to do and how we're trying to do it. With the way Tim left things, what can I tell you?" Jason shrugs. "It's pretty slow going."

When Emotional Vampires get caught, they start throwing out alternate realities faster than the Sci-Fi Channel. What should you remember in a situation like this? Two words: objective data. Rip open the curtains and let the daylight in.

"Well," Bill says, leaning back in his chair. "If you're having that much difficulty, I think we'd better make this reengineering into priority one."

Jason gives Bill the thumbs-up sign. "Can do, boss!"

"Oh, I don't expect you to do it by yourself," Bill says. "I'm willing to help."

"You've been a big help already. The example you set—"

"I intend to help with more than an example. Monday morning I want to meet with you and your whole department to see if we can work together to figure out what's going on. Have your people put together whatever data they have, and we'll go through it line by line."

The best way to keep from being hypnotized by Emotional Vampires is to recognize their tricks and not be taken in. As we've seen thus far, this is no small task. Not only do you have to understand vampires, you have to understand yourself as well.

In the rest of the book we'll look closely at the enticements that vampires may offer to draw you into their dark and predatory dance. When you recognize their subtle footwork as hypnosis, it will be lot easier to turn them down.

Here are few final rules to remember about job interviews of all sorts. Simple and obvious they may be, but if you follow them, they may save your neck:

1. *If a deal seems too good to be true, it is.*
2. *Patterns repeat.* The best predictor of what a person will do in the future is what he or she has done in the past. Always check references.
3. *Never bend rules on the spur of the moment.* First, discuss your decision with a couple of people you trust. Few things cost more and deliver less than impulsive decisions that the rules you've always followed don't apply.
4. *Anyone can be a chicken.* If you think you can't be hypnotized, you probably are already.

 Lovable Rogues

The Antisocial Types

Casually, the vampire shakes a cigarette out of the pack and puts it between his lips; then he smiles. His dimples would make him look boyish if it weren't for the fangs. He lights his cigarette and takes a deep drag. "The night is young," he says, patting the backseat of his Harley. "Why don't we go see what's out there?" The back of his jacket reads: "Live fast, die young, and leave a beautiful corpse."

Antisocials are the simplest of vampires, also the most dangerous. All they want out of life is a good time, a little action, and immediate gratification of their every desire. If they can use you to accomplish these goals, nobody is more exciting, charming, or seductive. If you stand in their way, you're dogmeat. Antisocials, like all vampires, are immature. On their best days, they function at the level of early teenagers. On their worst, they can give infants a run for their money—which, come to think of it, is true of teenagers also.

To be technically correct, we're talking about people who have tendencies in the direction of **Antisocial personality disorder.** Antisocial, in this case, means unsocialized—heedless of normal social constraints. The name is unfortunate. Like its predecessor, *sociopath,* it harks back to the days when psychiatric diagnoses were moral judgments rather than personality descriptions. A hundred or so years ago when this diagnosis was first formulated, it was considered to be the personality type of criminals. It still is. Of all the Emotional Vampires, Antisocials are the most likely to be involved in illegal behavior.

As we'll see in the following chapters, illegal behavior is only a small part of the picture, especially in the Antisocial vampires you see on a daily basis. Personality disorders exist along a continuum. At one end are criminals. At the other are exciting, adventurous, grown-up teenagers still heavily into sex, drugs, and rock 'n' roll.

The other problem with the name is that the colloquial meaning of *antisocial* suggests people who don't like parties. This is definitely not true of Antisocial vampires. They like being around people, and they love parties for all the opportunities they present. Wherever there's fun, you'll find Antisocials.

In another sense, however, Antisocials are loners. They have a hard time making any sort of commitment because they don't really trust anybody. Antisocials are convinced that the only human motivation is self-interest. They are predators to the core, and proud of it. They are perfectly comfortable with selfishness because they don't think there's any other form of motivation.

Antisocials are often damnably attractive, and a hell of a lot of fun. Imagine taking a regular person, doubling the energy level, tripling the love of excitement, then switching off the circuitry for worry.

Everybody has felt like that once or twice. Remember prom night when you were dressed to kill, and the air tingled with the scent of carnations and contraband beer. What if every day were filled with those kinds of possibilities? What if there were no little voice inside your head spoiling your fun by reminding you of the terrible things that could happen if you let yourself get *too* wild? Compared with a life of prom nights, it would be pretty hard to get excited about your day job.

THE FERRARI-TOYOTA DILEMMA

In the last chapter, I pointed out that many social interactions are like job interviews for various positions in your life—friend, lover, colleague, employee, or perhaps even nemesis. If you were placing an advertisement for people to hire into your life enterprise, what would it look like? I put together a composite of employment ads that I believe sums up many people's fantasy of the ideal employee:

> High-energy, enthusiastic self-starter wanted. We're looking for an independent person who doesn't need to be told what to do every minute of the day, someone with an entrepreneurial spirit who creates his or her own security by being quick, decisive, flexible, and able to think outside the box. Good social skills and political savvy a must. Apply only if you can turn setbacks into opportunities, and are willing to handle a little risk in return for big rewards. No whiners.

If in your mind you can see this applicant standing there with a big smile, a firm handshake, and a two-stroke handicap, what you're looking at is an Antisocial vampire. A Ferrari in a world of Toyotas.

Toyotas are safe and practical, but not much fun. Ferraris are dangerously powerful, fabulously expensive, and in the shop more than they are on the road. Still, they're what we dream about when we buy Toyotas.

After a few months on the job, the person hired from the above ad might get a performance review that looks like this:

> Unreliable and at times even dishonest. Does not accept being told what to do! Convinced that most rules are silly, confining, and made to be broken. Easily bored with day-to-day routine to the point that he or she often cuts corners and leaves important tasks undone. Takes advantage of others and often throws tantrums to get his or her way. Little ability to plan ahead or learn from mistakes. On the personal side, is going through divorce, has financial difficulties, and is rumored to have problems with alcohol and drugs.

The most important thing to remember about Antisocials is that the ad and the evaluation represent two parts of the same personality. Vampires' traits, both positive and negative, hang together in identifiable clusters. This book is full of descriptions, examples, and checklists that will teach you more than you ever wanted to know about which traits goes with which personality type.

It may not make any difference. Impractical as Ferraris are, people want them. Those who own Ferraris love them enough to pretend that they're sensible. Aficionados may talk themselves into believing that the Ferrari-Toyota dilemma doesn't really exist, or is the result of an anomaly that can easily be corrected by a skillful enough mechanic. I know that this is true because, for the past 25 years in my work as a therapist and business consultant, people have brought me countless human Ferraris to repair. They think I can somehow get rid of the bad parts and keep the good. I tell them it isn't possible, but most of the time they don't believe me.

In making your own existential choices between Ferraris and Toyotas, it doesn't matter so much which one you pick, only that you know the difference. The favorite prey of all Emotional Vampires are people who believe they can have the have the speed and exhilaration of a Ferrari with the safety and reliability of a Toyota.

HOW TO RECOGNIZE AN ANTISOCIAL VAMPIRE

Now we come to our first vampire identification checklist. I'll be the first to admit that the test is crude in that it relies more on opinions, impressions, and value judgments than on objective fact. The purpose of the checklists is not to make a medical diagnosis, but to help you recognize emotionally draining people before they suck you dry. Your first line of defense is always your own subjective impression that something is amiss. If you're in doubt, check out your intuitions with other people. This is a good idea even if you are absolutely certain.

Remember the rule from Chapter 2: *Nobody is all or none.* Nobody fits a category completely or not at all. Everybody is made of a set of characteristics that make him or her unique, and some of those unique people are considerably more emotionally draining than others.

THE ANTISOCIAL EMOTIONAL VAMPIRE CHECKLIST: LISTENING TO THE CALL OF THE WILD

True or false: Score one point for each *true* answer.

1.	This person believes that rules were made to be broken.	T	F
2.	This person is adept at using excuses to avoid doing what he or she doesn't want to do.	T	F
3.	This person has had legal problems.	T	F
4.	This person regularly engages in dangerous activities for their thrill value.	T	F
5.	This person can turn on brilliant bursts of charm to get his or her way.	T	F
6.	This person is not very good at managing his or her finances.	T	F
7.	This person smokes without apology.	T	F
8.	This person has one or more other addictions.	T	F
9.	This person has had more sex partners than most people.	T	F
10.	This person seldom worries.	T	F
11.	This person actually believes that some problems can be settled with a fistfight.	T	F
12.	This person sees no problem with lying to achieve a goal.	T	F
13.	This person justifies doing bad things to people because others would do them too if they had the chance.	T	F
14.	This person can consciously throw a tantrum to get his or her way.	T	F
15.	This person doesn't understand the concept of looking before you leap.	T	F
16.	This person believes in having fun first and doing the work later.	T	F
17.	This person has been fired from a job or has quit impulsively.	T	F
18.	This person refuses to comply with any sort of dress code.	T	F
19.	This person regularly makes promises that he or she never keeps.	T	F
20.	Despite all these faults, this person is still one of the most exciting people I have ever met.	T	F

Scoring: Five or more true answers qualifies the person as an Antisocial Emotional Vampire, though not necessarily for a diagnosis of antisocial personality disorder. If the person scores higher than 10, hold onto your wallet, and your heart.

WHAT THE QUESTIONS MEASURE

The specific behaviors covered on the checklist relate to several underlying personality characteristics that define an Antisocial Emotional Vampire.

High Need for Stimulation

At the core of the Antisocial's personality is a lust for stimulation of all sorts. All the other characteristics seem to arise from that central drive for excitement. At any crossroad, Antisocials will usually choose the path that leads to the most excitement in the least time. They themselves may be completely unaware of this dynamic, yet it serves to explain a good deal of their behavior.

On the positive side, Antisocials are not held back by doubt and worry. They embrace risks and challenges that terrify ordinary people. Most of history's great deeds of exploration, financial daring, and physical courage have been done by people who would meet the criteria set down here for Antisocial vampires. From the beginning of time we have loved them, thrilled to their exploits, and built monuments to honor their names. We just can't live with them. Heroes are often as dangerous to their friends as they are to the enemy.

The same drive that leads to courage on battlefields, in sports arenas, and on trading floors leads to boredom with everyday life. The landscape of the Antisocial world is made of scattered peaks of pulse-pounding exhilaration with wide deserts of mind-numbing boredom in between. Throughout the long hours when socialized people content themselves with delaying gratification in order to live up to their obligations, Antisocials are pacing like trapped beasts looking for any way to escape. The day-to-day rules that provide structure and meaning in our lives are merely the bars of their cages. Antisocials don't see themselves as looking for trouble, only for the chance to be free. Freedom for them, however, means trouble for everybody else.

In their search for constant stimulation, Antisocials are drawn to all things addictive like lemmings to cliffs. Sex and drugs are always popular, as are gambling, credit cards, and risky investments with other people's money. The drug of choice may vary, but the purpose is the same. Under the skin all addictions are alike in that they provide a rapid change in neurochemistry that is the central striving in Antisocial lives.

Impulsiveness

Antisocials seldom reflect on why they do the things they do; they just do them. Planning or consideration of alternatives, to them, is unnecessary and boring. On battlefields and playing fields, they are more beautiful than any of us could hope to be because they are free of the worry and doubt that slow us down.

Only over time does it become apparent that most Antisocial decisions are simply a roll of the dice. From the inside, Antisocials don't see themselves as making decisions at all. Life to them is a series of inevitable reactions to whatever is happening at the moment. Give them what they want, they're cheerful. Frustrate them, they throw a tantrum. Put them in a boring situation, they stir up a fuss. They truly believe that their actions are caused by what you do. This belief frees them from responsibility and guilt, but it also robs them of the perception of control over their own lives—a view that is one of the essentials for mental health. Worry and doubt may slow us down, but they also provide meaning and continuity to our lives.

Charm

Despite their faults, Antisocial vampires are lovable. You'd think that such predatory people would be hated and shunned, but that is far from the case. Immaturity is the wellspring of attraction, and the source of all charm. Vampires make their emotional living by using other people. To survive, they have to be very good at convincing you that they have exactly what you want. They *do* have what you want, but seldom for as long as you want it.

Our own immaturity can persuade us that a Ferrari is every bit as practical as a Toyota. Funny how it's usually the most messed up part of our personalities that makes the most important decisions.

REBELS WITHOUT A CAUSE

Do these vampires sound suspiciously like your teenage kids? They should, because the Antisocial pattern is quite similar to normal adolescence. With luck, your kids will grow out of it in their mid-twenties. Antisocial vampires seldom mature much until they hit 50, and then it's often only age and excess that slow them down.

5 Vampire Daredevils

**Sexy, thrilling, and definitely
bad for your health.**

If you like excitement and fun, you'll love this manifestation of the Antisocial vampire. Be careful that you don't love Daredevils too much; they can be addictive.

The most salient characteristic of Daredevils is their own addiction to excitement, which, as we have just seen, is the central dynamic of all Antisocials. The other two Antisocial types are partial to darker thrills: Used Car Salesmen to deception, and Bullies to aggression. Daredevils like excitement for its own sake, a trait that makes them the most socially acceptable of the Antisocials. At least they're not actively trying to hurt you or take advantage of you.

THE PHYSIOLOGY OF EXCITEMENT

Excitement, in a physiological sense, is nothing more than rapid changes in brain and body chemistry that can be achieved by jumping out of an airplane, having wild sex, playing the stock market, drinking a martini, or buying stuff on the Home Shopping Channel. We're talking drugs here, even though the substances in question are hormones, endorphins, and neurotransmitters. Daredevils also have strong proclivities for drugs that are manufactured outside the body. Whatever the source, the overriding goal of most Daredevil behavior is to get the biggest jolt in the shortest amount of time.

Daredevils do very little worrying. They have far more important things to think about than deadlines, obligations, or how you'll feel if they break a promise. Daredevils regularly lose jobs, spend money they don't have, and break the hearts of the people who care about them. Everyday reality is no match for the heart-pounding, gut-wrenching thrill of living a fantasy.

Drugs, whether bought from a dealer or squeezed out of the endocrine system by risky behavior, cause a second problem as well. Over time it takes more and more to do less and less. The huge jolts that Daredevils love so much inevitably deplete their brains of the smaller amounts of chemicals required to maintain day-to-day equilibrium. In the wide dry spaces between thrills, Antisocials of all types feel depressed, irritable, and empty.

This is where you come in. In addition to playmates, Antisocials usually need somebody to take care of them, clean up after them, and get them back on track. They will offer the world for these services, and pay nothing. Codependents don't even get gratitude. Still, when Daredevils are up and running, the ride is awfully sweet. Now that you know what's under the hood, you still have to choose: Ferrari or Toyota?

DAREDEVIL HYPNOSIS

Chemical or behavioral, at whatever level you think about their drive, Daredevils offer a wild ride that pulls you out of your workaday world and into their alternate reality of fun and adventure. Without even trying, they are superb hypnotists. It always starts small.

"Yo, David. Vampire Brian here with the ski report. Twenty-one new inches of powder last night, with more falling as we speak. If we drive up tonight we can beat the crowds to the lifts in the morning."

"Brian, tomorrow's Friday. I'm working. How did you manage to get the day off?"

Suddenly, Brian's voice sounds weak and raspy, as if he had to struggle to draw a breath. "I've got that flu that's going around. It's really hit me hard. I tried to get out of bed this morning, but I just can't seem to . . ." Brian's voice fades into a weak cough.

"Jeez, you really do sound sick. How are you doing that?"

Brian answers in the same faltering voice. "It's simple; just lie down and blow most of the air out of your lungs. It makes you sound like you're about to die. Try it."

David leans back in his chair and ties to imitate Brian's sickly voice. "I have a bad case of the flu—"

"Really lame, David."

"How's this? Do I sound sick enough now?" David chokes out the words.

"Right on the money." Brian's laughter turns into a fit of ersatz coughing that ends in a wheezing gasp.

Daredevils are great at spotting people who could use a little fun, especially fun that involves rebellion against authority. As hypnotists, they speak to the teenager inside us, and describe all the wonderful possibilities that life holds if we're just willing to take a risk. The bind they put us in is a dare, simple and effective: Do it, or kiss the opportunity goodbye and admit you didn't have the guts.

There's nothing wrong with calling in sick to go skiing if you only do it once in a while. The problem with Daredevils is that they don't know when to stop. They have a real gift for pulling other people along further than they wanted to go.

"It's called an IPO," Brian says, tapping the prospectus on the table next to the pitcher of beer. He has to shout to be heard over the happy-hour crowd. "They just opened IPOs up to regular guys who aren't like Warren Buffett. You buy in right before the stock goes public. Then, whoom!" Brian's hand becomes a rocket. "Four, five hundred percent on the first day."

David laughs. "Yeah right, Brian. Why don't we just buy a few lottery tickets?"

Brian shoves the prospectus across the table. "Hey, don't dis the idea till you look at the numbers on a few of these puppies." As David reads, Brian freshens up their beers; then he takes a couple of cigars out of his jacket pocket, and hands one to David.

Absently, David lights his cigar. "How much?"

"It costs a hundred thou to play, and we're splitting it five ways. You, me, Devin, Sheryl, and Rashid."

David takes a long pull on his beer. "You're not kidding about this, are you?"

"No way. We're going for the gold whether you come or not."

"I don't have $20,000 to invest."

"No? Have you looked at the balance of your retirement account lately?"

"Sure, there are all kinds of tax penalties if I take that money out."

"Yeah, but what kind of rate is that money earning? Eight percent or something? This could yield 800!"

"But the risk—"

Brian makes a face. *"What about the risk of staying in a dead-end job for 30K a year? Think about it, Dave-man. This is a once in a lifetime opportunity!"*

"But—"

"What about the equity in your house? It's really easy to refinance."

What is David to do in response to Brian's investment scheme?

First, we need to point out an important distinction. A Daredevil like Brian may talk you into taking a risk in which he stands an equal chance of losing his money and doesn't get anything more if you invest. As we'll see in the next chapter, a Used Car Salesman may try to talk you into a scheme in which you bear far more risk because he or she gets some of your money right off the top.

The thing to remember is that Daredevils are in the game for the risk as much as the gain. Losing big is also a powerful source of stimulation. An interesting point to consider is the well-known research finding that people diagnosed as having antisocial personality disorder don't learn very well from their mistakes, or from punishment of any sort. More than any other group, they have the capacity to pick themselves up, dust themselves off, and do the same stupid thing all over again.

You can know how reliable a person's business ideas are only by examining his or her track record over a long period of time, not by being dazzled over a recent spectacular success. It will take force of will to do this, because we are wired to pay more attention to recency and intensity than to what makes most sense in the long run.

HOW VAMPIRES KEEP YOU COMING BACK FOR MORE

Until now, we've talked about how vampires use hypnotic techniques to influence a single decision, like hiring, investing, or calling in sick for a day of skiing. In the real world, vampires prey on people by becoming a part of their lives and influencing them to make one questionable decision after another. Nowhere are the mechanics of this process more visible than in a romantic relationship.

Speaking of romance, do you remember Vampire Alec, the smooth operator in Chapter 4, who swept slightly clutzy Leeanne off her feet by seeing her as a dancer?

For a while, they were quite a thing. That is, until . . . Well, maybe I'm getting ahead of myself. Let's go back to the moment the affair really began. They'd seen each other a couple of times but hadn't slept together. At first, Alec was attentive, but in the last day or so he'd become almost cool. That night was the kicker. Leeanne was sure they'd made plans to see a movie, but Alec never showed.

The intercom buzzes, long and loud in the darkness. Leeanne looks at the clock: 2 a.m. "Who is it?" she shouts, as she pads through the bedroom door.

"Alec." His voice sounds tinny in the ancient speaker. Like somebody from an old radio show.

"Alec?"

"I'm sorry, Leeanne. I . . . Can I come up just for a minute?"

"Alec, it's two o'clock."

"Leeanne, I'm so sorry. I was, like, I don't know, scared or something. It was just that . . . Damn it, if I don't tell you now, I'll never have the courage again."

His words are cut short by the buzz and click of the lobby door.

This is definitely not like me, Leeanne thinks, as she listens to Alec bounding up the stairs.

The dark force that caused sensible Leeanne to open her door to a guy who'd just stood her up sets the pattern for the rest of the relationship. Alec taught her how good it can feel to be bad. Now she thinks that maybe she can teach him a thing or two.

The process is called *grooming,* a slow, seductive dance that leads you to behave like your own evil twin by crossing one little line at a time. Vampires can't get you to do anything really outrageous without having convinced you to make many little concessions in the past. When the dance is done well, it's easy to lose track of who's leading and who's following.

One week later, alone with Alec on the way to the twelfth floor, Leeanne flashes her best Meg Ryan smile and says, "Know what? I'm having this awesome fantasy about making love right here."

Alec's hand trembles so hard he can barely press the stop button. The elevator jerks to a halt.

"Alec, what are you doing?"

"Stopping the elevator. I figure we've got about five minutes until anybody notices."

"Alec, I didn't mean really—it's just a fantasy. I . . ."
He smothers out her words with a kiss.
"Okay," Leeanne whispers, "Let's do it quick."

Guerrilla sex is as exciting as drugs because it *is* drugs—adrenaline, serotonin, hormones, and endorphins, all in doses strong enough to be sold on street corners. Before you get too carried away, remember that fried egg in the television commercial.

A sex difference comes into play here: Women in love like to increase intimacy by sharing their thoughts and fantasies. Men have a hard time understanding why anyone would talk about something without actually wanting to do it.

Chemistry isn't the only reason people have a hard time just saying no. Peer pressure is pretty potent stuff too. When vampires don't get their way, they're pretty quick to throw tantrums. In the case of Daredevils, the tantrums often involve just walking away. If their designated playmate isn't enough fun, they're less likely to yell about it than they are to drift off in the direction of someone else. The prospect of imminent loss makes anything seem more valuable. People may find themselves unconsciously working very hard to keep the vampires in their lives satisfied, even when they know them to be a bad influence.

If Leeanne looked at her own behavior, she'd see all the warning signs of hypnosis. The relationship started with instant rapport. From day one she's been deviating from one standard procedure after another because Alec is the *most exciting* person she's ever met. Leeanne is confused about the relationship, but reluctant to talk about it with anybody, because she already knows what people would say.

Leanne's confusion increases, clouded by hypnosis and spurred on by drugs. The possibility that your lover may lose interest is the world's most powerful aphrodisiac.

It's that critical moment, just after making love, when Leeanne knows that Alec is deciding whether to go home or spend the night. She crosses her fingers under the pillow.

Alec rolls over, but makes no move to get up. Leeanne dares to imagine him relaxing, talking for a while, and drifting off to sleep next to her. The perfect night.

He tucks his hands behind his head and smiles. "I've had this idea," he says. "Wouldn't it be cool to do it right in the middle of old Sanford J.'s desk?"

Omigod no! Leeanne thinks. In the second that it takes to catch her breath, Alec slides his arm around her shoulders and pulls her close. "Maybe," she says.

Everything was going great until the janitor flicked on the light.

On a cold Monday morning, Leeanne looks through the want ads and wonders how she ever allowed herself to get into such a mess. Then she remembers Alec's devil-may-care smile and the warm thrill of his touch. She knows.

THE 10 ELEMENTS OF VAMPIRE FIGHTING STRATEGY: RESISTING THE FORBIDDEN FRUIT
Dealing with Daredevils takes a little willpower.

1. KNOW THEM, KNOW THEIR HISTORY, AND KNOW YOUR GOAL

Your best defense against vampires is to understand the hungers that move them. Daredevils are in the game for excitement rather than financial gain or everlasting love. That part of them will probably not change. If it did, they'd be different and far less interesting people. The way to enjoy them is to live for the moment and the good times you share.

As with any vampire, it's not possible to know what Daredevils are likely to do without knowing their history. The best predictor of what people will do in the future is what they have done in the past. Don't expect vampires to do something different unless there is some vast change in the situation, like they've suffered an enormous loss as a result of their actions, or they've been clean and sober for a year or more. Even then, don't push your luck. Antisocials like themselves the way they are and seldom learn from their mistakes.

Being clear with yourself about your own goals will help prevent you from making mistakes that you will have to learn from. The number one way that Daredevils drain other people emotionally is not really the poor vampires' fault at all. Their victims drive themselves crazy trying to get Daredevils to keep their charm, and be more reliable at the same time. Don't even think of it. You can't make a Toyota out of a Ferrari.

Your safest bet is to use Daredevils for what they're best at: fun, and jobs that scare the hell out of everybody else. Daredevils excel at hazardous duty whether the hazards be physical or emotional. They don't hurt easily, and when they are hurt they bounce back quickly. If by chance you are fighting a war, they're the best people to send.

If you aren't fighting a war, it's still a good idea to learn from the military, which from time immemorial has been the most successful employer of Daredevils. One word: structure. Have rules and procedures for everything, especially safety. Make Daredevils follow the chain of command and have strict sanctions for noncompliance. When the shooting starts, however, step out of the way and let them do their stuff. They'll handle the situation better than you will.

Daredevils also make some of the world's best salespeople. They are motivated by challenge, they don't get deflated by being told no, and their innate charm makes customers like and trust them. Unlike Used Car Salesmen, who may sell more in the short run by using out-and-out deception, Daredevils keep their customers coming back for more.

2. GET OUTSIDE VERIFICATION

Antisocials in particular may lie through their teeth. Daredevils usually won't try to deceive you for the fun of it, as Used Car Salesmen will do. They'll tell you a version of events that you (or they) would like to hear, rather than the way things are. This is especially true when Daredevils talk about sex, drugs, money, what they've done in the past, and what they intend to do in the future. If you can help it, never take their word for anything without some sort of external corroboration.

3. DO WHAT THEY DON'T

Daredevils don't worry. If you are going to hang out with them, you'll need to worry, because they don't. Worry for yourself, not for them. Protecting Daredevils from themselves is a full-time job with no pay and no results.

4. PAY ATTENTION TO ACTIONS, NOT WORDS

Give vampires full credit for doing what you ask them to do, even if they're only doing it to get you off their case. This rule works the other way around as well. Give credit only for performance, never for excuses or explanations. This is especially important when you'd rather believe the excuses.

At work, hold Antisocials accountable for specific deliverables at specified times. Forget about improving their attitude.

5. IDENTIFY HYPNOTIC STRATEGY

Daredevils can hypnotize you without breaking a sweat. Just saying "cluck, cluck"—implying that you're the cowardly kind of chicken—is one of the shortest and most effective hypnotic inductions known to science. Add devil-may-care charm and an alternate reality that's all fun and excitement with nobody having to pay the bills, and you'll know why Daredevils can have you hooked faster than you can say "adolescent fantasy." Speaking of adolescents, the Daredevil's favorite prey are people who have some doubts about how cool they are, the kinds of people who are especially sensitive to dares.

If there's a Daredevil in your life, make sure you recognize the warning signs of hypnosis: instant rapport, deviating from standard procedure, thinking in superlatives, discounting objective information, and confusion. I will repeat these signs so often throughout the book that I'm tempted to make up a catchy acronym. I'll spare us both the indignity, if you'll promise to remember.

6. PICK YOUR BATTLES

The battle you need to win with Daredevils is the one with substances. Their own brain chemistry is already intoxicating enough to impair their judgment. Under the influence of alcohol or drugs, they can become a real menace. They'll do absolutely anything, and they seldom have even the vaguest notion about when to stop. If you are going to draw any lines in the sand with a Daredevil, they should be around substance abuse.

Before you hire a Daredevil for any position in your life or your business, know where he or she stands with addictions. The big ones are chemicals, gambling, spending, and sex. At least one, and possibly all, have been or remain a problem for Daredevils. Know how they've dealt with their addiction problems. There is a vast difference in the amount of harm Daredevils can do depending on whether they're actively abusing versus actively involved in efforts (preferably some sort of structured program) to control abuse.

Never believe that making Daredevils, or any Antisocials, feel guilty will have any sort of positive effect. They are who they are and are not ashamed of it. Neither will you be able to "teach them a lesson" by doing the same thing to them that they do to you. They'll see such attacks as an invitation to a free-for-all, which they will win.

7. LET CONTINGENCIES DO THE WORK

The basic form for a contingency is: *If you do X, then Y will happen.* Y has to be something that really makes a difference to a Daredevil, not something you think *should* make a difference, like hurting your feelings.

Don't threaten firing or leaving the relationship unless you're absolutely sure that's what you want to do. If you aren't, Daredevils will surely push you to see how far you'll go. Brinkmanship is the Daredevil's all-time favorite game.

The more automatic the contingency, the better. Then you don't have to be the bad guy. The vampires have to choose whether to follow the rule or face the consequence. A good model is: If you don't turn in your time sheet, the computer doesn't print out a check.

The only way Daredevils ever learn anything is by facing the natural consequences of their actions. Never stand in the way of consequences, no matter how good the excuse. You'll only be providing advanced training in how to get around the rules.

8. CHOOSE YOUR WORDS AS CAREFULLY AS YOU PICK YOUR BATTLES

First and foremost, don't attempt to explain the concept of responsibility to a Daredevil. Believe me, it's been tried, and it doesn't work. As soon as you're gone, any Antisocial worth his or her salt will be mimicking your attempts at inspiration behind your back.

What you do need to say to Daredevils is *no* when you mean it. Do not expect them to pick up on the subtle nuances of *maybe.*

If you want Antisocials to do something, ask directly and let them know what you'll do if they don't. Never bluff; they're way better at it than you are. Ditto deception of any kind. They'll see through it immediately.

Don't bother asking Antisocials to feel what you want them to feel, or read your mind. Never discuss your relationship; they'll tune you out in under 15 seconds. If you want Daredevils to listen to you, avoid saying anything that isn't entertaining.

9. IGNORE TANTRUMS

Daredevil tantrums can vary from hot-blooded anger to cold indifference. The indifference is the most effective, because their anger is almost fun, an exciting diversion to distract you from whatever they don't want you to see. Usually, the worst they do is fling out a few gambits in the hope of getting a reaction. The more vehement you are, the longer they'll play. The worst epithet they can hurl is that you are chicken, or that you're old, dull, stodgy, or otherwise uninteresting. Don't argue the point; you'll lose. Instead, admit to whatever they accuse you of. No matter how unattractive you think it looks on your foot, if the shoe fits wear it. With pride. To a Daredevil, all responsible people are chicken.

When Daredevils get bored, the situation is more ominous, because you know they really will leave. Any attempt to hold on will push them away even further.

10. KNOW YOUR OWN LIMITS

Daredevils don't know where to stop. If there are any limits to be set, you will have to set them. Eventually, no matter what you do, Daredevils will leave. Prepare in your heart to let them drift away like the snows of yesteryear.

If by some chance they stay, congratulations. I guess.

6 Vampire Used Car Salesmen

**Slicker than cheap polyester, so always remember to
read the fine print.**

It's not my intention to impugn the dignity of men and women who actually
sell cars for a living. I'm sure most of them are upstanding citizens. The used
car salesmen that lend their name to the vampires in this section are those
archetypal personifications of verbal chicanery who, clad in pinky rings and
plaid polyester jackets, tinker with odometers and claim that their war-
ranties cover *everything*. Except anything that breaks.

Antisocials of all kinds love excitement. Used Car Salesmen are partial
to the shadowy thrill of deception. It is not so much that they get off on lying
for its own sake; it's more that they want the things they want so much that
they don't mind lying to get them. To their prey, the distinction is immaterial. You have it, they want it, and they'll happily lie, cheat, or steal to get it.

Used Car Salesmen have the terrifying ability to imitate human warmth
without feeling anything but desire for something you have. If you think
that the worst they can do is trick you into paying a lot of money for a piece
of junk, you may be in serious danger.

*The VP of marketing—Vampire Adrian—flashes a smile that could
light up a city street. "Sheila, it's great to see you! Are you still running this department single-handed?" He glances in the direction of
Sheila's boss's office and snorts dismissively. "Single-brained is more
like it." Adrian's gaze sweeps across Sheila's desk and comes to rest
on the gold-framed picture of her teenage daughter. "How's that
wonderful little girl of yours? Uh, what was her name—"*

"Courtney," Sheila says.

"Of course, Courtney. Is she still making all those A's?"

"She's doing fine," Sheila answers, blushing with parental pride. "Great, actually. Might even be salutatorian of her class."

Adrian nods as he picks up the picture to look at it more closely. "Gorgeous too." He holds Courtney's photo up next to Sheila's face and looks back and forth from one to the other. "You know, you could almost be sisters."

Despite herself, Sheila feels flattered. The manipulation alarm is clanging away inside her head, but she's just not paying attention.

As Adrian returns Courtney's picture, he moves aside a folder and looks at it with an expression of surprise. "Oh, is this the printout on the Ventex expenses?" He picks up the folder and flips it open. "I'd been meaning to check these figures out before they go to the board. Charlie Ryder was saying that there might be a couple of computer errors . . ." Adrian's voice trails off as he reads.

After a second or two, he frowns. "Oh yeah, I see exactly what he was talking about. Good thing I caught it before you sent it upstairs."

Adrian waves the folder as he strides down the hall. "I'll just take this with me and fix the problem. I'll drop it back just before the meeting, okay?"

Adrian is gone before Sheila can answer. She had spent all morning putting those figures together for the board meeting. There weren't any errors.

It's a little thing handing over a folder, but somewhere in her mind Sheila knows that Adrian is going to alter the numbers, not correct an error. In an interchange so fast that in a blink she'd have missed it, Adrian put Sheila in a terrible bind. Should she demand that the vice president return the folder or let him keep the printout, making her an unindicted coconspirator?

Adrian is counting on Sheila to be polite and helpful, rather than think about the implications of her actions. So Sheila goes along. This is how Used Car Salesmen operate. They maneuver you into a position where the ordinary, socially acceptable response is the one that gets you in trouble.

There's also the grooming phenomenon to think about. Now that Adrian has gotten Sheila to cross this line, she will be more vulnerable in the future. If he plays his cards right, she may be willing to keep things quiet, or even actively participate in a cover-up.

And Sheila was just trying to be nice!

It is this automatic niceness in people that Used Car Salesmen exploit. They're nice, you try to be nice back, and before you know it, you've been sucked dry. Used Car Salesmen are dangerous. If you don't recognize them and understand their tricks, they can hurt you badly. They can even turn you into a vampire yourself. This chapter will teach you how to spot Used Car Salesmen even without their polyester jackets. When you see them, remember whom you're dealing with. Pay attention to what's going on, be careful, and for heaven's sake don't be nice!

USED CAR HYPNOSIS

As you can imagine, Used Car Salesmen are masters of using hypnosis for their own personal gain. Their interpersonal world is one sales pitch after another. In their element they twist and twirl, graceful as figure skaters and venomous as snakes.

It's not all that easy to recognize a sales pitch. The best ones go by so quickly that the ink on the contract is dry, and the paper safely filed away, before you know you've bought anything. Most sales pitches are based on built-in polite responses—the vampire gives you something, and before you know it you're offering a bite of your neck, just to be nice.

My discussion of various kinds of sales pitches is strongly influenced by the work of social psychologist Robert Cialdini,* who has made a career of understanding the ways that people influence one another. He points out that there are only a limited number of possible pitches, but an infinite variety of ways that each may be used. All the patterns rely on people choosing the automatic, socially acceptable response, rather than thinking closely about what they're being asked to do.

Vampire sales pitches usually follow one of seven basic patterns.

Do It Because You Like Me

It's easy to like a vampire. In that short period of time when there is some doubt as to whether you are going to give them what they want, Used Car Salesmen can sparkle with wit and glow and synthetic kindness. The display usually ends three seconds after you give in, but while it lasts it smells sweet

---

*Robert B. Cialdini, *Influence: The Psychology Persuasion,* rev. ed. New York: Quill, 1993.

as cherry blossoms on a warm spring day. No one on the face of the earth is half as charming as a vampire who wants something.

It's not just charm that makes you like Used Car Salesmen. The main reason that people like other people is that they perceive them to be similar to themselves. Used Car Salesmen usually begin their pitch by establishing a perception of similarity. They watch you closely. They ask questions about who you are, what you like, and what you think, then profess to like and believe in the same sorts of things. Unless you're paying attention, their probes and ploys can seem like innocuous chit-chat.

> It's 7 a.m. Mark unlocks the office and goes straight to the coffee room to get a pot started. As it brews, he checks his e-mail. When he comes back to pour himself a mug, he runs into his new boss, Vampire Twyla.
>
> "Great coffee," she says, taking a sip. "You're the only person in this office who makes it strong enough." She fills a mug and hands it to him.
>
> "I guess I'm just a caffeine junkie," Mark says.
>
> "You know it. So am I," Twyla says. "I usually drink two or three of these in the morning just to get my heart started. Of course, when you make it I can get by on one."
>
> "I'm glad somebody else likes it," Mark says. "Not everybody is so complimentary. A lot of the reps call it 'Mark's mud.' "
>
> "Know what I really like?" Twyla says. "I like that coffee they make in New Orleans—you know, with that stuff in it."
>
> "You mean chicory?" Mark says. "I was raised on it. Grew up in Shreveport."
>
> "Well, I knew you were from the South." Twyla takes another sip of coffee. "It's not just the accent, it's an attitude. A work ethic. I grew up in Memphis myself, and—well, just look around you and see who's here at seven o'clock in the morning."
>
> They both laugh.

A friendly conversation, or the beginning of a sales pitch? Sometimes there's no way of knowing. Vampire hypnosis is hardly distinguishable from what ordinary people do when they like you. To make things even more confusing, remember that the vampires themselves are not choosing the details of their pitch consciously; they're just pretending to be your friend in case they need something from you.

Often, the only way to recognize the "like me" sales pitch for sure is to identify a repeating theme. Over a period of time, a vampire might unconsciously attempt to establish similarity in a number of different areas. If casual conversations keep drifting back to how much you're alike, it's either an amazing coincidence or a Used Car Salesman softening you up for his or her next pitch.

To protect yourself, remember that just because you like certain people or share some background, you don't have to agree with them or do what they say.

Do It to Reciprocate

Used Car Salesmen would have you believe that because they gave you something, you owe them something back. In their view, compliments are like the free samples those motherly types hand out in grocery stores. The purpose is not to nourish you, but to get you to buy.

> *Twyla and Mark have gone back to her office to discuss his new marketing position over a second cup of coffee.*
>
> *"I don't have to tell you that Sharon isn't completely sold on this marketing stuff," Twyla says. "But you know how she is—anything that doesn't improve the bottom line in 10 seconds flat is not worth doing."*
>
> *Mark sits up straighter in his chair. "That's the whole idea of marketing research—to give our reps a clearer idea about what clients want, so they can be more effective in their cold calls."*
>
> *Twyla smiles. "Good point. That's exactly what I'll tell her. In, let's say, six weeks you'll present her with some ideas from your research for improving sales rate."*
>
> *Mark swallows hard. "Six weeks might be a little bit soon to develop a decent survey, analyze it, and come up with specific ideas."*
>
> *Twyla frowns and shakes her head. "Sharon is going to be breathing down my neck pretty hard by then. You know how much she likes to see results."*
>
> *"I guess I could work faster, but—"*
>
> *"What do you say we do this? You can set up a few focus groups, then come up with something to sell Sharon on this marketing project."*
>
> *"But the whole idea of marketing is you don't start making changes until you've done research."*

"I know that, Mark. I'm the one who backed you for this project from the beginning. We're talking about politics here. If we're going to bring in these new ideas at all, we have to do it in just the right way." Twyla laughs. "I don't have to tell that to an old southern boy like you, do I? Of course not. You'll know what to do. That's why I picked you for the job."

What does Mark owe Twyla for supporting him? She is trying to sell him an alternate reality in which he owes her something more than trying to do the best job he can. She has put him in a bind in which pushing to do the job the way he thinks it should be done is somehow unwise and maybe even disloyal. Twyla is implying that the department might be closed down if she and Mark don't come up with some quick and dirty results. The polite response is for Mark to scurry off, do what he's told, and not ask questions.

What he really needs to do at this point is ask a lot of questions.

First, he needs to ask himself if what Twyla is implying really makes sense. Would Sharon create a marketing department, then shut it down in disgust if it actually did marketing? If he really believes that, maybe he ought to think twice about working in such a bizarre environment. Next, he needs to ask Twyla if what he's hearing is what she's actually saying. This requires an understanding of both tactics and tact. Mark might ask Twyla how long they have to come up with something before Sharon pulls the plug.

There are several ways that Twyla might respond to such a question; each would give Mark valuable information. Twyla could answer with a number—say, three months—and thus confirm that she actually thinks that Sharon would close them down. If this were the case, however, why would Twyla have bothered implying something she could have said straight out?

It is far more likely that Twyla would answer the question by toning down the level of imminent danger, thereby giving Mark room to negotiate a more realistic time line. The other possibility—far more likely for a vampire—is that Twyla would answer by becoming irritated, thus implying that Mark is either ungrateful or politically naive for questioning the alternate reality that she is trying to sell. This response would alert Mark that he is being set up for something.

Do It Because Everybody Else Is Doing It

Remember Brian, the Daredevil investor in the last chapter? Even though he wasn't technically a Used Car Salesman, like most Antisocials, he had an instinctive grasp of the sales pitch. By saying that Devin, Sheryl, and Rashid were in on the venture, Brian created a bandwagon for David to jump on.

The mental answer to this pitch is simple. You heard it a thousand times from your mother: If Devin, Sheryl, and Rashid jumped off a cliff, would you do it too?

This Offer Good for a Limited Time Only

Brian also made good use of the scarcity of both time and options for buying into the IPO. If David thought about it too long, he'd miss the boat. Vampires know that anything scarce takes on a value far beyond its intrinsic worth. Call it the Beanie Baby effect.

Do It to Be Consistent

Cognitive dissonance, that amazing force that bends reality to conform to the choices we have already made, is what Emerson would call foolish consistency. Used Car Salesmen call it a gold mine. They're all too ready to sic the hobgoblin of small minds on you until you do what they want.

Foolish consistency is the psychological principle that makes grooming possible. People try to maintain an internal sense of consistency between their actions and beliefs. This is hard enough to do with careful thought. It's almost impossible with a vampire trying to confuse your perceptions about who you are and what you believe by making you cross one little line after another.

Let's return to the story of Mark and Vampire Twyla. As it turned out, Mark set himself up to get drained because he didn't ask questions.

Against his better judgment, he went ahead and did a few focus groups as Twyla suggested. Mark figured he'd make the best of a bad deal, and give the project his best shot. He interviewed clients and sales reps, and discovered that the two main reasons cited by clients for investing were to have money for their own retirement and to improve their children's future. He came up with a sales presentation that addressed both issues, complete with graphs of how much money regular monthly investments could yield when clients were ready to retire or send the kids to college. Twyla was less impressed than Mark had hoped.

"Mark, let's think outside the box here. People believe in saving for their retirement or their children's future. They mean to save, but

when it comes time to plunk down the money, there's always some-thing else they can spend it on. According to your research, these folks want to feel like they're being responsible. That's what we have to capitalize on. What if we get the reps to tell people that the only way they can be responsible investors is to be absolutely sure they're getting the best possible return on their money? Otherwise, they're screwing over their own children."

"Uh, there's a little problem with that. The clients aren't sure they're getting the best possible return on their money, and, to tell the truth, in a lot of cases they aren't."

Twyla ignores Mark's comment about honesty. "Don't we have computer programs that show clients the returns they're getting?"

"Yes, but the reps are having some problems with the programs. They think they're a little bit deceptive. A lot of the time it seems like they're adding percentage points that aren't really there."

Twyla is beginning to look a little irritated. Mark wonders if he should go on. He decides that honesty is the best policy and that it makes sense to get everything out on the table. "The reps also feel that the sales quotas are so high that there's a lot of pressure on them to churn their present accounts, to sell stuff and buy stuff unnecessarily just to make enough commission to live on."

The anger Mark expects doesn't materialize. Instead, Twyla settles back in her chair and lets out a huge sigh. "Welcome to management," she says. "The first thing you'll discover is that there are a lot of peo-ple out there who just can't cut it, so they always blame the system."

Mark is about to speak, but Twyla waves her hand in the air to stop him. "No," she says. "You don't have to tell me. All I want to know is this. You have always made more commission than most people in this department. Did you ever have to misrepresent the facts or churn an account to make a sale?"

Mark looks into his own heart, debating between the correct answer and the one Twyla expects. "No," he says, finally.

Twyla's welcome to management points out that Mark, like most of us, is not completely pure. He probably did do a little churning to keep his totals up. Twyla implies that in the world of management everybody does it, but nobody admits it, and Mark buys right in by not admitting. What else can he do? If he tells the truth, he shows that he's not management material.

By being on what Twyla defines as the management side of the line, Mark has to discount the views of the sales reps as being unsophisticated. It is the fatal bite that changes him.

Mark should have remembered the rule about not letting a vampire be your only source of information. He could have searched his own soul, or asked other people what they thought of Twyla's views on business ethics. Instead, he jumped on the vampire management bandwagon and let it carry him away into the night.

You Can Believe Me—I'm an Authority

Vampires know that people are likely to do what authority figures tell them. Regardless.

In the most chilling social psychology experiment of all time, Stanley Milgram* demonstrated that average people would administer what they believed were potentially lethal electric shocks because someone in a white coat told them it was okay.

On the other hand, all societies are built around trust in authority. Most of the time that trust is justified. Everyone can cite exceptions to this general rule, but the fact remains that people who have some knowledge of what they're talking about usually give you better advice than, say, your brother-in-law.

Used Car Salesmen never ignore a chance to abuse trust.

Do It or Else

How can you blame Mark for buying into Twyla's schemes? It was either that or get fired. At least that's how he saw it. Or how he was hypnotized into seeing it. One of the main reasons people listen to an authority figure is the fear that they will be punished if they don't.

Would Twyla really have fired Mark? Who knows? Vampires with power usually threaten far more than they will actually do. They know that people who are trying to keep their jobs safe often expose other parts of their lives to far greater danger. Mark is a living example. All he wanted was to be a good person and do a good job. In the space of a few short conversations, Twyla twisted that motivation and used it to change Mark from

---

*Stanley Milgram, *Obedience to Authority,* New York: Harper and Row, 1974.

whatever he was to someone more like her. You know what happens when a vampire bites you.

IS HONESTY REALLY THE BEST POLICY?

It depends on what you mean by *best*. If you mean does honesty yield the most internal rewards, then the answer is yes. Absolutely. If you mean is honesty the best way to become successful in business or politics—well, no.

HOW DO YOU TELL IF SOMEBODY IS LYING?

There's no sure way to know whether somebody is lying, unless it's about something that can be independently verified. Forget about lie detectors and those little things on phones that flash in different colors. The theory behind those devices is that people become more physically aroused when they lie. Usually, only small-time liars worry enough to have it change their physiology. Bigger liars can do it in cold blood. The most dangerous liars don't have to lie at all. They groom somebody else to do it for them.

Nevertheless, if you are willing to tolerate a little uncertainty, there are a few guidelines that may come in handy for discriminating truth from falsehood. Use them with care.

1. *Lies are sometimes vaguer than the truth.* The fewer specifics you have, the harder it is to check up. Usually the vagueness increases as you get closer to the center of the issue. Beware of people who don't answer questions directly.
2. *Sometimes lies are more complicated than the truth.* Liars may include superfluous peripheral details, even while they're being vague about central issues. Liars know that people like stories, and that if theirs is good enough, others may buy in. Sometimes they try too hard.
3. *Only a liar swears to be is telling the truth.* People who are actually telling the truth seldom think that you might not believe them.
4. *Liars are perfectly capable of looking you in the eye.* The research is absolutely clear on this point. Liars are likely to exploit this widespread misconception by making more eye contact than people who are telling the truth.
5. *Liars generally benefit from their lies.* Why would people make up a story if there was nothing to be gained from doing so? The more

someone will gain from your credence, the more careful you have to be.

6. *If something sounds too good to be true, it is.* Remember this one from the discussion of hypnosis in Chapter 4? It's the most reliable method of distinguishing truth from falsehood but the one least often employed.

7. *Most liars are repeat offenders.* You know the saying: Fool me once, shame on you; fool me twice, shame on me.

THE 10 ELEMENTS OF VAMPIRE FIGHTING STRATEGY: PROTECT YOURSELF FROM PREDATORS IN POLYESTER
Just say no to Used Car Salesmen.

1. KNOW THEM, KNOW THEIR HISTORY, AND KNOW YOUR GOAL

Let the buyer beware. Used Car Salesmen don't all wear polyester jackets, but most of them have been running the same confidence games throughout their lives. Always find out as much about their previous performance as you possibly can. In hiring, always contact previous employers, and always do a check of police records unless there is some legal reason that you shouldn't. Make it your standard procedure and stand by it, even if the vampire acts hurt or offended. If you are being hired, try to get some inside stories on your employer from suppliers, customers, and current employees. Also, it couldn't hurt to check with the Better Business Bureau.

With Used Car Salesmen, the most important goal is to recognize them and prevent them from taking advantage of you at the outset. Once they've bitten you, there's not much you can do except not let it happen again.

In your day-to-day dealings with vampires, your best strategy is to use your confusion as a cue to stop and analyze what's going on. Think hard before you take the next step, especially if you feel uneasy. Ask questions, and if the answers don't make sense, say no.

There is a downside to this strategy, however.

Vampires with power grant privileges and promotions to the people they see as most likely to do their will. When you say no to them, they may stop bothering you, but you will no longer be a part of their inner circle. The promotions will stop. Don't think for a minute that these vampires will respect you for standing up to them, or reward you for virtue. The best deal you can get is being left alone. Consider a transfer to another department or another company. Used Car Salesmen typically don't actively retaliate against people who say no, but they do toss people aside when they can't use them any more.

Don't expect Used Car Salesmen to change. It's not that they never do, or that you should never trust them. Just don't trust them to take care of your interests as well as they take care of their own.

2. GET OUTSIDE VERIFICATION

Dealing with Used Car Salesmen without checking the facts is like going to Carfax Abbey at midnight without a crucifix. Always read the fine print and check the numbers.

More than any other vampires, Used Car Salesmen can turn your perceptions upside down. The most important concerns to talk over with someone you trust are the ones you'd rather not talk about. The worst danger comes from keeping your fears in darkness because they don't show you in a good light.

Mark's experience with Twyla is a fairly typical example of what can happen if you let a vampire be your guide. One small step at a time, you'll find yourself moving away from what you believe in.

3. DO WHAT THEY DON'T

Be straightforward. Don't try to hide your reservations out of politeness or fear of consequences. That's what vampires want you to do.

Don't try to fool Used Car Salesmen. When it comes to deception, you're just not in their league.

If you have to manage slippery vampires, don't be slippery yourself. Deal with them directly, face to face. Ignoring them will send the wrong message to everybody else. Cowardly attempts to trap vampires by redesigning general policy will always fail. The vampires will find the loophole, and the honest people will feel justly insulted. Your best employees will judge you by how you treat your worst.

4. PAY ATTENTION TO ACTIONS, NOT WORDS

Vampires will make every attempt to distort your perception of reality. That's what their sales pitches are all about. All the while they're sucking you dry, they keep congratulating you on what a good deal you're getting. Sometimes it's easier to believe what a smooth-talking vampire tells you than what you see with your own eyes, or feel in your own gut.

To know what's really happening, think carefully about the history of your relationship. Imagine it as a series of transactions entered in a ledger as credits and debits. Pay less attention to the words and more to who did what *for* whom, and who did what *to* whom. See who's coming out ahead. Often it helps to have somebody else audit the books. There may be a few entries you have been hypnotized into ignoring. As we'll see in Part 3, the transaction approach also works well with Narcissistic vampires.

With Used Car Salesmen, in addition to actions rather than words, you need to pay attention to words rather than innuendoes. When vampires seem to be hinting at something, ask questions to clarify what they are actually saying. Get as much as possible on the record. Used Car Salesmen hate accountability as much as they hate sunlight.

Management by objectives, taken seriously, is the ideal tool for dealing with Used Car Salesmen—whether you're an employer, an employee, a friend, or a spouse. Specify the goals in advance and check the performance.

5. IDENTIFY HYPNOTIC STRATEGY

Watch and listen for the seven basic patterns of persuasion. When you recognize them, use them as a reminder to think for yourself rather than just giving the vampire the automatic polite response. Here are the patterns along with a few ideas about what you might think instead.

Do It Because You Like Me.   Always remember that you're free to like the person and hate the product. Just because a person is similar to you in some ways, it doesn't mean he or she has your best interests at heart.

Do It to Reciprocate.   Beware of vampires bearing gifts. They usually have big, sticky strings attached. Their idea of fair is to give you something small and hope you'll reciprocate with something bigger. Much bigger.

Try to pay off obligations in kind—lunch for lunch, compliment for compliment—rather than favor for favor.

When vampires offer you something, always ask the cost. If they say there is none, say "thank you" and think no more about it. A gift is a gift. Be suspicious of people who imply that you owe them unless they have a signed contract for a specific dollar amount.

Do It Because Everybody Else Is Doing It. If you remember what your mother said, you'll never get caught by this one.

This Offer Good for a Limited Time Only. If you don't have time to think, you don't have time to buy.

Do It to Be Consistent. Avoid the hobgoblin of small minds. Don't let your past mistakes trap you into making more in the future.

You Can Believe Me—I'm an Authority. Most often, what vampire authorities know best is how to take advantage of people who trust them.

Do It or Else. Ponder this one carefully. You may fare better if you choose the *or else.*

6. PICK YOUR BATTLES

The most common battle you have to fight with Used Car Salesman is the one to avoid being cheated. The most important battle is the one to keep them from compromising your values. The battle you'll seldom win is to show the world what big liars they are.

The one you'll never win is showing *them* anything.

Don't ever think you can beat vampires at their own game. Only lawyers have the requisite training.

7. LET CONTINGENCIES DO THE WORK

If you manage Used Car Salesmen, the unbreakable rule must be: *Follow the rules or face the consequences.* Needless to say, excuses from vampires aren't worth the hot air they're made of.

Again, the watchword is accountability, and the ideal tool is management by objectives. Try to negotiate contingencies about process as well as product.

8. CHOOSE YOUR WORDS AS CAREFULLY AS YOU PICK YOUR BATTLES

No is the most important word you can say to a Used Car Salesman. Say it often. In fact it's a good idea to use it even before it's needed. Think of it as a diagnostic tool. If you tell normal people no, they will usually respect it. Vampires are more likely to respond to being told no by turning up the charm or turning on a tantrum. It's against the vampire code to take no for an answer.

Never say yes just to be nice, and figure you can work it out later. It will be harder later, believe me.

Tell vampires what your standard procedures are, then follow them to the letter. If they want you to buy something, have your accountant check the figures. If they want you to sign something, show it to your lawyer. Both the delay and the independent advice will serve you well.

Don't waste your breath trying to convince a vampire that he or she is lying. All you'll ever get is a denial or an excuse.

9. IGNORE TANTRUMS

Used Car Salesmen are usually too smooth to throw big, noisy tantrums. That doesn't mean that they won't make comments that sting. If you don't give them their way, they're likely to imply in offhand comments that you are naive or stupid, or don't have what it takes to make it in the real world. When they start acting like that, it means you're winning. The stupidest thing you can do is get mad and try to convince them how smart and sophisticated you are.

Sometimes, Used Car Salesmen will feign anger for effect. If they do, the best way to handle their tantrums is in exactly the same way you handle people who really are angry. The next chapter, on Bullies, is loaded with ideas about how to do that.

10. KNOW YOUR OWN LIMITS

With Used Car Salesmen, as with any vampires, you have to decide where to draw the line. Try not to get so caught up in the moment that you forget who you are and what you believe in. There's no need to shout it from rooftops. Just know. If you lose your bearings, talk it over with someone you trust.

A final word on Used Car Salesmen, since the world is full of them. It's not that you can't trust them at all. You just have to trust them to be what they are. *Caveat emptor.*

7 Vampire Bullies

Big, scary, powerful, and stupid as the guys who used to take lunch money.

There are few experiences more emotionally draining than being yelled at. If you've met a vampire Bully, you know.

Like the rest of the Antisocial types, Bullies are hooked on excitement. Their drug of choice is anger. Rage transports them into a simple and bloody alternate reality in which only the strong survive. In their own minds, they are the strong. In reality, their anger may be the source of their strength, but it's also their greatest weakness.

Vampire Bullies like power, but they don't understand it. They aren't interested in the sedate, gray-flannel ways of real power, in which strength is measured by what you *might* do. For Bullies, the excitement comes from actually doing it. No amount of real power can match the raw thrill of confrontation and the sweet, feral scent of fear.

Vampire Bullies are animals. Well, we all are, but Bullies are more in touch with their animal nature than most people. They use that primitive power to manipulate the animal in you.

THE INSTINCT FOR AGGRESSION

By animal nature, I mean the older parts of the brain that have come down to us virtually unchanged from the time of the dinosaurs. The patterns for anger and fear are hardwired into our souls.

"F---ing Garbage!" Vampire Richard snarls, throwing the brief down on the glass top of his desk. "A first-year law student with half

a brain could do a better job than this. And I thought you were sup-posed to be some big-time genius from Harvard. What do you have to say for yourself?"

Ethan's heart flutters like a butterfly impaled on a pin. "Uh . . ."

Richard shakes his head in disgust. "Let me tell you something, Mr. Harvard hot shot," he says, leaning forward and pointing his fin-ger. "If you ever hand me another piece of dreck like this, I'm gonna shove it right down your throat."

Now Ethan feels himself getting mad. Stand up to the bastard, damn it! he shouts to himself, inside his head. Richard's nothing but an old man. You can take him.

Then Ethan imagines what would happen if he actually started a fight with a senior partner. Shock at his own impulse hits him like a blow to the gut. Ethan's mind won't work; still he forces himself to answer. "What's wrong with the brief?" he finally gasps. He wants to say more, but seems to have run out of air.

Richard stands up, rising to his full five-and-a-half feet. Ethan involuntarily shrinks down in his chair. "If you don't know," Richard says, "there's no point in telling you."

It's called the *fight or flight response.* Our ancestors needed it as a way to shift to overdrive in response to physical threat. Without it, they wouldn't have lived long enough to become our ancestors. The rules were simpler back then. If the danger is smaller than you, kill it and eat it. If it's bigger, run away before it eats you.

Richard's attack neatly transported Ethan to an alternate reality that looked a lot like Jurassic Park. In that world, Richard was completely at home, and Ethan was little more than a babe in the woods, Harvard Law notwithstanding. Even though law school is no place for the squeamish, the aggression there is a bit more subtle.

Richard's simple and transparent actions didn't fool Ethan for a sec-ond, but they did fool his brain. The crude attack to his ego was misread as a physical threat, and presto, Ethan's physiology was ready for a race or a fistfight, a state hardly conducive to intellectual riposte.

Never in a million years would Ethan actually throw a punch, but in that one instant, he considered it. Then everything went blank.

Ethan's own brain betrayed him. By the time he figured things out, Richard was already thumping his chest in victory.

VAMPIRE BULLY HYPNOSIS

Bully hypnosis is crude, but extremely effective. Bullies just attack and let your own nervous system do the rest. A Bully assault can bypass the rational part of your brain and set you down in a prehistoric alternate reality where there are only three choices: fight back, run away, or stand still and be eaten. It's the perfect bind; no matter which one you choose, you lose. The newer, smarter parts of your brain may realize what's happening, but they're so awash in chemicals and primitive impulses that they can do nothing but watch in horror as the grim drama unfolds.

A common experience when Bullies attack is not being able to think and not knowing what to say. This happens because the parts of your brain that control thinking and language have been short-circuited. There is no greater isolation than being separated from your own mind.

A Bully's anger elicits dumb, brutish fear. Like all hypnotists, Bullies know exactly what they want, and what they have to do to get it.

Fear leads to avoidance. After a couple of attacks, Bullies usually don't have to do anything to maintain their hypnotic control except snarl once in a while. People let them do whatever they want, because it's easier than confronting them.

Bullies are angry people who have discovered, to their delight, that anger—which they would engage in anyway for its thrill value—also gets them power and control, at least in the short run. In the long run, Bullies' anger destroys them. So what? Knowing that the vampire who's browbeating you right now will eventually get his or her comeuppance offers little comfort and no protection.

The hypnotic relationship between anger and fear has stood the test of time, and will continue until you do something about it. But what?

WHAT TO DO ABOUT BULLIES

Lots of people have given you advice on how to deal with Bullies.

Your mom probably said to ignore them and they'd go away, but you couldn't and they didn't. They'd walk along beside you, poking, prodding, and teasing until you felt like you'd explode or, worse, cry. "Sticks and stones can break your bones, but words can never hurt you," mom said. As each new taunt burned its way into your psyche, you wondered what planet your mother grew up on.

Maybe your dad told you to fight back. If you followed his advice, you learned what abject terror feels like. You and the Bully, circling on the playground, your adversary enjoying the sport, you frightening yourself even more by imagining worst-case scenarios.

The assistant principal, also somewhat of a Bully, made it perfectly clear that fighting would not be tolerated on *this* playground. If you fight, you get expelled. Should anybody hit you, take no action on your own. Report to the office for further instructions.

As an adult, you've probably scanned the self-help shelves in bookstores, looking for some more useful answers. Stand up for yourself, the books say. Don't take a Bully's anger personally. Be assertive, but not aggressive. It may be good advice, but it's harder to follow than the instructions for programming a VCR.

Everybody tells you something different. How do you decide what to do?

What you've heard is both right and wrong. Any of the strategies might work, depending on the situation. They also might not.

Rather than looking for specific advice, remember one rule only: *The place to defeat a Bully is not in the dust of playground, but in your own mind.* If you stay in contact with the part of your brain that thinks, even though you're scared to death, you win. The important thing is what happens inside your head. All that's required externally is that you disrupt the ancient hypnotic pattern by doing the unexpected.

"I don't know if I can handle working with him any more," Ethan says. His voice trembles as he tells Kathy and Ramon about his encounter in Richard's office.

"You can't take it personally," Kathy says. "He does it to everybody."

"You got it," Ramon says. "I don't know why they let that SOB get away with verbal harassment like that. A lot of associates have quit."

"Maybe you should talk to somebody," Kathy suggests.

"Who would I talk to?" Ethan asks. "Richard's a senior partner. The only person who outranks him is God."

"There's got to be somebody," Ramon says. "I've heard a few rumors that he's on the way out."

"Those rumors have been going around since I was an associate." The three of them look up to see Lorna, the head of the litigation

department, standing in the doorway. She turns to Ethan. "I heard about what happened with the brief. I thought I'd come by to see how you're doing."

"How do you think he's doing?" Kathy says. "Richard just kicked the crap out of him. Why do you guys let him get away with it?"

"Good question," Lorna says. "I think it has something to do with male psychology." She smiles at Kathy. "In case you haven't noticed, there are a number of attorneys in this firm who make very little distinction between the law and Marine boot camp. They think that a successful legal career depends more on how tough you are than on what you know. A lot of people, especially in the old guard, think Richard's temper is a good way to toughen up tender little associates."

"Give me a break," Kathy says.

"I know," Lorna says. "I didn't say that I agreed. I think his behavior is hurting us more than some people realize, but those people are convinced only by the bottom line, which, in Richard's case is still pretty respectable."

"So, what you're saying is that nobody is going to do anything."

"Well, you could look at it that way, but I think you'd be missing something important. Not about Richard, but about yourself. What he does works only if you play along."

"What are you talking about?" Kathy asks.

"You said it yourself. I heard you as I came in. 'You can't take it personally. He does it to everybody.' "

Ramon leans forward in his chair. "Easy for you to say."

Lorna shakes her head. "No, it's not easy. It wasn't easy at all."

HOW TO DO THE UNEXPECTED

For a change, let's look at the situation from the vampire's point of view.

First and foremost, Bullies are angry people. If you asked them, they'd say they hate their anger. They know that, like an addiction, it can give them heart attacks, destroy their careers, and drive away the people close to them.

Anger *is* an addiction with vampire Bullies. They don't stop because they're always getting caught up in the rush of chemicals to their brains. Bullies don't know that anger is something they're doing; they think it's being done to them. They think that they're just trying to go about their business, when some idiot does something stupid that messes up their day. From that point on, the rest is automatic. Bullies experience the adrenaline rush of the fight or flight response just as you do, but they choose to fight.

Bullies say that they're not looking for an altercation; it's just that they can't allow other people to push them around. Actually, when they're angry, which is most of the time, they don't see other people as people at all, but as obstacles. Or worse, people are threats to their dignity. Throughout history, the worst aggression has been done in the name of defending a reputation.

As you can imagine, with a world view like this, Bullies get involved in a lot of fights. Eventually they get good at them. When regular people get angry, they distrust their own feelings and hold themselves back. Not Bullies. They lean into their anger and swing it hard to achieve the maximum impact. Later they may be sorry, but in the heat of the moment, they give themselves over to the primitive excitement of battle.

Not only do Bullies give themselves over to the excitement, they actively court it, whether they know it or not. If you look at Bullies' lives, you'll see that time and again, they go out of their way to get into fights. Many of them abuse substances, which lower their threshold for anger. Invariably, they will say that they're getting high to relax.

Always remember that Bullies are fighting to achieve an altered state of consciousness, rather than to get you to *do* anything in particular. Any of the three responses dictated by the primitive brain centers is perfectly acceptable. Bullies will be equally happy if you fight back, run away, or cringe in fear. The way to win is to do something unexpected that will jolt Bullies out of their familiar, primitive pattern and make them think about what's going on. They hate that, because it spoils their high.

Of course, in order to do the unexpected, you have to be able to think in the midst of an adrenaline rush. That's what all the advice is about, whether it comes from your mother, the assistant principal, or this book. You can follow any of it, so long as it keeps you in the thinking part of your brain.

I received a letter from a woman who attended one of my seminars. She said it had saved her life. On the way home from my talk, she was accosted in a parking garage by a man with a knife and a ski mask. Instead of panicking, she asked herself, "What would Dr. Bernstein do in this situation?" She decided to scream at the top of her lungs and run toward a group of people at the other end of the garage. This was not a technique I taught in the seminar. What saved her, she said, was thinking about what to do instead of descending into the fight or flight response. Responsible or not, I was happy to take credit for her new-found bravery.

What do you do if you meet a Bully on the road and you can't fight back, run away, or freeze in terror? The first thing you do is question your assumptions. Who says you have only three choices?

Richard comes storming down the hall, red-eyed and wild. Kathy's stomach begins to quiver. Since she was little, she could always tell when someone was about to yell at her.

"Who the hell set up for a deposition in the conference room?" Richard bellows.

Kathy tries to keep her voice calm. "I signed up for it two weeks ago. Is there a problem?"

Richard extends his hands toward heaven in mock supplication. "A problem, she says! Yes, there's a goddamn problem! I've got six heavy hitters from Yoshitomo coming over in 10 minutes for a contract review. You know how those guys are. Unless they get the big conference room, they're insulted; it's like they lose face or something. So, if all you're going to do is a take a piddly little deposition, you need to get your stuff out of there and into one of the smaller rooms down the hall. Right now!"

Kathy's muscles clench so tightly she fears her bones may break. Needles of ice jab at her spine. By sheer force of will she pushes a breath past the band of iron around her chest.

What to do next?

The primitive part of your own brain tells you that angry people are big, powerful, and dangerous. They may be, but they're also really stupid. This is true, no matter how smart they are in other areas of their lives. If you use the thinking part of your brain and they're operating on primitive instinct, you'll have an advantage of about 50 IQ points. If you can't win with an advantage like that, you ought not to play.

Thinking, however, isn't all that easy when a bully attacks.

In that one awful second, everything Kathy has been and done in 36 years comes rushing down on her in a torrent of conflicting emotions.

It's not fair! I signed up for the room! *Objection overruled by the darker law that says whoever is biggest, strongest, and maddest gets his way.*

Be nice, dear. Do what he wants. Her mother's all-purpose smile shines out like a beacon, luring her to the false safety of shallow water.

Don't take it personally. Advice she's heard a thousand times plays in the background like a song in another language. Just a string of words.

Hide and it will all go away. A sad little voice wails just as talons of shame drag her out from under the bed.

WHAT HE DOES TO YOU IF YOU SAY SOMETHING WILL BE NOTHING COMPARED WITH WHAT I'LL DO IF YOU DON'T.

But can I afford to make an enemy of a senior partner?

DO SOMETHING, NOW.

Don't take it personally. Yeah, right.

Maybe I could work at a smaller firm where it's less stressful.

DON'T LET THAT MAN ABUSE YOU!

THIS IS ABOUT WHO YOU ARE!

No it isn't.

Slowly, creaking like a rusty hinge on a seldom used gate, Kathy's mind swings open. *It's not about who I am. It's about him.*

As her focus moves from herself to Richard, she sees a pitiful old man making a scene because his carelessness might blow his image with a big client. His bullying has nothing to do with her. Unless she completely loses it, her reputation isn't at stake here. His is.

Don't take it personally.

Suddenly, the words have meaning. Kathy feels them tingling and fizzing in her body, like giggles.

For some silly reason, she remembers a verse from Dr. Seuss:

What happened then?

Well, in Who-ville they say the Grinch's small heart grew six sizes that day.

Giggles are the sound a heart makes when it's growing. Kathy knows. Richard's piddly little tantrum is no longer a problem.

She smiles in the face of wrath. *"I think I hear you asking for a favor, counselor, but I'm not sure. Maybe you could rephrase?"*

Here, in one small vignette, is the whole reason that there are therapists and books full of helpful advice. It's not what we tell you to do—you've probably heard the same advice a thousand times before. It's the knowing you can do it.

The purpose of all the explanations and examples is in helping you understand difficult situations well enough to recognize other possibilities. Your heart grows when you step out of an old pattern and do something new and unexpected, even if it's scary and difficult.

Especially when it's scary and difficult. If you don't believe me, ask Kathy.

THE 10 ELEMENTS OF VAMPIRE FIGHTING STRATEGY: DON'T LET VAMPIRES KICK SAND IN YOUR FACE
Martial arts don't work with Bullies.

1. KNOW THEM, KNOW THEIR HISTORY, AND KNOW YOUR GOAL

Vampire Bullies advertise. Whether they're wearing corporate uniforms or greasy denims and Harley-Davidson T-shirts, everything about them—their gruff manner, their sharp tone of voice, their air of smug superiority—says: *Don't mess with me, I'm tough.*

The only place Bullies are hard to recognize is beneath you in an organizational chart. Bullies understand dominance. They usually kiss up to the people above them so they can prey undisturbed on those below. What you hear about them is about one-tenth of what's going on, if that.

Think about it. If your boss is a Bully, would you risk his or her wrath by reporting the problem to the boss's boss, who may be an even bigger Bully? If you suspect that somebody below you is using bullying tactics, the only way you'll know for sure is to ask the person's subordinates directly, and give a firm promise of immunity from retaliation. If you hear of one or two incidents, it usually indicates there's a pattern. Don't ask unless you intend to take action. If you ignore what you hear, you'll be implicitly approving.

No matter what your father told you, you can't free yourself from Bullies by fighting. Even if you win a round, they'll be back, even angrier. The only way to win is by not engaging in the first place. Easy to say, hard to do, especially since Bullies love to sneak up and ambush you.

The goal you will not be able to accomplish is getting a Bully to care how bad his or her anger makes you feel. All vampires are deficient in empathy, Bullies especially so.

If you ever find yourself thinking about hurting a Bully, instead of acting on the impulse, learn from it. Fantasizing about revenge is a firsthand example of how your primitive brain tries to sneak its agenda into your behavior.

You can't outbully a Bully, but you can outthink one. The goal you may be able to achieve is to deflect attacks. Even though your primitive brain centers may be screaming at you to fight back or run away, the only effective strategy is to stay with the part of your brain that reasons, and be reasonable. The Bully will do you less damage, and may even calm down and participate in a rational discussion. Or maybe not. Count yourself lucky if the Bully just goes away and vents that anger somewhere else.

Always remember that you can't disengage from a Bully and retaliate at the same time. One hostile word can send you all the way back to the jungle. If your goal is to control a vampire, first you must be in control of yourself.

2. GET OUTSIDE VERIFICATION

Check out your perceptions of Bullies' anger and your response. Do this carefully, and read between the lines. Someone may be trying to tell you tactfully that you're being too sensitive.

Or not sensitive enough. The last thing you need is a so-called friend with a grudge against the Bully, someone who works you up to an aggressive response and then fires you off like a guided missile.

Vampire Bullies get a lot of mileage out of threats. It may be helpful to find out whether the vampire in question has the power to make good on threats, and whether he or she has actually taken documented retaliatory action. Take the stories you hear with a grain of salt, and perhaps a little garlic.

If a vampire's threats of firing people have been empty in the past, they may still be. When it comes to getting rid of people, vampire Bullies are far less likely to fire people than they are to drive them to quit. It is more difficult to be driven out of a job if you don't participate in the process.

If you have to deal with Bullies, it's helpful to find out as much as possible about their previous modus operandi. They are seldom creative enough to come up with something new.

Outside verification is also the only way you can find out if you have Bullies working for you. If you ask them, they'll say they never hear any complaints. Is that because people are happy or intimidated? You won't know until you ask.

3. DO WHAT THEY DON'T

To defeat Bullies, you have to do what they don't. Namely, stay cool and keep your wits about you. Here's some advice that may help.

Ask for Time to Think.   Only in the primitive jungle do you have to respond to attacks immediately. That's where the vampire wants to send you, but there's no law saying that you have to go.

Normal people don't get angrier at you if you ask for a minute to think things over. By your actions you are communicating that you take the situation seriously and want to handle it well. Vampires may try some other device to get you to respond in an immediate, emotional manner. They want a fight, not a rational discussion. They may mistake your silence for freezing up with terror, which you may be, but you don't have to let them know it.

Whatever you're feeling, just asking for a couple of minutes to think things over is usually so unexpected that you may be able to end the confrontation right there. No matter what, take your time and think before you respond.

Think About What You Want to Happen.   While you're taking your minute to think, consider the possible outcomes. Immediately discard any that involve making the Bully back down and admit that you're right. You cannot be right and effective at the same time. Don't even try.

Get the Bully to Stop Yelling.   Actually, this is easier than you might think. Just keeping your own voice soft may do the trick. Bullies expect you to yell back; don't oblige them. If either of you is yelling, nothing reasonable will be said.

Another unexpected way to get a Bully to stop yelling is by saying, "Please speak more slowly. I'd like to understand." Often people will comply with this request without thinking about it. Reducing the speed will also reduce the volume. Have you ever tried to yell slowly? This strategy works particularly well on the phone.

On the phone, also remember the "uh-huh" rule. We usually respond with "uh-huh" when the other person takes a breath. If you go three breaths without saying "uh-huh," the other person will stop and ask, "Are you there?" Following this technique will allow you to interrupt without saying a word.

Whatever You Do, Don't Explain.   If you are ever attacked by a vampire Bully, you may feel a powerful urge to explain the whys and wherefores of your own actions. Don't do it! Explanations are the way that primitive responses sneak down from your reptile brain and out your mouth. Explanations are usually a disguised form of fighting back or running away. The typical explanation boils down to "If you know all the facts, you will see that I am right and you are wrong" or "It wasn't my fault; you should be mad at somebody else." Never mind that your explanations seem true and reasonable to you. Bullies always recognize the primitive patterns for dealing with aggression. They will see your explanation as an invitation to go for the jugular.

Ask, "What Would You Like Me to Do?"   Nothing stops a vampire attack dead in its tracks like this simple little unexpected question. Vampires either do not know or will not admit what they want you to do. Bullies just want you to stand there while they yell at you, but it sounds awfully silly if they have to ask for it.

When you ask vampires what they want you to do, they'll have to stop and think. This may be enough to move them into the more rational part of their brains, which can only help you. If vampires are trying to conceal their real motivation, they'll have to ask you for something more acceptable than what they really want. Give it to them, and vanish into the night, unscathed.

Don't Take Criticism Personally.   This is the hard one. To follow this advice, you have to understand what it means to take things personally.

All of us have external things—our children, our pets, our favorite sports teams, our opinions, and our creations at work—that we experience as if they were parts of our bodies. Psychologically, we make little distinction between verbal disparagement of these things and physical attacks to our vital organs. That doesn't mean we have to respond to every criticism with an instinctive kill-or-be-killed counterattack.

If you're attacked by a Bully, it's time to employ the vampire fighter's number one strategy—*use your confusion as a cue to stop and think about what's actually going on.* With vampires, how it feels is seldom what it is. Bully attacks *are not* personal. Bullies yell at everybody. If you think about it, the attacks actually say more about who and what Bullies are than they do about you. To keep from taking an attack personally, you have to look beyond your initial emotional response to see the pattern, then step out of it.

Learn from Criticism. Every criticism contains useful information as well as an attack. If you don't hear anything useful at first, keep listening until you do. Not everyone who criticizes you is a vampire. Be especially alert when you hear the same thing from several sources. My grandfather used to say, "If three people call you a horse, buy a saddle."

If you make it a practice to wait 24 hours before you answer criticisms, it will drive vampires crazy. Other people will be impressed by your maturity and reasonableness. You may even learn something.

Reverse these roles if you have to criticize someone with a penchant for taking things too personally. Structure the situation so that the other person doesn't have to admit wrongdoing by accepting what you have to say. Always offer a face-saving option. Make it clear in your comments that you understand how a reasonable and honorable person might do what he or she did. Direct your advice toward improving the situation rather than pointing out mistakes. *Focus on what you want to happen rather than on what's wrong with what has already happened.* As we'll see in later chapters, this technique will prove invaluable if you want to criticize vampires in a way that they can hear and accept.

4. PAY ATTENTION TO ACTIONS, NOT WORDS

This is tricky, because the behaviors you have to pay attention to with vampire Bullies are all made of words. You have to focus on what the words *do,* as opposed to what they say. In a verbal altercation, if you pay attention to the content, you almost *have* to give the kind of fight-back-or-run-away response that automatically heats up the situation. This is why arguments with vampires so often escalate and so seldom solve anything.

If you were to transcribe several different arguments and analyze their content, you'd discover that, though the participants and the subjects differ, the pattern remains remarkably constant. The content of each statement seems to evoke an inevitable response, like lines in a well-rehearsed play. The transition from one step to another makes perfectly good sense, but the overall pattern moves away from a solution instead of toward one.

The process bogs down because both parties are trying to advance their view of the past—that their actions were right and the other person's were wrong—rather than planning for a future in which similar problems are averted. Many people seem to believe that you have to agree on what happened in the past in order to solve a problem. This may be true in a court of law, but not in real life.

If you want to keep your discussions from turning into arguments, the most effective approach is to avoid the temptation to explain what happened in the past. Instead, negotiate for what you want to happen in the future.

5. IDENTIFY HYPNOTIC STRATEGY

Vampire Bully hypnosis attempts to transport you to the steamy jungles of your genetic past. If you don't go, you discover that there are many more options than kill or be killed.

6. PICK YOUR BATTLES

Amen. Don't think you have to indulge vampires by getting bent out of shape over their slightest insults. Make them work hard to start a fight with you.

7. LET CONTINGENCIES DO THE WORK

The contingency that most people think about with Bullies is getting a big friend to beat them up. It could happen. If you do report the situation to an authority figure, state the facts and avoid any attempt to interpret or exaggerate. Really powerful friends disappear at the slightest hint of overreaction. No matter how reasonable you sound, you may still discover that your only friends are people with no more power than you who would love it if you took care of the Bully for them. Or lawyers.

Don't waste too much time looking for big friends. Revenge fantasy is a form of self-hypnosis that can make you believe that the important battle is out there, rather than in your own head.

If you have to work or live with a Bully, the most effective contingency is stating that you will not be yelled at (or called names, or whatever) and will immediately leave for a specified length of time. Then do it, without further explanation. It's always a good idea to go to a public place where you're less likely to be followed. If you insist on delivering a parting shot before you leave, you deserve whatever you get.

8. CHOOSE YOUR WORDS AS CAREFULLY AS YOU PICK YOUR BATTLES

Always think carefully before you say anything to a Bully. Screen your words for disguised forms of fighting back. The Bully will recognize disparagement in any form, so you should too. There's no point in starting a fight by accident.

Be very specific about what you call a Bully's attacks. Understate rather than exaggerate. Don't use terms like *harassment* or *abuse* unless you're filing suit. Your goal is getting Bullies to stop picking on you, not to acknowledge how much it hurts to be picked on.

9. IGNORE TANTRUMS

Vampire Bullies expect you to treat their tantrums as if they were threats to life and limb. Do the unexpected.

10. KNOW YOUR OWN LIMITS

Nobody deserves to be yelled at. Most of the time, the only person who can enforce that rule is you. It's always better to get away before you're goaded into doing or saying something you'll regret later. Or, sometimes, it's better just to get away.

THERAPY FOR ANTISOCIAL VAMPIRES

What should you do if you see signs of Antisocial behavior in yourself or someone you care about? This section provides a thumbnail sketch of the sorts of self-help and professional therapeutic approaches that might be beneficial. Always remember that attempting psychotherapy on someone you know will make you both sicker.

THE GOAL

The basic goal of treatment for Antisocial Emotional Vampires is overcoming the addiction to excitement (and any other addictions). Socialization means learning how to delay gratification, endure boredom, and live by someone else's rules.

PROFESSIONAL HELP

Twelve-step programs and Antisocials were made for each other. Literally. Alcoholics Anonymous was created by Antisocials for Antisocials, and nobody has yet devised a better system for dealing with substance abuse in the thrill-seeking personality. The structure, social stimulation, constant reminders of behavioral consequences, and sponsors who can be called in a moment of weakness are all just what the doctor ordered. Actually, they're better than most things that doctors come up with.

The only people whom Antisocials might remotely consider trusting are other Antisocials; they see virtually everyone else as hypocritical. Addictions are one of the few exceptions to the general rule that says a therapist should never treat anybody for what he or she has or is recovering from.

SELF-HELP

If you recognize Antisocial tendencies in yourself, the following exercises will be very difficult for you, but they will make a difference.

Learn to Endure Boredom. This is essential. If you can't stand the long stretches of boredom that come with being a responsible adult, you'll never be one. Don't believe for a minute that shifting your addiction to a more socially acceptable form of excitement will change anything. Addicts usually go back to their drug of choice.

Live by the Letter of the Law. This means every law, not just the ones you agree with. Start with turning in your paperwork on time and driving within the speed limit. Even if other people break a few rules here and there, you can't. If you do, accept the consequences without trying to talk your way out of them. You have to learn to be straighter than the straight people.

Laboriously Consider the Effects of Your Actions. Recognize that you don't live in a vacuum. Every time you break a rule, it hurts someone else. If you can't figure out how, sit there until you can.

Avoid Name-Calling or Raising Your Voice. Think of it as the duct-tape solution to temper problems. Until you learn to express your anger in a constructive way, don't express it at all.

Keep Promises. Don't make *any* promises to *anyone* unless you're absolutely sure you can keep them.

WHAT WILL HURT

Emotional Vampires tend to select approaches to improving themselves that make them worse rather than better. Antisocials should stay away from extensive examination of family-of-origin issues and approaches that emphasize expression of feelings over learning to control feelings. Antisocials have enough excuses already, and insight into the past seldom affects their behavior in the present. Beware of nice therapists who write letters to get Antisocials out of things because of extenuating circumstances. With Antisocials, there are no extenuating circumstances.

Antisocial vampires *do not* need advocates to help them escape the repercussions of their behavior. If there are Antisocials in your life, the best thing you can do is stand aside and let them face their own consequences.

2 Show Business, Vampire Style

The Histrionic Types

*Sparkling with jewels and trailing clouds of expensive perfume, the vampire enters, laughing. She scans the room, and when she sees you, her smile brightens enough to light up a fair-sized town. "Darling! It's so good to see you!" she says, kissing the air next to your cheek. "You look absolutely **scrumptious** in that new outfit. I could just **eat** you up!"*

Just as Antisocial vampires like excitement, Histrionics love attention and approval. They're willing to work hard to get it. Given half a chance, they'll sing and dance their way into your heart. They invented musical comedy. They do more subtle performances too. Histrionics are virtuosos of polite conversation, so interested that they make you feel interesting. One of their finest inventions is small talk, the miracle glue that holds conversations together. They also invented gossip.

Histrionics have what it takes to get hired into your business or your life. You want good looks? They've got them (or they'll spend hours trying to get them). They bubble with enthusiasm, sparkle with wit, and sometimes tingle with sexual excitement. Be careful. *Histrionic* means dramatic; what you see is all a show, and definitely not what you get.

Histrionics are always acting. Mostly, they try to do cheerful sitcoms, but the performance can change before your eyes into a sordid, overacted soap opera with you as a part of the cast. Or a medical drama. Or a seamy talk show. Or even professional wrestling.

These vampire performers have tendencies toward **Histrionic personality disorder.** The condition is old, but the name is new, an attempt to replace the less politically correct *hysterical.* Ancient Greek physicians like Galen and Hippocrates thought that the dramatic emotional shifts and vague physical complaints they saw in Histrionics were caused by the migration of a childless womb (hystericum) to other parts of the body.

Histrionic personality has for centuries been considered primarily a disorder of women. This misperception arises from the fact that the Histrionic types most often seen in clinics are stereotypically feminine.

There are plenty of Histrionic men as well. They tend to seek approval and acceptability more than attention. Their roles are masculine stereotypes—fifties dad, avid sports fan, joke-telling raconteur, or highly motivated businessman. Histrionic men also play at being tough guys; professional wrestlers are a good example. They can sometimes be misdiagnosed as Antisocial, but if you look more closely you can see that the violence is faked, and the real goal is trying to put on a good show. In the next chapter we'll look more closely at male-pattern Histrionics.

Histrionics were Freud's favorite patients. They gave him the idea that much of human experience occurs outside awareness. If you spend any time with Histrionics, you too will believe in the unconscious.

The internal landscape of Histrionic vampires is foggier than a Transylvanian night. They can get lost in whatever role they happen to be playing. They can forget who they really are and what they really feel. Or think. Or anything. Their true feelings come out in body language, the sound of their voices, and their unintentionally revealing choice of words. Histrionics also invented the Freudian slip.

WHAT IT'S LIKE TO BE HISTRIONIC

Histrionics' desire for attention and approval is so strong that, in their minds, they divide themselves into the parts people like, and the parts that aren't there. When Histrionics are forced to confront those unacceptable missing parts, everything falls to pieces.

Imagine walking into a party in a brand-new outfit that you couldn't have worn only 10 pounds ago. You're feeling turned on, toned up, trimmed down, and decked out. You can sense people's eyes following you. For a few minutes, life is exactly the way it's supposed to be. You feel marvelous! Then you pass a full-length mirror and see in excruciating detail what it means to be 5 pounds from your goal. This is the agony of the Histrionic.

In normal people there's a little voice that says: *It's who you are, not what you look like.* Histrionics do not hear that voice. Seeing themselves as unacceptable in any way unleashes a storm of emotions that requires hours of reassurance to abate. Reassurance may not be enough. Sometimes they feel compelled to intensify the performance to fever pitch, or to engage in bizarre and destructive actions to regain their sense of equilibrium. Histrionics also invented crimes of passion. Ditto anorexia and bulimia.

It's also possible that the emotional storm won't be expressed outwardly, that it will be forced into a dark cupboard in the mind where it will roil and seethe, mixing with other unacceptable impulses until some tiny slight blows the door off the cupboard and unleashes a hurricane.

When it comes to the three elements of psychological health—sense of control, connection to something larger than oneself, and pursuit of challenge—Histrionics are all over the map. Their beliefs and abilities change with their moods. The world of Histrionics is a mass of contradictions—cheery sunshine one minute, fog and lightning the next. You never know what's going to happen, and neither do they.

One thing is sure. If you're close to a Histrionic vampire, you'll be the one who has to clean up after the storm.

The favorite prey of Histrionic Emotional Vampires is someone who will rescue them from themselves and from the complexities of everyday life. They hate boring details worse than a stake through the heart. What they offer in return is a really good show and promises they just can't seem to keep.

THE HISTRIONIC DILEMMA

If Antisocials are Ferraris in a world of Toyotas, Histrionics are more like those beautiful little model cars that have all the moving parts but do nothing except sit there and look good. Actually, they're less like cars and more like rare and beautiful flowers that require an enormous amount of maintenance, but still fade in a day. The dilemma they present is simple, though fiendishly difficult to resolve: Either you supply the maintenance or someone else will.

THE HISTRIONIC VAMPIRE CHECKLIST: LIVING A SOAP OPERA

True or false: Score one point for each *true* answer.

1.	This person usually stands out in a crowd by virtue of looks, dress, or personality.	T	F
2.	This person is friendly, enthusiastic, entertaining, and absolutely wonderful in social situations.	T	F
3.	This person treats superficial acquaintances as if they were close friends.	T	F
4.	This person may become visibly upset when forced to share the spotlight.	T	F
5.	This person frequently changes his or her style of dress and overall look.	T	F
6.	This person loves to talk, gossip, and tell stories.	T	F
7.	This person's stories usually become more exaggerated and dramatic with each retelling.	T	F
8.	This person has a good fashion sense, but perhaps a bit too much concern with his or her appearance.	T	F
9.	This person can become very upset over relatively small social slights.	T	F
10.	This person seldom admits to being angry, even when his or her anger is quite apparent to other people.	T	F
11.	This person has very little memory for day-to-day details.	T	F

12. This person believes in supernatural entities, like angels,   T   F
deities, or benevolent spirits who regularly intervene in
everyday life.

13. This person has one or more unusual ailments that come   T   F
and go according to no discernible pattern.

14. This person has some problems doing regular chores like   T   F
paperwork, housecleaning, and paying bills.

15. This person has been known to get sick to avoid doing   T   F
something unpleasant.

16. This person fervently follows several television shows or   T   F
sports teams.

17. This person's communication, though highly colored, is   T   F
often indirect and vague.

18. This person requires more maintenance than a rare orchid,   T   F
but believes he or she is the easiest person in the world to
get along with.

19. This person often seems seductive, though he or she may   T   F
not admit to it.

20. Despite all the problems, this person is always in demand   T   F
and more popular than most people could ever hope to be.

Scoring: Five or more true answers qualifies the person as a Histrionic Emotional Vampire, though not necessarily for a diagnosis of histrionic personality disorder. If the person scores higher than 10, be careful that you don't inadvertently join the cast of his or her soap opera.

WHAT THE QUESTIONS MEASURE

The specific behaviors covered on the checklist relate to several underlying personality characteristics that define a Histrionic Emotional Vampire.

Sociability

First and foremost, Histrionic vampires are social creatures. They enjoy other people's company, and most of the time they are enjoyable to be with. They can be cheerful, cordial, witty, sexy, exciting, or anything else you want, except substantial. Without Histrionics, the world would be a less friendly place, all business, devoid of drama and style.

Need for Attention

Attention is the lifeblood of Histrionics. If they don't get enough of it, they feel themselves start to shrivel up and die. Histrionics always seek out the most appreciative audience. This tendency can destroy relationships. If anybody flirts with them, Histrionic vampires will usually flirt back, regardless of their intentions.

If their bosses and coworkers don't give them enough attention, these vampires will just go down the hall and get some. Where they go is immaterial to them, but it may play havoc with the chain of command. They might drop into the CEO's office for a little chat, or pick up the phone and gossip with a customer about all the problems the company is having. They don't mean to cause trouble, but they always seem to create far more than their share.

Need for Approval

Histrionic vampires prefer that all the attention they get be positive. They strive for social acceptability, and work hard to live up to everyone's expectations.

Histrionic vampires hope everybody thinks they're wonderful. They regard criticism either as meaningless grumpiness to be charmed away or as an affront to natural law. Either way, they will not hear anything but unqualified praise. Pity the poor manager who tries to write something in the *needs to improve* box on a Histrionic vampire's annual review.

Emotionality

Histrionics live in a world of emotions. Their reality is defined by what they feel, rather than what they think or know. This emotionality can be disconcerting to anyone who tries to reason with them. A butterfly flapping its wings in China is sufficient to change a Histrionic's mood. Even less is required to change his or her mind.

Histrionics are famous for their selective memories. They can tell you how exciting a meeting was, who came, what they wore, and who was mad at whom, but not what topics were discussed.

Dependency

No matter what role they're playing, beneath the makeup. Histrionics feel incompetent. They are easily overwhelmed by all those little details that they have such a hard time remembering. The whole purpose of their incessant showmanship is to cajole some big, strong, competent person to like them enough to take care of them, and maybe change all those annoying little rules. Usually, the strategy works.

Concern with Appearance

Looks are the stock-in-trade of Histrionics. They devote a good deal of energy to keeping them up. About as much as you put into your career. On the whole, it's not a bad investment. Physical attractiveness beats everything else hands down when it comes to predicting who will succeed. Needless to say, Histrionics invented aerobics, face-lifts, and liposuction.

No creature of the night is more desperate than a Histrionic vampire whose looks are beginning to fade.

Suggestibility

Histrionic vampires are such good shape shifters that it almost seems as if they have no permanent form of their own. They automatically start becoming what you want as soon as they sense that you want it. They are superb hypnotists. They don't have to create an alternate reality; they are one. They can easily talk to plants, meditate on their past lives, and see angels. Histrionics invented New Age everything.

Lack of Insight

Histrionics know how to get looked at, but they don't have a clue about how to look at themselves. They often know less about their own history and motivation than about those of their favorite television characters.

Histrionics' selective memories make their lives into a series of vivid but unconnected events, no more related to one another than the programs broadcast on a given night.

Physical Symptoms

Histrionics invented the undiagnosable illness. Their lives are confusions of reality and fantasy, obsession and repression, impulse and inhibition. When they feel bad, they express it with their bodies. Illness is an art form. Histrionic diseases have to be interpreted like poems as well as treated with medicine and surgery. Histrionics get backaches when they can't stand up to somebody. Or constipation when they can't take any more crap.

Just giving them pills is missing the point. We will explore the uses of illness as metaphor in Chapter 9 when we examine Passive-Aggressive vampires.

HOW TO PROTECT YOURSELF FROM HISTRIONIC VAMPIRES

In a sentence, know them better than they know themselves.

8 Vampires Who Ham It Up

Whether it's sex, sickness, or secrets of success, there's only one show business.

Vampire Hams will do absolutely anything for attention. Overdo it, actually. Histrionic Hams are typically not great artists. Their ploys for getting people to notice them are often crude, transparent, and superficial. To their intended audience, however, they're riveting.

> *Damon hears Vampire Shandra's laughter in the hallway. He looks away from his computer screen, toward the door. He doesn't notice it, but every other man in the accounting office is looking in the same direction.*
>
> *Enter Shandra, wearing a slinky red dress that reveals some spectacular cleavage. She smiles, nods, and waves at people as if she were walking into a party. She turns toward Damon. He feels his heart speed up as their eyes meet.*
>
> *Shandra stops cold, eyes and mouth open in pleasant surprise. "Damon," she says, rushing up to his desk. "Is that really you? You look so different without that old beard."*
>
> *Shandra's perfume smells like flowers and spice all mixed together. It takes Damon's breath away as she leans over his desk to touch his face. "I didn't know you were so handsome under there!" she says. Her fingertips lightly graze his now smooth cheek.*
>
> *Damon's face burns. Through sheer force of will, he keeps his eyes from glancing downward. "I, uh, thought it was, like, you know, time for a change," he says.*
>
> *Shandra tilts her head and smiles as if it were the most interesting thing she'd heard all day. "You look so cute! I bet girls just follow you around the office."*

"I wish." Damon says.

Shandra laughs. "Oh, you! You're just trying to be modest." She pokes at him with a long red nail as she lays a stack of folders on his desk. "Mr. Doyle asked me to see if I could get somebody to work these figures up today. Do you think . . . ?"

Damon pushes a deskful of projects aside and pulls the folders toward his heart. "No problemo," he says.

Damon is smitten. Nobody else is fooled for a minute, especially other women.

Later, in the break room, Jen, with a towel stuffed under her sweater, regales Brandy and Elise with her Shandra imitation. "Oh, Damon, you look soooo cute without that icky old beard." Jen speaks in a breathless, Marilyn Monroe voice and a fake southern accent. She leans over in front of Elise as if she were Damon. "See anything you like?" she says, batting her eyelashes.

Elise is laughing so hard she almost falls over.

"You should have seen Damon's face!" Jen says shaking her head. "He never knew what hit him."

"How can men be so stupid?" Brandy asks.

Good question. How *can* men be so stupid? Are they so blind from testosterone poisoning that they can't see through phony and manipulative Ham-it-up vampires like Shandra?

It's not just men.

Lest we assume that these sexual caricatures are all female and their dopey victims are all male, let's run the clock back a few months to the weekend that Jen, Elise, Brandy, and some of the other folks from the office spent in Aspen. There was this ski instructor named Wolfgang, tall, blond, and still tanned from his summer of surfing and bodybuilding in Hawaii.

Last winter, Damon was doing Wolfgang imitations in the break room.

If we look closely at these little vignettes, we can begin to see the dark and enigmatic power that Histrionic vampires wield. To begin with, their victims are not the people they are trying so transparently to manipulate. People like Damon are usually quite willing to be used in return for an enjoyable illusion. *It is the people watching the process who are most annoyed, and in the end they are the ones the vampire is draining.*

Remember that vampire Hams are trying to get the most attention possible, and they don't care whether it's positive or negative. To people who spend most of their lives trying to look good, it takes no effort at all to get people of the opposite sex to drool over them. Their real audience is much larger. The attention that seductive vampire Hams crave is from everyone with whom they are competing for attention, and beating hands down.

Getting noticed is a competitive sport, and vampire Hams are the real pros. Boy toys, drag queens, death rockers, outrageous athletes, foul-mouthed deejays, and all the unsung small-time seducers like Shandra and Wolfgang have discovered that if you're flagrant enough, you can get twice as much attention from the people who hate you as from your adoring fans.

Unless the people with whom they play their sexual games are very naive, seductive vampire Hams present very little danger to them. Like prostitutes, these vampires offer a simple business transaction—I put on a show to make you feel attractive and sexy; you pay me with attention and little favors. The real problem these vampires cause is the disruption of the social order. Ham-it-up Histrionics invented sexual harassment, both doing it and suing for it. One theatrical vampire can turn an entire office into a battlefield.

Other people competing for the same attention and favors using less effective tools, like brains, talent, and hard work, resent the fact that Histrionics get special treatment because they're obnoxiously sexy or just plain obnoxious. It isn't fair!

No it isn't. It *is* show business.

HAM-IT-UP HYPNOSIS

Ham-it-up Histrionics are the kinds of hypnotists who get people to cluck like chickens and enjoy doing it. Hypnosis is a show, and these vampires have an instinctive ability to work an audience.

The alternate reality that Ham-it-up Histrionics offer is themselves. They already live in the magical world of show business, where everything is bigger and better than life, but simpler and easier to understand. Boy meets girl, good guys fight bad guys, knights in shining armor rescue maidens—we all know the stories and love them. Histrionic hypnotists offer the chance to live them.

Ham-it-up vampires invite you to go on stage and live out their fantasy with them. You can either be a good guy and play along or a spoilsport bad guy, full of criticism and negative vibes. Either way, you're part of the show.

Histrionic vampires spend most of their lives in a hypnotic trance. When they're about, it's almost impossible *not* to be hypnotized. To understand them, and to protect yourself, you must pay close attention to those danger signs.

Deviating from Standard Procedures

Ham-it-up vampires hope you'll be so enthralled by their performances that you'll relieve them of their tedious day-to-day responsibilities. The most common strategy is to hypnotize you into believing they are too ditzy to take care of things themselves. Vampires unconsciously structure the situation so that it seems much easier for you to do things for them than it is to get them to do things for themselves. If you find yourself running around madly trying to get someone out of the preposterous messes he or she has stumbled into, that person is either your child or a Histrionic vampire. Or both.

Thinking in Superlatives

Histrionics prefer brightly colored emotional impressions to thought. Their world is made mostly of superlatives and hyperbole, so it is no wonder that they should elicit the same from you. You either love them or hate them, but you just can't ignore them.

Instant Rapport

Histrionics invented love at first sight. If they don't get you with their first impression, they probably won't get you at all.

Seeing the Person or Situation as Special

Histrionic vampires offer a devious and dirty deal. Here they are, attractive, exciting, and needy. It's easy to imagine that if you take care of a few trifling details for them, they will be sooo grateful that they will continue to shower you with attention and love. You might even believe you can pick up a relationship with a really attractive person at a bargain price, just by being a little nicer than all those other meanies.

Dream on. Ham-it-up vampires may be a lot of things, but they are never a bargain. Like all skilled hypnotists, they use your own hidden needs to control you. If you find yourself engaging in pleasant fantasies of rescue and eternal gratitude, wake up and rescue yourself.

Lack of Concern with Objective Information

If people you used to trust tell you that you are being played for a fool, and you think they're just jealous, hope that God will have mercy on your soul because the vampire won't.

Confusion

With Histrionics, the play's the thing, and you can't *not* play. Sometimes it's easy to see that you're being manipulated, but devilishly difficult to figure out what to do about it. Theater is the secret of Histrionic power and vulnerability. If you have to deal with a Ham-it-up Histrionic, your best defense is to write a role for yourself that keeps you at a safe distance. The only way to fight show business is with more show business.

WRITING A SAFE ROLE FOR YOURSELF

The closer you get to Ham-it-up Histrionics, the more dangerous they are.

If you become their main audience, you'll discover that the price for their performances is extremely high—your complete attention, and taking care of their every need. If you let them down even slightly, the script will shift from light comedy to horror. Unappreciated Histrionic vampires instantly explode into rage, sadness, or whatever it takes to regain the center of attention. You'll never know what got into them or what hit you.

Your best defense is not to get taken in by their performance in the first place. The way to do that is by writing a simple, easily understood role for yourself that puts you outside the sweep of Histrionic drama.

On the job, the simplest way to protect yourself is to play the role of a boring person who is all work and no fun. When you see a Ham-it-up vampire coming, conspicuously pay attention to the nearest computer screen or spreadsheet. It's kind of like not making eye contact with a panhandler. If you talk, stick to business. Turn yourself into one of the extras on the set, just doing your job and not worthy of notice. Your primitive brain may be screaming "notice me," but the rest of you will fare better for not listening. It may take a good deal of effort to stay in character, especially if you are a charming and friendly person yourself. Imagine being one of those stone-faced guards at Buckingham Palace.

ILLNESS AS THEATER

Histrionics have a limited amount of energy. The downside of their enthusiasm is a vague feeling of lassitude and general malaise when life gets too complicated. Trust their vivid imaginations and instinctive flair for the dramatic to turn not feeling like performing into a performance. Burned-out Ham-it-up vampires can change their life scripts to medical dramas when they discover how much attention they get for being sick. You can bet that their maladies will be as draining to you as they are to them. We will examine Histrionic illness in more detail in Chapter 9.

HISTRIONIC VAMPIRES AND MOTIVATION

Sex and medical drama are not the only commodities that Ham-it-up vampires offer. Wherever there is an audience, you'll find them. In the corporate world, they're drawn like moths to a flame by the eldritch cult that holds formless, transcendent enthusiasm to be the ultimate secret of life. They become its high priests and evangelists, motivational speakers.

Cleve Gower, vampire, former basketball player, and sports commentator, is already sweating beneath the hot lights of the convention center stage.

"I played against Chamberlain," Cleve thunders over the PA. "Wilt Chamberlain was my friend. A great athlete and an even greater human being. One day, Wilt Chamberlain and I were talking. 'Cleve,' he said, 'there are a lot of guys out there with talent. The ones that really make it are the guys with attitude.' "

*"Wilt Chamberlain lived what he preached. **He** had attitude. The question I'm here to ask today is if **you** have attitude." Cleve pauses for the question to sink in.*

*"It's like Wilt the Stilt said. "The ones who really make it are the guys with attitude. If **you** have attitude, no one is big enough to block your shot at excellence." There is a smattering of applause, but Cleve waves it away.*

"I wasn't born a successful athlete. I admit I had a little talent when I was growing up dirt poor in the slums of San Diego. That talent counted for absolutely nothing. Why? Because I had asthma. It was so serious that the doctor told my mother I wouldn't live to graduate from high school." Cleve nods gravely. "That's right; he said I wouldn't live through high school. But now that doctor is dead, and

here I am talking to you. Why? Because I had attitude!" The applause is louder this time. Cleve waves it away again.

*"I refused to believe that even asthma could hold me back. And that's why I'm here today. To tell you that **attitude is everything!"** Now the cheering starts.*

Motivational speakers retell the central heroic myth of sports and business: Attitude is everything. If you have the right attitude, anything is possible. The concept is indispensable for success, but it is metaphor and not literal fact. Attitude is not really everything. Training, ability, specific knowledge, and clear direction all count for something. In the minds of Histrionics, however, metaphors are always preferable to boring details. These vampires truly believe that being motivated enough to put on a good show can exempt them from having to pay attention to tedious day-to-day technicalities. It is a simple, comforting alternate reality, very easy to buy into, especially if your job involves the difficult and confusing task of managing other people. It's much easier to tell subordinates what they're supposed to feel than what they're supposed to do and how to do it.

Because of their enthusiasm, team spirit, and ability to make great presentations, Ham-it-up Histrionics can be promoted beyond their level of competence, into management. Management is hard work that requires a good deal of specific communication and attention to detail, neither of which is a particular strength of Histrionics. As managers, they often prefer to gloss over the particulars in favor of trying to instill motivation.

At the 7:30 Monday morning pep rally, Vampire Gene is, as usual, playing a motivational tape. Today it's Cleve Gower, one of his favorites. Every time the speaker makes a good point, Gene writes it on the electronic blackboard. In quotes and underlined. At the end of the meeting each member of the team will get a printout.

The tape is over and Gene is talking. "Continuous Quality Improvement is the way we become a full-time, customer-driven, learning organization. Creativity! Flexibility! Always on the lookout for ways to do more with less. Improving our already excellent customer service, while improving our sales performance with self-monitored goals."

Steve holds up his hand. "How much improvement, exactly?"

"No more than we can handle, big guy," Gene answers. "If we just learn to work smarter instead of harder."

> *Jamal chimes in. "But how much smarter are we talking about?"*
>
> *"I'll be honest with you," Gene says, shaking his head. "Corpo-rate doesn't think you can do it. They said it was way too—what did they call it—ambitious."*
>
> *Get to the point, already, Gwen thinks. She lets out a sigh and raises her hand. "I assume there is an actual amount—"*
>
> *"You know, that could be the problem right there," Gene says. He gets up and writes the word ASSUME on the board, then draws lines on either side of the U, so that it reads ASS/U/ME. "When you assume, you make an ASS out of U and ME."*

Ham-it-up managers like Gene make metaphors come to life and walk cor-porate hallways like an army of cheerful, highly motivated zombies. These vampires drain their employees of the ability to think for themselves by labeling critical comments as evidence of a bad attitude. They are also likely to withhold controversial information for fear of demotivating people.

Gene's style is fairly typical of the male theatrical Histrionic. He loves to share motivational homilies, sports talk, and incessant jokes, many of which are off-color.

His world is simple, being made up of good guys who can do their jobs without requiring much from Gene besides pep talks and an occasional attaboy. Bad guys are bad listeners. They don't laugh at jokes, and they ask too many embarrassing questions. Gwen is just about to cross the line into bad-guy territory.

Histrionic vampires think you're wonderful until they think you're ter-rible. Then the battle begins. Usually the fighting doesn't involve direct con-frontations, at least not at first. Perhaps Gwen will find a few extra motivational tracts in her mailbox. If she doesn't get the message, there will be gossip and snide comments about how difficult she is. Gene will write a role for her as a troublemaker, then trick her into playing it in front of an audience. One well-timed sexist comment ought to do the trick. All she has to do to fall into the trap is lose her cool.

Battles with Hams must be fought on stage. The only way Gwen can win is by creating a new role for herself, neither good guy nor bad guy. The role of fiscal conservative might work well. She can present herself as single-mindedly devoted to the bottom line. Gene may even answer a few ques-tions if he thinks they're directed at making money for the company. The more numbers Gwen throws around, the better. Histrionic vampires usually hate math worse than holy water. If Gwen plays it right, she can demonstrate her motivation in a way that Gene can't criticize—because he doesn't understand it. The worst he can do is call her a boring old bean counter. He is likely to leave her alone, or maybe even rely on her skill in his area of ignorance.

THE 10 ELEMENTS OF VAMPIRE FIGHTING STRATEGY: HOW TO KEEP FROM JOINING THE CAST
Step out of vampire Hams' never-ending drama with a new script.

1. KNOW THEM, KNOW THEIR HISTORY, AND KNOW YOUR GOAL

Ham-it-up Histrionics are usually ridiculously easy to spot. They're right at the center of attention. Look for sexual stereotypes; listen for jokes, juicy gossip, mindless effervescence, motivational talks, or maybe even heart-rending sobs.

If you ask other people about these vampires, you'll hear many different and contradictory stories. This is because they are, each of them, many different and contradictory people.

Your goal with Ham-it-up Histrionics is to keep from being drawn into their drama. This is difficult. At first, they'll treat you as if you were the most wonderful person on earth. They may compare you with other people who have been mean, cruel, unappreciative, unmotivated, or whatever. Let the fact that their world is filled with good guys and bad guys alert you before you step into their fantasy. If you let them down, you can easily be transferred from one group to the other.

If you pass up the flattery, you can avoid emotional turmoil later on. Your best bet is to write yourself a role that allows you to stand on the sidelines and just watch the show. Avoid the impulse to become a critic, because sooner or later, that will turn the spotlight on you.

Ham-it-up Histrionics are outrageous. If you allow yourself to be outraged, you will be the one who gets drained.

If you are involved with a Ham-it-up Histrionic, expect to provide a great deal of maintenance for an occasional great performance. If you expect consistency or reciprocity, you will only get a headache, either in the vampire's head or in yours. The effects will be pretty much the same.

Histrionic vampires of both sexes invite sexual harassment and sexual harassment suits. Think long and hard before you embark on either of these paths. Ham-it-up vampires sometimes give their greatest performances on the witness stand.

2. GET OUTSIDE VERIFICATION

Histrionics prefer to give their emotional impressions of events rather than facts. Their stories are interesting and entertaining, but very short on accurate information, and often quite biased. They expect you to believe them, and will regard it as a slight if you don't. Risk their displeasure by asking someone else's opinion. You'll be glad you did. Remember the rule about not letting a vampire be your source of information.

3. DO WHAT THEY DON'T

Be boring. Be consistent. Plan ahead. Let the facts rather than your emotions determine your response. Learn to keep your mind open and your mouth shut.

4. PAY ATTENTION TO ACTIONS, NOT WORDS

As with all vampires, you have to hold Histrionics responsible for what they do rather than what they say. With Ham-it-up vampires, the do and say distinction begins with listening to the actual content of their words. These vampires seldom lie, but they seldom tell the whole truth, except when it slips out between the lines.

Pay attention to detail. Ask questions to determine the who, what, when, where, and why of situations before assuming you know what's going on.

5. IDENTIFY HYPNOTIC STRATEGY

With Histrionics, it may be more productive to identify what *isn't* a hypnotic strategy. Whatever you want, that's what they are. Even they believe it. Histrionics are blatantly seductive, though it's not always clear who is seducing whom for what purpose.

One thing is sure: If you forget to pay attention to the warning signs of hypnosis, you'll be the one getting screwed.

6. PICK YOUR BATTLES

Always remember that the battle to win with Ham-it-up vampires is the one to avoid being cast as the person whose emotions are drained. They can drain you by wearing you out with their endless dependency or, just as surely, by making you angry at them.

You have to decide when Ham-it-up vampires' erratic and sometimes obnoxious dramatics cross the line and require retaliatory action. If you are going to fight back, be sure that you've got your own act together.

Never take action when you're angry. Histrionics will perform far better in the heat of any moment than you will. Plan carefully, and check out your ideas with other people before you say something that you'll regret.

The most thankless task you can possibly take on is trying to explain Histrionics to themselves. Ham-it-up vampires are quite unaware of their own motivations even when everybody else sees them clearly. You'll be astounded at how much they can ignore. You won't believe that they can't see how obvious their manipulations are. Spare yourself an enormous amount of trouble by remembering Histrionics really *are unaware of what they are doing and why they are doing it.* They invented denial.

Not only do Histrionics not understand themselves; they don't have a clue why anyone does anything. Their understanding of psychology and physics is often tinged with magic. They may believe that things happen because of the alignment of stars, the vibrations of crystals, or the intervention of guardian angels. If you suggest otherwise, they'll just think you're crazy.

Speaking of crazy, the last thing you want to do is engage a Histrionic in a battle over dress code.

7. LET CONTINGENCIES DO THE WORK

The best kinds of behavior control programs for Ham-it-up vampires are the same ones that work for obstreperous children. Be as clear as possible about the exact behaviors you want to see, and structure all contingencies so that vampire Hams get more attention for doing things right than they do for doing them wrong.

Histrionics have chronic problems with day-to-day tasks. They forget to pay bills, run errands, or do enough advance planning to get anywhere on time. There is no record of a Ham-it-up Histrionic ever having balanced a checkbook. It will seem easier to do for them rather than making them do for themselves. Indeed, the implicit deal they try to make is that performing should exempt them from all other duties.

To get Ham-it-up vampires to do anything they find unpleasant, you'll have to set strict limits and stick by them in the face of all manner of dramatic distractions. Never let performances of any sort get Histrionic vampires out of their responsibilities.

That's the theory, anyway. In practice, consistency with Ham-it-up vampires is almost impossible. Sometimes they'll just wear you out. They can put on a two-hour performance to get out of a five-minute task.

All contingencies should revolve around things Ham-it-up vampires are supposed to do, rather than how they're supposed to act around other people. You won't get very far with rules about flirting, off-color jokes, or other annoying behaviors because Ham-it-up Histrionics are constitutionally unable to see their own behavior as anything but charming and appropriate. That's why educational seminars on sexual harassment and cultural sensitivity seldom work on the worst offenders.

You'll get further by using Histrionics' acting ability to direct them toward more productive roles. If you give them a sexual harassment lecture, they may ask, "What do you want me to do, act like some kind of saint or something?

Say, "Yes, exactly."

The very best contingency with Ham-it-up vampires is to sneak up on them when they're being good and praise the hell out of them.

8. CHOOSE YOUR WORDS AS CAREFULLY AS YOU PICK YOUR BATTLES

This one is simple. If you want to get anywhere with Ham-it-up Histrionics, use praise and flattery in sugared doses that would put a normal person into diabetic coma. Regular praise for even the smallest of accomplishments is the only thing that keeps Ham-it-up Histrionics anywhere near copacetic.

Don't waste your breath on criticism of any sort. Histrionics will always believe that the problem is with your perception rather than their behavior.

Anyway, if you remember the praise, you can pretty much forget about everything else.

9. IGNORE TANTRUMS

If you criticize or forget the praise, there will be tantrums. Their forms will be as wild and various as the vampires who throw them. Ham-it-up Histrionics use emotional outbursts in the same way Afghan rebels use Kalishnikovs as weapons and threats, or simply as expressions of general exuberance.

Tears, however, are the Histrionic's specialty.

For a civilized human being, another person's pain requires action. It is almost impossible to watch others cry and do nothing to make them feel better—even when you know they're using tears to get around the rules.

To handle manipulative crying, use an old therapist's trick. Don't let the tears or the reason they're falling become the subject for discussion. When vampires cry, hand them a tissue and go on with whatever you were talking about. This technique takes practice, but it works.

10. KNOW YOUR OWN LIMITS

However much attention you have to give, Histrionics will need it all. They will draw it out of you at first with flattery. They put you in a special category all by yourself. Usually, the last thing you hear before Histrionic vampires start draining away your life force is, "You're the only person I can talk to."

Ham-it-up Histrionics do have useful talents and abilities. They can be good and entertaining friends and productive workers, especially when the job requires being dramatic and engaging. Histrionics can blossom, but they require as much care as a rare and beautiful orchid. Only you can decide how much a flower is worth.

9 Passive-Aggressive Vampires

**Deliver us from ghoulies and ghosties and people
who are only trying to help.**

Passive-Aggressive vampires hunger for approval. If you ask them, they're always doing what they're supposed to do, thinking what they're supposed to think, and feeling what they're supposed to feel. They're relentlessly obedient, cheerful, thrifty, brave, clean, and reverent. At least in their own estimation. You may wonder how such nice people could create problems for anyone. The answer, stated simply, is: What they don't know can hurt you.

What these aggressively nice vampires don't know is how real people operate. Like all Histrionics, Passive-Aggressives create a role for themselves and then become lost in it. Unlike their flamboyant Ham-it-up cousins, the role these vampires create is more internal than external. In their minds, they are good children—innocent, happy, eager to please, and always willing to do more than their share.

Real people are complex, full of base motivations and unacceptable desires as well as the stuff of angels. Passive-Aggressive Histrionics have the frightening capacity to deny any but the most superficial and attractive thoughts. They blithely ignore the ugly stuff even if it's plainly visible to everyone else. Histrionics are not perfectionists, they're more like perfectionist wannabes. They don't necessarily want to be perfect; they just want to *look* perfect. It is as if they are trying to be Barbie and Ken, without realizing that their role models are nothing but plastic dolls.

Since the role they're trying to play is impossible, no wonder they keep stepping out of character.

Vampire Meredith steps up to the counter to order her coffee. She eyes the double-fudge brownies in the case, but virtuously passes them up in favor of a container of yogurt. She makes quite a show of checking the nutritional labels. "Oh, look," she says. "This one is only 120 calories!"

"Come on, Meredith, live a little," Erin says. "Get one of these brownies. They're great!"

"Yeah right," Meredith says. "If I even like smell one of those, it goes right to my hips." She pats her rather ample derriere.

As Meredith sits down with her yogurt and nonfat latte, Erin shakes her head. "You've got more willpower than I do. I'd die without my daily chocolate fix."

Meredith shrugs. "It's like so not hard once you get used to it. I haven't had chocolate in such a long time, I hardly even remember what it tastes like."

"You're incredible," Erin says as she takes another bite of her brownie.

On the way home, Erin passes the coffee shop. Inside, she sees Meredith pointing at the double-fudge brownies in the case. The counter guy takes out four, bags them up, and hands them to her.

Erin, excited about catching her friend in the act of being human, hurries in and sneaks up behind Meredith. "If you give me one of those brownies, I won't tell anybody I saw you here," she says, giggling.

Meredith turns slowly. Her eyes seem unfocused. She looks at Erin for a second or two before appearing to recognize her. "Hi," she says. "I was just getting some brownies for my niece."

"Oh, okay," Erin says, feeling embarrassed. As she hurries out to catch her bus, she seems to remember Meredith saying that her niece lived in Chicago.

Erin thought she saw a regular person succumbing to the urge for a little illicit chocolate. To her, there was nothing unusual about it. She occasionally binges on brownies herself and jokes about it later. What Erin actually saw was a Histrionic vampire stepping out of her perfect role while hypnotizing herself to believe that she was still in it.

Meredith is operating as two people at the same time: as a person of exemplary willpower who always follows her diet, and as a regular person who occasionally binges on brownies. The one with willpower is the one she sees as herself. The other one she hardly sees at all.

This kind of splitting of the personality is the hallmark of Passive-Aggressive Histrionics. Please don't call it "schizophrenic." Schizophrenia is a biochemical psychotic disorder in which the splitting is from reality. Histrionics are the people who divide their personalities into acceptable and unacceptable parts, then do their best to ignore the unacceptable.

All vampires use self-hypnosis to avoid seeing themselves as they really are, but Histrionics are virtuosos of self-deception. Like stage magicians, they divert their own awareness away from the strings and wires that hold their personalities together. They simply do not see anything in themselves that they consider inappropriate or unlovable. Their image of themselves is like a series of attractive still photos, scenes from a movie with no overall plot to hold them together.

The real problem is not with brownies and diets. Had Erin pressed, Meredith would probably have admitted that the chocolate was for her. There are other things Meredith would be far less likely to recognize. At the top of the list are the aggressive impulses that such a confrontation would evoke.

To a psychologist, *aggression* refers to a continuum of thoughts and actions that have to do with imposing your own will onto the world. At one end is angry, assaultive behavior; at the other are simple attempts to act in your own self-interest and get your own way. Histrionics, who accept only the loving and giving in themselves, reject the whole continuum. They prefer to believe that they live their lives for others and never put themselves first. Many of them have problems acknowledging their sexual impulses as well.

The problem is that all people, Histrionic vampires included, are biologically hardwired for sex and aggression. We all want things for ourselves that may be embarrassing or inappropriate. Normal people recognize that they can't act on their impulses. Passive-Aggressive Histrionics try to believe that they have no inappropriate impulses to act on. This is what makes them dangerous.

Back to Meredith and Erin. At work, most people like Meredith, but they see her as a bit ding-y. They call her "Little Miss Perfect," knowing full well that she is neither little nor perfect. To Erin, catching Meredith *flagrante delicto* with a bag of brownies is wonderful material to share at coffee break. In a day or two the brownie story is all over the office. In a week it's forgotten, by everyone but Meredith.

Inside, Meredith feels hurt, misunderstood, betrayed, and angry, but she can't acknowledge these feelings even to herself, much less to Erin.

Not being aware of her anger doesn't stop Meredith from acting on it. Suddenly, she begins to realize that Erin is not really such a nice person. Meredith likes her and all, but she is a bit hypercritical and, well, bitchy. *Everybody* says so—especially a few disgruntled employees in Erin's department with whom Meredith finds herself spending more and more time.

Eventually, Meredith tries to help Erin by telling her in a very nice way that a lot of people don't like her. Not only does Erin not listen, she actually gets mad!

Meredith is frantic. The only person she can go to is Jane, the department manager.

"Knock, knock." Meredith taps tentatively on the fabric of Jane's cubicle. "Do you have a minute? I really need to ask you a question."

"Sure, come on in," Jane says.

Meredith sits down and opens her planner so she can take notes. "I need some ideas about how to work with Erin. I'm absolutely at my wit's end."

Jane waits a minute to see if there's more to the question. Apparently not. "Did something specific happen to make you feel that way?"

"It's just, well, everything. Since she came here, there's always been something. I mean I really like her as a person and all, but she's just so totally unpredictable. You never know when she's going to bite your head off for some little comment."

"Did you get into an argument with her?"

"I don't know if you could call it an argument. I mean, she was the one yelling. I was like just standing there with my mouth hanging open." Meredith demonstrates the astonished expression she wore at the time.

"Was there something in particular that Erin was upset about?"

"She said I was trying to undermine her authority." Meredith does her astonished face again. "Can you believe that? It is so not-like-me to try to undermine anybody. I was only trying to help."

"How were you trying to help?"

"I just told her that some of the people in her department were going on stress leave because they can't take her management style."

"Really? Who's going on stress leave?"

*"Well, nobody right now, but a lot of people are thinking about it. They come to me because they're afraid to talk to her. I just told Erin about it so she could maybe talk to them or something, but instead she went completely **ballistic**."*

Under the guise of being helpful and standing up for the poor underdogs who are too frightened to speak for themselves, Meredith mounts a Passive-Aggressive assault on Erin. There's a good possibility that everyone in the unit may be hurt as a result of a stupid bag of brownies.

GIVING UNTIL IT HURTS

Passive-Aggressive Histrionics love giving. Most of it is truly sincere, but some crosses the line into manipulation. They believe that the Golden Rule is a binding contract: If they do unto others, others are supposed to do back.

Everybody takes. Some people ask you for what they want. Passive-Aggressive vampires are more apt to give and give until you finally get the idea they want something. If you don't get the message, they'll keep on until they make themselves sick and make you sick of them. But, in their own minds at least, their accounts payable look great. Everybody wants something, and everybody gets angry at not getting it. This is a law of nature, but Passive-Aggressives keep thinking they can break it.

Many Histrionics also believe that the more you deny yourself, the better you are as a person. Viewed in this context, anorexia nervosa is the height of nobility.

Histrionics are also frustrated and angry. Not that they would admit it. They will, however, point out the well-documented fact that they do for everybody else, but nobody even listens to them. All they can do is keep giving, suffer in silence, and throw more fuel on the subterranean fires that keep them burning with resentment.

This pattern of pathological giving, though not specific to women by any means, does correspond to what has been expected of females throughout thousands of years of male domination. Pathological giving may also be the result of the mind-warping influences of a dysfunctional family. As always, however, knowing where a problem comes from is not the same as solving it.

It is possible to consider Passive-Aggressive vampires as victims of forces beyond their control. That's probably how they see themselves, and that in itself is a big part of the problem. Another law of nature is that victims victimize.

ILLNESS AS METAPHOR

Vampire Allison stands at Jim's doorway. "You wanted to see me?"

"Yes, I did," Jim says, already beginning to feel the blood pounding in his temples. He doesn't care for confrontations with employees, even when the issues are clear and indisputable. Far worse to have to talk to Allison about all the time she's missing because of one vague health complaint after another. Not that he thinks she's faking or anything, but Jim just can't see how one person can suffer so much unusual illness at so many inopportune times.

As Allison sits down, her eyes well up with tears. "I'm sorry," she sobs.

For a minute, Jim dares to hope. Maybe she finally understands how difficult her incessant illnesses have been for the whole department.

"The doctor called today," she says, as she pulls a crumpled tissue from the pocket of her sweater. "I have to have exploratory surgery. He thinks it could be—well, serious."

The chances are very good that Allison's surgery will discover nothing unequivocal. The sickness in her body is, at least partly, an expression of the tumult of unacknowledged hostile impulses in her mind. An Antisocial might tell you to take your job and shove it; a Passive-Aggressive Histrionic will say she loves the job, but make a show of being too sick to do it.

In addition to being medical phenomena, Histrionic illnesses are a form of self-expression. They are metaphors for what Histrionics feel about themselves and their world. These vampires feel confused and overwhelmed; therefore their disorders are confusing and overwhelming to the Histrionics themselves, and to the people who have to treat them. Even more distressing is having to live and work with sick Histrionics.

Histrionics favor vague maladies that are as debilitating as they are hard to diagnose. Allergies are big, as are all forms of gastrointestinal disorder. Also popular are designer diseases, like hypoglycemia and malevolent yeasts.

Let me make this perfectly clear: *Histrionics' ailments are not all in their heads.* No self-respecting Passive-Aggressive Histrionics would *ever* fake an illness. They really are sick. How they get sick is the unanswerable question. Viruses may stalk them when their immune systems are down, or perhaps they use unconscious self-hypnosis to unbalance the chemistry of their own bodies and brains.

Many Histrionic disorders are psychological, ranging from agitated depression to delayed posttraumatic stress. The symptoms are usually pervasive, confusing, and frustratingly sporadic. Some of the psychological epidemics of the 1980s, especially recovered memories of sexual abuse and multiple personality, may have been the result of mistaking Histrionic metaphors for actual reality. These disorders do exist, but not in the vast numbers diagnosed at the height of the "me" decade.

PASSIVE-AGGRESSIVE HYPNOSIS

Passive-Aggressives can cloud minds better than the Shadow in the old radio program. The only trouble is it's their own minds that they cloud. They create an alternate reality in which they are admired and loved by one and all because they never need anything for themselves, and they never, ever do anything bad. The logical contortions they go through to maintain this illusion are enough to make anybody's eyes glaze over.

If you listen closely to them, you'll find yourself entering another dimension, where everything is entertaining, but nothing makes much sense—*Alice in Wonderland* is a fairly realistic portrayal of a Histrionic's world.

People react differently to Passive-Aggressive hypnosis. Some are enchanted enough to want to rescue the poor waifs; others get a pounding headache. Everybody gets drained, especially the poor souls who keep trying to get Histrionics to admit that they really are angry.

PASSIVE-AGGRESSIVE BEHAVIOR IN RELATIONSHIPS

Think for a minute of the many subtle ways that a person close to you can signal that he or she is irritated. Sniffing, snorting, sighing, eye rolling, choosing words and phrases that imply criticism, or even saying nothing at all. The list is endless, and Passive-Aggressive vampires use everything on it to clobber unsuspecting friends, lovers, and family members. The most common pattern goes something like this:

Vampire:	*(Snorts, sniffs, or whatever.)*
Victim:	*What's wrong?*
Vampire:	*Nothing.*
Victim:	*What do you mean "nothing"? Whenever you make that sound, you're upset about something. So tell me, what's wrong?"*
Vampire:	*Nothing.*
Victim:	*(Growing agitated) You always do this. You snort and sniff and make faces, then say nothing's wrong. I know something is bothering you, so why don't you just tell me what it is?*
Vampire:	*(In a voice tinged with ice) I said nothing is wrong.*
Victim:	*(Shouting) I know something's wrong! I demand that you tell me what it is instead of doing what you always do, just sitting there making faces and saying nothing's wrong!*
Vampire:	*You really need to get control of your temper.*

Now look at the way to handle this kind of subtle attack.

Vampire:	*(Snorts, sniffs, or whatever.)*
Victim:	*What's wrong?*
Vampire:	*Nothing.*
Victim:	*Oh, okay. (Goes to another part of the house.)*

A relationship with a Passive-Aggressive vampire can be draining and difficult, a perpetual battle of the inarticulate against the indirect.

THE HIGH SELF-ESTEEM SYNDROME

Mary Wollstonecraft Shelley wrote a book about a sad and unintentionally dangerous creature sewn together from mismatched bits and pieces. She could have been describing another kind of monster created of the scraps of late twentieth-century pop psychology—the person with high self-esteem.

Self-esteem used to be the effect of success, but somehow it evolved into a cause for failure. Over the past 40 years, most human problems have been ascribed to the pernicious forces of low self-esteem. Self-esteem is taught in school, and people are advised to repeat affirmations under the assumption that raw good feeling can be shaped into any sort of achievement.

Self-esteem now seems to be regarded as an end unto itself, the prime mover of the human mind, like motivation in the world of business. There is a logical flaw in this concept: Anything that explains everything also explains nothing. The worst problem, however, is that many approaches to improving self-esteem are unwittingly teaching people to be more like Passive-Aggressive Histrionics.

The basic idea is to improve self-esteem by accentuating the positive and eliminating the negative, which is fine in theory. The only difficulty is that the negative isn't eliminated; it's merely plastered over with affirmations and often projected onto other people. It has become fashionable to see low self-esteem as the result of some form of abuse. People are supposed to get better by bringing their resentments out into the open. Everybody is loved and affirmed, except for abusers, and anything that makes good people feel bad is defined as abuse.

What's missing in this popular approach to psychology is the same thing that is missing in all Histrionic creations—namely, an attempt to go below the surface and deal with the self in all its complexity. The human psyche is constantly aswirl with contradictory thoughts and impulses. The great challenge we all face is to understand that roiling mass of instinct and emotion and organize it into moral and productive behavior.

Even if my concerns about popular psychology are prejudiced and unfounded, there are still problems with the idea of making people better and more successful by raising their self-esteem. As we'll see in the next chapter, on Narcissistic vampires, high self-esteem itself can be a destructive force.

THE 10 ELEMENTS OF VAMPIRE FIGHTING STRATEGY:
ENDURING THE TERRIBLE MEEK
Don't get mad at Passive-Aggressives.

1. KNOW THEM, KNOW THEIR HISTORY, AND KNOW YOUR GOAL

This chapter has attempted to describe the psychology of Passive-Aggressive Histrionics so you can recognize them by the underlying pattern of concealing their unacceptable impulses from themselves. The specific forms of concealment vary, changing according to whatever innocent, blameless role they're playing.

Often these vampires have a history of interpersonal problems that, according to them, come out of nowhere to plague them. Their world is two-dimensional, full of villains and victims. In an interview they will usually tell you about personality conflicts in their previous job. On a first date they will tell you about their last dysfunctional relationship because you're a nice person and will understand. Be warned. Nice person or not, in their next interview or on their next first date, they'll be saying the same things about you.

The more these hapless vampires like, respect, or fear you, the less able they are to say directly, "I'm angry" or "I don't want to do that." They have to rely on misunderstanding, forgetting, or falling apart to do the job for them. That's the way it is; accept it or pay the price. The most frequent cause of headaches is pursuing the one goal that is absolutely unattainable with Histrionic vampires—having them admit to their actual motives.

Even if Passive-Aggressives don't understand their motives, you should. Remember that they hunger for approval, and they cause the most trouble when they aren't getting it.

The most productive goal with these vampires is preventing their Passive-Aggressive outbursts by giving them the approval they want, but making it contingent on specific behaviors. Never let them guess what you want; the consequences are too great if they get it wrong. Tell Passive-Aggressives in explicit detail what it takes to please you and praise them profusely when they do it. The strategy is simple and almost foolproof, but it is seldom employed. It's hard to praise somebody who gives you headaches. Hard as it is, it's far easier than the alternative.

As long as they are getting explicit direction and plenty of praise for their successes, Passive-Aggressive vampires can perform most social tasks even better than normal people. They'll be caring friends, devoted lovers, and hardworking employees. They're happy to give and give as long as they're getting something back. But then it isn't giving, is it? Never mind. If you try to apply logic to the behavior of Passive-Aggressive Histrionics, you will always end up frustrated and confused. Instead, just love them and praise them. If you can't, stay away from them.

2. GET OUTSIDE VERIFICATION

Frustrated Passive-Aggressives will come to you with all kinds of stories about who said and did what to whom. It is important to remember that their perceptions are often distorted by their belief that they couldn't possibly do anything wrong. Histrionic tales may be dramatic and convincing, but you should never believe them without getting corroboration.

If they're out sick, require a doctor's note.

If Passive-Aggressive vampires tell you other people are upset with you, it means *they're* upset. The way these vampires ask for anything is by telling you that somebody else wants it.

If you're a manager, and Passive-Aggressives come to you reporting discord in their department, proceed carefully, especially if there are complaints about you. Don't make the mistake of thinking that just because these vampires overreact there is no validity in what they say. They are quite sensitive to what upsets people, and often they will be the first to tell you about real problems. Accept their inevitable assertion that *they* don't believe what people are saying, that they're just sharing it with you to be helpful.

If you charge in and demand that people tell you directly if they have any problems with you, they'll say you're wonderful. Passive-Aggressive or not, most people know enough to tell authority figures what they want to hear. If you want to know what people really think about you, ask general questions about what would make the office run better and listen between the lines. If the situation is sensitive, you might want to hire a professional consultant to go in and find out what is really going on.

Dealing with Passive-Aggressive vampires will teach you an important truth about the human condition—you can never know what is really going on, because there is no such thing as an objective source. People will see the same events differently, according to their own needs. Verification is, in the end, always a judgment call.

3. DO WHAT THEY DON'T

Understand yourself and your own motivations, both acceptable and unacceptable. Always assume you are acting in your own self-interest, and know what you expect to get for what you give.

Be direct. Tell people what you expect to get. Make it very clear what you feel and what you want. If you're angry, say so. Don't try to disguise attacks as constructive criticism. Better yet, wait until you're over your anger before you approach the problems that Passive-Aggressive Histrionics cause. As with all vampires, you should think about what you want to happen rather than what's wrong with what's already happened. Let your goals determine your actions. Easy to say, hard to do.

4. PAY ATTENTION TO ACTIONS, NOT WORDS

The maddening thing about Passive-Aggressives is that their words are so different from their actions. If you ask them what they want, they'll say they want to make you happy, even as they do things to make you miserable.

On the surface, their actions make no sense, but there is an underlying logic. If you want to understand Histrionics, read their actions as if they were sad, angry adolescent poems about how the expectations of others are a prison from which they can never escape.

If you're involved with Passive-Aggressive Histrionics, you cannot avoid being perceived as the person who is imprisoning them. Don't try. Instead, focus on your own behavior, and try to be a compassionate jailer.

5. IDENTIFY HYPNOTIC STRATEGY

Passive-Aggressive vampires live in an alternate reality in which they are givers who never ask for anything in return. The bind they put you in is neat and inescapable if you don't recognize it in advance. They draw you in by guessing your needs and giving you more than you ask for, because they are such nice people. It looks like they're handing you a blank check, but it's really a credit card. You never get to see the bill, but you'll definitely find out when you've fallen behind in your payments. If you quibble then, you're the ungrateful bad guy.

The only way out is to refrain from using the emotional credit cards that Passive-Aggressives are only too happy to offer. Always pay in cash. Return favor for favor and never run up a tab.

6. PICK YOUR BATTLES

Forget any attempt to make Passive-Aggressive vampires admit to what they really feel. It'll only make your headache worse. Don't make the mistake of demanding that they talk to you directly about problems. You might as well demand that they speak in rhyming couplets.

There really are no battles you can win with the Passive-Aggressive. Once the situation turns into a battle, you have already lost.

The battles you can win are all with yourself. Dealing with Passive-Aggressive Histrionics requires you to go beyond your own conceptions of how things ought to be done. This can be especially helpful if you are a manager.

With regular attention, Passive-Aggressive Histrionics can become exemplary employees. They are more likely to become problems, however, because the tactics required to keep them performing well are incompatible with many corporate cultures.

Success in the business world is often determined by the ability to discern and live by political rules that nobody ever specifically states. Passive-Aggressive Histrionics are strikingly bad at figuring out the unwritten rules. Unless you tell them otherwise, they will assume that what is written describes the way things actually are. For example, they might believe that management decisions are based on the corporate mission statement, or that their job descriptions define what they are and are not supposed to do. Punishment for this kind of political naivete is usually swift and, in the eyes of Histrionic vampires, totally unfair. They will retaliate by causing headaches for everyone. They may even call the friendly folks at the local regulatory agency.

To make good employees out of Passive-Aggressives, you have to step out of the confines of corporate culture and explain to people how things are really done. Once you take on that battle, you can gain something of lasting value if you win.

7. LET CONTINGENCIES DO THE WORK

At work or in relationships, Passive-Aggressive vampires want to be rated *excellent* on all performance reviews. You can use their powerful need for approval to teach them how to be less Passive-Aggressive. Here are some suggestions.

Always Pay Attention. If you ignore a creature whose major goal in life is to get your attention, there will be consequences. Remember, you aren't the only one using contingencies. Headaches are powerful tools for modifying your behavior. You'll get them if you forget to notice all the wonderful, helpful things the Passive-Aggressive vampire is doing.

Make Contingencies Explicit. Passive-Aggressive vampires want to please you, and hope that you'll please them in return. If you don't specify clearly what you want, these vampires will give you what they think you ought to want and expect you to shower them with what they want in return. If you value your sanity, never accept this sort of implicit deal, no matter how good it looks on the surface. If you take, you will pay, believe me. Your life and the vampire's will be much easier if nobody has to guess.

If you live or work with Passive-Aggressive Histrionics, you want them to do what they're supposed to do, and not feel criticized and abused. At least not enough to retaliate. To accomplish this formidable goal, you and the vampire have to relate on the basis of clear, explicit expectations rather than any sort of unspoken agreements. No matter how innocently they are offered, never take gifts from vampires without paying for them up front.

Always Give Lots of Positive Feedback. Explicit instructions, while absolutely necessary will not work as well as you think they ought. Passive-Aggressive vampires deal with the world by misunderstanding and by being misunderstood. The thing they never misunderstand is praise. Use gobs of it.

Ignore Irrelevancies. Passive-Aggressive vampires will always do whatever you pay most attention to. If you make a big deal out of forgetting, complaining, surliness, negative body language, or whatever, that's what you'll get. With Passive-Aggressives it is possible to waste considerable time and effort trying to get them to improve their attitude rather than getting the job done. Make sure your contingencies favor the behaviors you really want rather than the ones you find most annoying. What's the point in rewarding people for giving you headaches?

Avoid Punishment, Because It Never Works. Berating Passive-Aggressive vampires will make the situation worse, because they'll have more reason to fear you or get back at you. Criticism of any sort will elicit explanations rather than behavior change. If you try to induce guilt, you'll trigger an equal amount of resentment.

If there need to be negative consequences for breaking rules, the kind that work best are called *response costs*. They aren't punishments; they're more like raising the price of messing up. If people forget to do something or do it incorrectly, make them do it over, especially when it would be easier to do it yourself. Creative practitioners may raise the price of misbehavior still further by adding paperwork—incident reports, remediation plans for absences, or whatever else they can think up. The emphasis is on think. Response costs created in anger do more avenging than teaching.

With Passive-Aggressive vampires, it works better to tailor your strategy to fit their particular dynamics. Since many Histrionic behaviors are attempts to avoid confrontation, make Passive-Aggressives deal directly with the people they attack. Don't just tell them to do it, because they won't. Instead, call a meeting of the accuser and the accused to discuss the charges. Always demand objective evidence, but never make judgments; the meetings are a consequence, not a trial.

For all passive-aggressive behaviors, prevention is the best strategy. We have been through this before, but it's important enough to mention again. Most passive-aggressive people, vampires or not, feel chronically underappreciated. They need more praise than other people. Figure at least four times what you'd need (more if you're particularly macho).

Be Consistent. If the contingencies you set don't apply to everyone, all the time, they don't apply to anyone, any time.

Be Sensitive. If you discover the cause of hidden hostility, don't rub a Passive-Aggressive's nose in it. Instead, offer a positive way to resolve the problem. All these vampires really want is your approval.

8. CHOOSE YOUR WORDS AS CAREFULLY AS YOU PICK YOUR BATTLES

Telling Passive-Aggressives what they're doing and why it's wrong always makes the situation worse. Many people will assume that they just haven't explained the situation well enough, so they will go through it again, this time in more detail. Engineers and other left-brain types are particularly likely to persist in this kind of error. Their careful efforts get them nothing but bigger headaches.

Dealing effectively with Passive-Aggressive vampires is often a matter of semantics. Your words must reflect an understanding of their view of the world, rather than demanding that they accept yours. These vampires live in an alternate reality where their thoughts are pure, their motives are selfless, and all their mistakes are caused by misinterpretation. That is where you must go to have any meaningful communication with them.

Phrase everything in a way that doesn't assault their view of reality. Instead of criticizing, acknowledge that Passive-Aggressives were doing their best, then let them know how to do better. Don't even think of talking to them when you're angry. They'll see it as verbal abuse.

They will do better if you phrase instructions as a personal request for their help, and specify what you're willing to do to reciprocate. Forget about explaining; just ask and pay up.

If Passive-Aggressive vampires seem angry and you want to know why, you'll get more information by approaching the situation indirectly. Ask them what other people might be concerned about. Always use emotionally neutral words like *upset* or *concerned* to describe the emotional state. Passive-Aggressives will usually be only too happy to tell you the kinds of things that may be bothering somebody else. If they have a chance to voice their concerns, however indirectly, they may have less need to act out.

9. IGNORE TANTRUMS

Passive-Aggressive Histrionics throw passive tantrums. When they're upset with you, they show it by getting sick, misunderstanding your instructions, or talking about you to somebody else. If you get angry, they'll see you as an abuser and feel justified in taking further retaliatory action. In the short run it seems easier not to deal with them at all and just do whatever they were supposed to do yourself. Big mistake.

One of the reasons these vampires are so difficult is that most people deal with their passive tantrums passively, by absolving them of their responsibilities. This approach ensures that the next time there is something difficult to be done, Histrionics will again handle it by not being able to handle it.

Not only do these vampires escape the anxiety of doing something directly aggressive, they also get out of lots of unpleasant tasks. The technical term for this added benefit is *secondary gain*. It makes Histrionic behaviors particularly hard to change. Freud realized this, and you will too unless you set up contingencies in advance and stick with them consistently, no matter what creative challenges Passive-Aggressive vampires may throw at you.

10. KNOW YOUR OWN LIMITS

If you can't control your own temper, you should never even attempt to deal with Passive-Aggressive Histrionics. They'll make you hate them and yourself. If you feel angry at one of these vampires, walk away and cool down before you commit yourself to an action you'll regret.

Passive-Aggressive vampires cause far more trouble than they should. Their dynamics are simple, and they respond well to praise and attention. The problem is that their annoying behavior can distract you into fighting with them when the really important battles are with yourself.

THERAPY FOR HISTRIONIC VAMPIRES

What should you do if you see signs of Histrionic behavior in yourself or someone you care about? This section is a thumbnail sketch of the sorts of self-help and professional therapeutic approaches that might be beneficial. Always remember that attempting psychotherapy on someone you know will make you both sicker.

THE GOAL

The most important goal for Histrionics is to learn to take care of themselves rather than using their charm, devotion, or neediness to get other people to take care of them. They should also work on recognizing and expressing their negative emotions consciously. This usually requires the help of a professional.

PROFESSIONAL HELP

Histrionics profit from an approach that emphasizes thinking rather than aimless recounting of unconnected feelings. Many New Age approaches make Histrionics feel better by not requiring them to change a single thing about their wonderful selves. Consider therapy of this sort like going to a day spa. Calming, but very temporary.

More than any other kind of Emotional Vampires, Histrionics can benefit from an examination of their past. The focus should be on recognizing continuity in their own thoughts, feelings, and choices, rather than on cataloging the things that others have done to them.

SELF-HELP

If you recognize Histrionic tendencies in yourself, the following exercises will be very difficult for you, but they will make a difference.

Let Your Thoughts Be Your Guide. First, learn to recognize the difference between what you *think* and what you *feel.* Try to make more choices based on thinking.

Do Things for Yourself and by Yourself. Try it. You may come to like your own company.

Ask for What You Want. Everybody takes; it's a law of nature that no amount of good intentions can repeal. It's far better to be aware of what you want and ask other people to give it to you. It's not selfish if you say *please* and *thank you.*

Openly Disagree With Somebody Every Day. Say it nicely, but say it.

Banish the Phrase I Don't Know *from Your Vocabulary.* Try not to space out when people ask you tough questions. The things you need most to think about are always the ones that are most difficult.

WHAT WILL HURT

Emotional Vampires tend to select therapeutic approaches that make them worse rather than better. Histrionics would prefer medical treatment for their aches and pains rather than any examination of psychological issues that may be causing them. If two doctors say the problem is psychological, check with a psychiatrist or psychologist before looking for further physical remedies.

Many Histrionics have been damaged by "abuse" therapies that list the sorts of symptoms victims should experience and the stages that they *must* go through to be healed. Histrionics will happily do whatever is expected, even if it destroys them and all their relationships except the one with their therapist.

Histrionics probably shouldn't be treated by counselors who have what they have, or do what they do, even if the counselors purport to be recovering from it. Fellow sufferers sometimes forget that real recovery means growing out of the need to have people depend on you the way you depended on *your* therapist.

3 Big Egos, Small Everywhere Else

The Narcissistic Types

At the other end of the alley, a figure materializes from the mist.

He moves closer. Moonlight shines on his bared canines.

You back up, only to hit a wall. The vampire flashes an unholy smile.

Then, all of a sudden, his cell phone rings. He holds up a finger, then reaches into his cape, pulls the phone out, and flips it open. "Talk to me," he says.

The vampire listens, then shakes his head. "Does it have to be now?" he says to the phone. "I was just going to have a little nosh. Okay; wait a minute."

The vampire looks at you with red, glowing eyes. Your breath catches in your throat.

"I've got a problem," the vampire says. "I'd like to bite you and all, but there's this big meeting I have to get to and I'm a little pressed for time. Here's 20 bucks. Could you run down to the blood bank and pick me up a pint?"

Narcissistic vampires have a disorder that is both psychological and cosmological. They believe the universe revolves around them. Unlike Antisocials, who are addicted to excitement, or Histrionics, who crave attention, Narcissistic vampires just want to live out their fantasies of being the smartest, most talented, and all-around best people in the world.

Some Narcissistic vampires turn out to be little more than legends in their own minds, but a surprising number are adept enough to turn some of their grandiose fantasies into reality. There may be narcissism without greatness, but there is no greatness without narcissism. One thing is certain, however: In the eyes of other people, these vampires are never so great as they consider themselves to be.

Considering themselves is what Narcissistic vampires do best. The trait they most conspicuously lack is concern for the needs, thoughts, and feelings of other people.

These vampires have tendencies in the direction of **Narcissistic personality disorder.** The name derives from Narcissus, a Greek youth who fell in love with his own reflection. To outsiders, it looks as if Narcissists are in love with themselves because they think they're better than other people. The actual relationship is a bit more complex.

More than loving themselves, Narcissists are absorbed with themselves. They feel their own desires so acutely that they can't pay attention to anything else. Imagine their disorder as a pair of binoculars. Narcissists look at their own needs through the magnifying side, and the rest of the cosmos through the side that makes things small to the point of insignificance. It's not so much that these vampires think they're better than other people as that they hardly think of other people at all. Unless they need something.

Narcissistic need is tremendous. Just as sharks must continually swim to keep from drowning, Narcissists must constantly demonstrate that they are special, or they will sink like stones to the depths of depression. It may look as if they are trying to demonstrate their worth to other people, but their real audience is themselves.

Narcissists are experts at showing off. Everything they do is calculated to make the right impression. Conspicuous consumption is for them what religion is for other people. Narcissists pursue the symbols of wealth, status, and power with a fervor that is almost spiritual. They can talk for hours about objects they own, the great things they've done or are going to do, and the famous people they hang out with. Often, they exaggerate shamelessly, even when they have plenty of real achievements they could brag about.

Nothing is ever enough for them. That's why Narcissists want you, or at least your adulation. They'll try so hard to impress you that it's easy to believe that you're actually important to them. This can be a fatal mistake; it's not you they want, only your worship. They'll suck that out and throw the rest away.

To Narcissistic vampires, the objects, the achievements, and the high regard of other people mean nothing in themselves. They are fuel, like water forced across gills so that oxygen can be extracted. The technical term is *Narcissistic supplies*. If Narcissists don't constantly demonstrate their specialness to themselves, they drown.

WHAT IT'S LIKE TO BE NARCISSISTIC

To know how Narcissistic vampires experience life, imagine playing golf, tennis, or some other competitive sport and having the best day of your career. You feel great, but the mental wall between confidence and fear is thin as tissue paper. Everything is riding on the next shot, and then the one after that. For Narcissists, the game encompasses the whole world, and it is never over.

Imagine the pressure should the only meaningful goal in your life be proving that you are something more than human. Narcissistic vampires' greatest fear is of being ordinary. They can't feel connected to anything larger than themselves, because in their universe there *is* nothing larger. Beyond their frenetic attempts to prove the unprovable lies only a dark, unexplored void. You might be tempted to think of them as tragic figures if they weren't so petty and obnoxious.

Narcissistic vampires are usually talented and intelligent. They are also among the most inconsiderate creatures on earth. You'd think that such smart people would recognize the importance of paying attention to other people. Dream on.

Narcissists are so wrapped up in their own dreams that there is no room for anything else. It is an ironic coincidence that sometimes the realization of Narcissistic dreams benefits all humanity. Narcissists invented art, science, sports, business, and everything else you can compete at. They invented sainthood too, for that matter. Our lives are better because of Narcissists' attempts to prove themselves better than we are.

THE NARCISSISTIC DILEMMA

More than any other vampire type, Narcissists evoke mixed feelings. We love their accomplishments, but hate their conceit. We deplore the way they ignore our needs, yet unconsciously we respond to the infants inside them that need us so much.

And we need them. Without Narcissists, who would lead us? Or who, for that matter, would think themselves wise enough to say where leadership ends and narcissism begins?

There's no doubt that too much narcissism is a dangerous thing. But how much is too much?

And what is narcissism anyway? To live at all we must have some instinct to put our own needs first. Narcissism may be the power behind all motivation. To live as human beings, we must balance that power with responsibility. Struggling with the Narcissistic dilemma is what being human is all about. The great rabbi Hillel summed it up like this:

If I am not for myself, who will be for me?
If I am only for myself, what am I?
If not now, when?

Emotional Vampires are people who have for one reason or another abandoned the struggle with the Narcissistic dilemma. Antisocials ignore it because it's no fun. Histrionics pretend that they never act in their own self-interest, and Narcissists believe that what's good for them is all that exists. Vampires are forced to prey on other people for the answer that the rest of us must struggle to find within ourselves.

What's the answer? Another great rabbi summed that up:

Do unto others as you would have them do unto you.

Narcissistic vampires break the Golden Rule without so much as a thought. Does this make them evil, or oblivious? Your answer will determine how much damage they do to you.

The easiest way to get drained is to take Narcissists' inconsideration personally, to get upset over what they must be thinking of you to treat you the way they do. *The most important thing to remember is that Narcissistic vampires are not thinking of you at all.*

NARCISSISM AND SELF-ESTEEM

Narcissism is not the same thing as high self-esteem. Self-esteem is a concept that has meaning primarily to people who don't have it. Narcissists don't need a concept to explain why they are special any more than sharks need a concept to explain water.

You might argue that their constant need for Narcissistic supplies to buoy them up is evidence that the whole purpose of their life is to compensate for low self-esteem. This may lead you into the mistaken belief that all it takes to fix Narcissists is to teach them how to feel good about who they are inside, so they can just relax and let themselves be regular people. As we'll see in the next chapter, which covers Narcissistic Legends in their own minds, it's possible to waste your whole life pursuing this futile goal.

THE NARCISSISTIC VAMPIRE CHECKLIST: IDENTIFYING THE SMARTEST, MOST TALENTED, ALL-AROUND BEST PERSON IN THE WORLD

True or false: Score one point for each *true* answer.

1. This person has achieved more than most people his or her age.   T   F
2. This person is firmly convinced that he or she is better, smarter, or more talented than other people.   T   F
3. This person loves competition, but is a poor loser.   T   F
4. This person has fantasies of doing something great or being famous, and often expects to be treated as if these fantasies had already come true.   T   F
5. This person has very little interest in what other people are thinking or feeling, unless he or she wants something from them.   T   F
6. This person is a name dropper.   T   F
7. To this person it is very important to live in the right place and associate with the right people.   T   F
8. This person takes advantage of other people to achieve his or her own goals.   T   F
9. This person usually manages to be in a category by himself or herself.   T   F
10. This person often feels put upon when asked to take care of his or her responsibilities to family, friends, or coworkers.   T   F
11. This person regularly disregards rules or expects them to be changed because he or she is in some way special.   T   F

12. This person becomes irritated when other people don't   T   F
    automatically do what he or she wants them to do, even
    when they have a good reason for not complying.
13. This person reviews sports, art, and literature by telling you T   F
    what he or she would have done instead.
14. This person thinks most criticisms of him or her are   T   F
    motivated by jealousy.
15. This person regards anything short of worship to be rejection. T   F
16. This person suffers from a congenital inability to recognize
    his or her own mistakes. On the rare occasions that this   T   F
    person does recognize a mistake, even the slightest error
    can precipitate a major depression.
17. This person often explains why people who are better   T   F
    known than he or she is are not really all that great.
18. This person often complains of being mistreated or   T   F
    misunderstood.
19. People either love or hate this person.   T   F
20. Despite an overly high opinion of himself or herself, this   T   F
    person is really quite intelligent and talented.

Scoring: Five or more true answers qualifies the person as a Narcissistic Emotional Vampire, though not necessarily for a diagnosis of narcissistic personality disorder. If the person scores higher than 10, and is not a member of the royal family, be careful that you aren't mistaken for one of the servants.

WHAT THE QUESTIONS MEASURE

The specific behaviors covered on the checklist relate to several underlying personality characteristics that define a Narcissistic Emotional Vampire.

Well-Advertised Talent and Intelligence

The first thing you'll hear about Narcissistic vampires is that they are extremely intelligent and talented. You'll probably hear this from the vampires directly, since they are not the least bit shy in saying good things about themselves.

A surprising number of Narcissistic vampires know their numerical IQ scores and share them with new acquaintances. You may also hear about famous people whom these vampires have met and in some way impressed.

At seminars and meetings, Narcissistic vampires often have their hands in the air, but they never ask real questions. They make comments to demonstrate to everyone that they know at least as much and probably more than the person at the front of the room.

The pattern of trying to dazzle you with their talent and intelligence persists with Narcissistic vampires long after they make their first impression. They'll keep on until you're no longer visibly awed, then they'll ignore you completely.

Achievement

Most Narcissistic vampires have achievements to back up their high opinion of themselves. Unlike other vampire types who are just as happy to pretend, Narcissists are quite willing to work hard to glorify themselves.

In their careers, these vampires are usually focused and goal-directed. Many are workaholics, but unlike Histrionic people pleasers who'll work themselves half to death for approval and love, Narcissists take on only those tasks that pay off in money, fame, or power.

Grandiosity

Narcissistic vampires are absolutely shameless in their fantasies about how great they are and how much everybody admires them, or should.

If you press them, they'll admit that they consider themselves the best in the world at something. Actually, you won't have to press very hard.

Entitlement

Narcissistic vampires believe they are so special that the rules don't apply to them. They expect the red carpet to be rolled out for them wherever they go, and if it isn't, they get quite surly.

They don't wait, they don't recycle, they don't pay retail, they don't stand in line, they don't clean up after themselves, they don't let other people get in front of them in traffic, and their income taxes rival great works of fiction. Illness or even death is no excuse for other people not immediately jumping up to meet their needs. They aren't the least bit ashamed of using other people and systems for their own personal gain. They boast about how they take advantage of just about everybody.

Competitiveness

Narcissistic vampires love to compete, but only when they win. Usually, they'll do whatever it takes to win, whether it be practice or stacking the deck in their favor.

Narcissistic vampires are obsessively concerned with status and power. They'll fight to the death over a corner office, not because they want a nice view, but because they know what a corner office means in the organizational hierarchy. They know what everything means in every hierarchy. What they wear, what they drive, where they live, and who they're seen with are not random choices based on something so silly as what they like. Everything Narcissistic vampires do is a move in the great game of self-aggrandizement, which is their main reason for living.

Conspicuous Boredom

Unless the subject of the conversation is how great they are, Narcissistic vampires will become visibly bored. One of the main reasons Narcissists wear expensive watches is so they can look at them when someone else is talking.

Besides boredom, Narcissistic vampires have only two other emotional states. They're either on top of the world or on the bottom of the garbage heap. The slightest frustration can burst their balloon and send them crashing to the depths.

Lack of Empathy

To a Narcissistic vampire, other people are either prospective purveyors of Narcissistic supplies or invisible. More than any other vampire type, Narcissists are incapable of seeing their fellow humans as having wants, needs, talents, and desires of their own. Needless to say, this lack of empathy is the source of untold amounts of pain to the people who love them.

But for their lack of human warmth, there is a lot about these vampires to love. Many people destroy themselves by believing that it's their fault that Narcissists don't love them back. They will work hard and long, sometimes for their whole lives, without realizing that these vampires can't give what they don't have.

A particularly scary trait that Narcissists share with Antisocials is the ability to feign empathy when they want something. Narcissists are the best flatterers on the planet. They give great ego massages even as they're draining people dry. Needless to say, this talent makes them great at politics. Even though Antisocials and Histrionics can be sexy, all the best seducers are Narcissists.

Inability to Accept Criticism

Narcissistic vampires' greatest fear is of being ordinary. God forbid they should do something as mundane as making a mistake. Even the smallest criticisms feel like stakes through the heart. If you reprimand Narcissistic vampires, the least they'll do is explain in great detail why your opinion is wrong. If you're right, the situation will be much worse. They will melt before your eyes into pitiful, dependent infants who need enormous amounts of reassurance and praise just to draw their next breath. You can't win. There's no such thing as a Narcissistic vampire being objective about his or her faults.

Ambivalence in Other People

Other people usually feel strongly about Narcissistic vampires. They either love them for their talents or hate their guts for their blatant selfishness. Or both. It's hard to say what does most damage—the selfishness, the hatred, or the love.

Narcissistic vampires always know what they want from you. They won't be the least bit reticent about asking for it or just taking it. To deal effectively with these self-absorbed children of the night, you must be equally certain about what you want from them. Always drive a hard bargain, and always make them pay *before* they get what they want from you. Remember this rule, and there's not much else you need to know.

Well, maybe one more thing: Unless you want your heart broken, never make Narcissistic vampires choose between you and their first love, themselves.

10 Vampires Who Are Legends in Their Own Minds

With talent like theirs, who needs performance?

Narcissism carries within itself the seeds of both success and failure. Grandiose dreams of being special and unique can be used as goads to get ahead, or as rationalizations for not having to do what success requires.

Many Narcissists push themselves to succeed. They recognize that they can get at least some of the supplies they need just from having an office with a name on the door and making lots of money. Those hapless Narcissists who don't do well in their careers have to scramble harder to get the admiration they feel they deserve.

Narcissistic vampires who can't turn their grandiose dreams into reality may turn their reality into dreams. They become legends in their own minds.

With no objective support whatsoever, Narcissistic Legends see themselves as more talented and intelligent than other people. They are expert in finding small ponds that will let them be big fish, and extorting Narcissistic supplies from people whose need to be needed is as great as their vampiric need to be adored.

The house is silent but for the rattling of keys on Vampire Tyler's computer.

"Tyler, it's two o'clock. Are you still on the Internet?" Rachel calls from the bedroom.

"I'm almost done," Tyler says. "I'll come to bed soon."

"Come on, honey, get some rest. The Internet will still be there in the morning."

"I know, I know. I'll be there soon. I'm closing a big sale with a guy in Norway."

Closing a sale! Rachel's heart soars. For the past six months, since Tyler started Netmarket.com, there have been no sales, even though he's been working on it night and day. The project is a great idea. It's a subscription purchasing network for small businesses, in which Tyler can match up customers and suppliers anywhere in the world. The earning potential is enormous. Rachel has seen the projections.

But then again, all Tyler's ideas are great. His creativity is one of the main things Rachel admires about him. Just talking to him makes her see the world differently.

But interesting conversations don't put bread on the table. Rachel hopes against hope that Netmarket will. Tyler says it's only a matter of time until things fall into place.

Rachel can't help worrying that time is running out. Lying in bed listening to the soft clatter of keys, she dares to hope that tonight is the night. It would be so wonderful if Tyler could make his project pay off. They could use the money. Not that she'd put any pressure on him. Since she got promoted at work, they've been able to make it on her salary. Just barely. Mostly, she wants this project to work out for Tyler. He could use a little good luck for a change.

Half an hour later, the keys are still clattering. If this is Tyler's big moment, maybe she should be there to support him. She drags herself out of bed and pads softly into the office to stand by her man.

Tyler is a Narcissistic Legend in his own mind. He really does know quite a bit about the art and science of purchasing. Ask him. He won't be the least bit shy about telling you that he knows more than most business school professors, not to mention the heads of the five or six purchasing departments where he's worked and been let go. He'll go to great lengths explaining that his ideas are so radical that a lot of people just don't understand how great they are.

Rachel tries to understand. She loves Tyler, and wants to help him succeed. She knows how hard he works, how much he worries, and how depressed he gets when things don't go right. In Tyler's mind, helping him means relieving him of anything that might distract him from working on his project. That's why Rachel earns the money, does the housework, and takes care of the kids. She feels it will all be worthwhile if it helps Tyler get his business off the ground. More than that, Rachel hopes Tyler will see that her sacrifices for him mean that there's someone who believes in him and cares for him. Maybe that will help him believe in himself and do what he needs to do to pull himself out of this terrible slump. Late at night, she sometimes wonders if what she's doing is actually helping.

It isn't. Rachel's nurturing is no more noticeable to Tyler than the air he breathes. He may need it, but he never thinks about it. Like most Narcissistic vampires, he pays attention only to what he feels he might lose. Rachel is there for him, loving, solid, and therefore pretty much ignored. It hurts Rachel that Tyler seldom acknowledges her efforts, but making demands and playing hard to get are not part of her nature. If she were down, she'd want somebody to stand behind her.

Rachel is making the most dangerous mistake possible in dealing with Emotional Vampires. She's assuming that she understands Tyler based on what she knows about herself. Rachel sometimes has problems with low self-esteem. When she messes up on something, even on something little, she feels like a failure. Rachel imagines that Tyler feels as low as she would if she'd been fired from jobs and couldn't make any money. So, following the Golden Rule, she tries to give him what would help her.

When other people give Rachel affection, support, and encouragement, she can feel good enough about herself to get up and do what needs to be done. In this respect, Rachel is like most people, but she's not like a Narcissistic vampire.

Narcissism is definitely *not* a problem with low self-esteem. Despite the setbacks, Tyler has no doubts about his self-worth. When Tyler broods, he's not blaming himself. It's more likely that he's feeling hurt and abused because people are not immediately recognizing the quality of his ideas and moving him to the head of the class, where he thinks he belongs. The last thing a Narcissistic Legend is likely to consider is that setbacks are the result of his own behavior. Even when he goes through periods of depression, during which he talks about what a terrible person he is, what Tyler is looking for is not advice on how to do things better, but someone to reassure him of what he knows in his heart—that he's just fine the way he is. Unfortunately, that's just what Rachel does.

What should Rachel do instead? To answer that question, we have to look more closely at what prevents talented and intelligent Narcissistic Legends from achieving their potential.

HOW NARCISSISTIC LEGENDS PREVENT THEMSELVES FROM SUCCEEDING

Often, Narcissistic Legends are bright and creative, but it takes more than that to succeed at a career. Specifically, two other things are required: *the ability to do things you don't want to do because the job requires them, and the ability to sell yourself and your ideas to other people.* Narcissism stands in the way of learning and practicing both of these skills.

In order to succeed in any system, you have to be perceived as a part of it. This usually means going through an initiation period of doing pointless work because somebody more firmly entrenched in the system wants it done. There's no way around paying your dues. Narcissistic Legends are quick to note that the work they're being asked to do is pointless and generally believe that they, because of their superior intelligence, are the first to discover this amazing fact. Often, they will use this pseudo-insight as justification for not doing what they consider unimportant.

There are two problems with this approach. First, Narcissistic Legends are apt to confuse what they don't like with what is unimportant. Whether it's making cold calls, playing politics, or checking facts and figures, every job requires doing things that you'd rather not do. The first step toward success comes from learning to do them anyway, regardless of how you feel.

The second problem with the Narcissistic approach to menial tasks is that what's unimportant to Narcissists may be of critical importance to everybody else. To someone who's climbed an organizational ladder for 20 years, paying dues at every rung, it's inconceivable that a new hire who never gets paperwork in on time should expect the business to be reengineered in his or her own image.

Besides the forbearance to do necessary but uninteresting work, success requires the ability to sell. Selling, first and foremost, means paying enough attention to other people to know what they will buy. Narcissistic Legends could care less about what other people want. They believe that they're better mousetraps, and that people should be beating a path to their door. This makes them terrible at selling. Their idea of a sales pitch is sketching out their idea and acting as if it would be stupid to consider anything else.

Narcissistic Legends' disregard of how they affect other people makes them blind to the real contingencies in their lives. Like Antisocials, they can make the same mistakes over and over and still not learn from them. Narcissists *can* change their behavior when they find out it's preventing them from getting what they want. The funny thing is that they seldom find out, because other people don't explain the problem to them in a way they can understand.

NARCISSISTIC LEGEND HYPNOSIS

Narcissistic Legends create alternate realities that push powerful people away and attract the weak.

Narcissists know that they're the best. People who doubt themselves are attracted to Narcissistic certainty. When these vampires want someone, they can make that person feel like the second most special being on the planet.

In the dark hallway, on her way to Tyler's office, Rachel remembers how it was when she and Tyler first met. He sent actual handwritten notes in the mail every day; it was before e-mail. He wrote her poetry. It was awful, but she loved it anyway. He gave her flowers and those dippy stuffed animals that she still keeps on the dresser. They stared into each other's eyes over candlelit dinners (she cooked them and Tyler brought the candles), talking far into the night about his big ideas and wonderful dreams. Rachel had never known such an intelligent person. And Tyler loved her; he said it all the time. More than that, he needed her. She knew that from the moment she saw that pig sty of an apartment he lived in.

Since that time, the love has been buried under the ruins of one big idea after another, but still, Tyler needs her.

Narcissists who want something are willing to work hard and single-mindedly to get it. In the early stages of a relationship, when it's new and uncertain, these vampires can be enthusiastic, if not adept, at courtship. Their lack of grace doesn't matter. What really draws their victims in is Narcissistic need.

Prospective victims see Narcissistic Legends as talented intelligent people who need someone to take care of them. These poor benighted souls dare to hope that in return for their hard work and affection, the vampires will feel enough gratitude to love them back.

Narcissistic Legends are blissfully unaware that anyone could see them as less than perfect. Once the relationship is certain, they stop making an effort. The Narcissist expects other people to be so thrilled by even a little attention that they will happily give anything for the pleasure of associating with such a superior person. Victims do little to discourage the idea.

In the beginning, both vampire and victim see each other as bargains. For a while, their relationship seems to be a very sweet deal. Then it slowly goes sour.

No matter how hard victims work, Narcissistic Legends feel very little gratitude. They expect their victims to be grateful to them. After a while, even the most caring victims get sick of having their needs ignored. Then they create their own hypnotic bind. Either they keep on giving, and thereby continue to be good but exploited people, or they nag or leave or otherwise act in ways that they themselves consider selfish and hurtful. They can't win, so most often they do nothing but hurt inside.

If victims do allow themselves to ask for anything at all, it's usually something vague and after the fact, like appreciation. The victims never think of demanding specific behaviors with specific consequences for not complying. Unfortunately, ultimatums and contingencies, the very things that might help the relationship, are as alien to the victims as appreciation is to the vampire.

The situation continues to get worse. The vampires do less and want more, because that's precisely what their victims have inadvertently taught them to expect. The relationship is marked by one crisis after another each time victims realize that, yet again, they've been had.

Rachel gets out of bed to be with Tyler as he makes his first sale. On bare feet she tiptoes into the office. Tyler, as usual, is hunched over the keyboard. He doesn't see Rachel until she's standing right behind him. He seems to be studying an aerial view of a castle with an army of skeletons swarming over it.

"Tyler, what is this? It's one of those games, isn't it?"

He turns toward her, grinning like a little boy caught with his hand in the cookie jar. As he does, he hits a key and the Netmarket.com logo appears on the monitor. "Just taking a little break while I'm waiting for

Bjorn in Norway to message me back. Thought I'd check out the old castle. Bjorn said he'd get right back to me."

The instant messenger pops up. "See, this must be him now," Tyler says.

The message scrolls across the screen in capital letters as if someone very far away were shouting to be heard.

"TROLLMEISTER, GET ON THE STICK. IT'S YOUR MOVE!"

Rachel feels a million things at once, none of them charitable. "You haven't been working at all," she says. The cold fury in her voice frightens even her. "You've been playing those stupid games again."

"No, You don't understand. I was just—"

"You don't have to lie about it, Tyler. From here on out, you can play all the computer games you want."

"What do you mean?" he asks. His voice is barely above a whisper.

For a long time Rachel stares at him and says nothing. She's never spoken the words before tonight. Tears fill her eyes and she begins gasping for breath. "I think maybe you should get a place of your own."

Tyler's lip quivers as he speaks. "Honey, please don't. I'm sorry. I'll do anything."

If you're applauding Rachel for finally throwing the bum out, you probably don't understand her or Tyler very well. Rachel loves Tyler, and she believes strongly in the power and obligation of love. By turning her back on Tyler after all these years of hoping and helping, she is repudiating what, until this moment, has been the most important force in her life.

Tyler is inconsiderate and he can't seem to earn much of a living, but he's not a bad man. He doesn't drink, run around, or beat her. The kids love him; when he has time for them, they play Nintendo together. What right does Rachel have to abandon him for playing a computer game in the middle of the night? Wouldn't that be more selfish than anything Tyler has done?

The chances are good that Rachel will let Tyler stay in return for a few vague promises to do better. This would be a huge mistake. Letting Tyler stay isn't the mistake; it's the vagueness of the promises. What Rachel needs to do is make their relationship contingent on Tyler doing some very specific things. As I said earlier in the chapter, Narcissistic vampires can learn to act differently, but they're usually not taught very well. There are two elements to effective teaching: a good lesson plan, which we'll discuss later in the chapter, and sufficient motivation for learning. The only thing that reliably provides enough motivation for Narcissistic vampires to change is the imminent loss of something they value.

Narcissists are insensitive, but they're not stupid. They may fume and fuss, but they do respond to ultimatums. If you tell them to shape up or ship out, and they believe you're serious, you'll have their attention in a way that is impossible to achieve by any other means. Obviously, they don't always shape up, but a clear ultimatum, contingent upon very specific behaviors, is the best, and only, chance you're going to get.

Why bother? Wouldn't it be better to divorce or fire a Narcissist and get on with your life? I can't answer that for you; the question brings up one more Narcissistic dilemma.

ANOTHER NARCISSISTIC DILEMMA

Narcissists, annoying as they are, add something to the world—creativity.

Narcissists need to be different and special. As we've seen, this can play havoc with the sense of connection to other people and anything else larger than the vampire's own oversized ego. Narcissists are, by definition, outsiders. If you think about it, however, *outside* is the only place that creativity can possibly come from. Emotional Vampires, because of their driving and insatiable needs, have far more motivation to be creative than do normal people, whose lives are in better balance. Contentment seldom motivates new ideas.

Of all the vampire types, the most creative are the Narcissists, with their intelligence and need to be special, and the Paranoids, whom we'll meet later in this book, with their profound sense of alienation.

Most people think creativity is a good thing, but few of them, even the ones who have it, really understand what it is.

Not too long ago I was asked to speak at a business seminar titled "Awaking the Creative Genius Inside You." Experts were enlisted to give peppy little talks about how to get creative juices flowing in order to develop a new marketing plan. The fact that the people putting together the seminar thought that new ideas could be turned on and off like a faucet was my first clue that they had never experienced creativity firsthand.

Creativity is a mental aberration that might be more of a curse than a blessing in the typical corporate setting.

To begin with, the process is called "creativity" only when it generates ideas that are useful, convenient, and cost-effective. The rest of the time it's called "being weird" or "having a bad attitude." Creativity grows from the same roots as rebellion. People who like things the way they are just aren't motivated to think of anything new. Nor are they well disposed to new ideas that change the way they do things.

Creativity means seeing things differently than other people, and it means believing that your vision is better than what's already there. Nothing could be more insensitive, irreverent, annoying, threatening, and well, Narcissistic.

Without Narcissists around you, you'll experience far fewer creative ideas in your business or in your life. Whether that's good or bad, you'll have to decide for yourself. There is, however, an alternative to accepting Narcissists the way they are, or getting rid of them.

HOW TO SOCIALIZE NARCISSISTIC LEGENDS

With powerful enough motivation and a good lesson plan, it's possible to teach Narcissistic Legends to act in a more socialized manner. You may not be able to change their basic narcissism, but you can get them to act in ways that are not so destructive to relationships and careers.
First, the contingencies have to be crystal clear:

> *"You're saying you'll do anything to stay in this marriage?" Rachel asks Tyler at the end of a long and tearful night.*
>
> *"Anything." Tyler says.*
>
> *"All right," Rachel says. "Here are my terms. First, you can go on with the Netmarket project for three more months. If you aren't making the equivalent of minimum wage by then, I want you to get a real job and do whatever it takes to hold it for at least a year."*
>
> *"Three months? But it takes longer than that to get a thing like this off the ground."*
>
> *"Then work on it in your spare time. After you've done two hours of work around the house every day."*
>
> *"But—"*
>
> *"No buts. Take it or leave it."*

You're probably thinking that Rachel would never say those things in a million years, and you're right. It's what she *should* say, because it's the only approach that will have a ghost of a chance with a Narcissistic Legend like

ortunately, it flies in the face of the kindness and unconditional
p___. gard that Rachel thinks are essential to a loving relationship.

Can she be this cold and calculating, even to save her marriage? That's
up to her. We leave Rachel struggling with her Narcissistic vampire and her
own personal demons.

The only way to teach Narcissists basic human skills is to clearly show
them that it is in their own self-interest to act differently. A strong contingency is essential. They can put out considerable effort if they believe that it
is the only way they can avoid getting divorced, being fired, terminating a
friendship, or going to jail. Most other contingencies are not compelling
enough. Once the contingency is in place, you have to direct the effort
toward two specific goals:

1. Narcissistic Legends have to learn to make themselves do things
   they don't want to do.
2. Narcissistic Legends have to learn to sell themselves and their ideas
   by paying enough attention to other people to know what they're
   likely to buy.

Be clear that in offering suggestions for change, you're acting in your
own self-interest rather than as the agent of a higher moral authority or out
of simple kindness. Narcissists don't believe in your altruism. Most of them
would argue that Mother Teresa's saintliness was at least in part an ego trip.

THE 10 ELEMENTS OF VAMPIRE FIGHTING STRATEGY: GETTING GENIUSES TO DO SOMETHING USEFUL FOR A CHANGE
Teach Narcissistic Legends a little work ethic.

1. KNOW THEM, KNOW THEIR HISTORY, AND KNOW YOUR GOAL

Narcissistic Legends are people who have trouble living up to their potential. You can find them everywhere, in break rooms at work and in chat
rooms on the Internet. They're always talking about how much brighter and
more talented they are than people who are merely rich and famous.

Often they really are smart, but if you're considering hiring them into your life, you need to know more than their IQ numbers. Carefully examine their track record, and expect their future behavior to be similar to what they've done in the past. Narcissistic Legends are quick to explain that *this* time things will be different. They are slow to grasp how their own hang-ups ensure that everything will stay the same. All they seem to learn from mistakes is that other people make them.

Your goal with Narcissistic Legends is, as with all vampires, to keep them from draining you. This is difficult, because they can drain you in so many different ways. Legends can dash your hopes or suck out every drop of support and affection you have, and still expect more. They can whip you into a froth of self-destructive outrage at their insensitivity, or they can alienate you to the point that you reject a really good idea just because it came from them. The list is endless, and Narcissists take no responsibility for any of it. Narcissism means never having to say you're sorry.

Narcissistic Legends demand a lot. Your most important goal is to make sure you're getting something back for what you give.

2. GET OUTSIDE VERIFICATION

Narcissistic Legends can tell wonderful stories about the great things they've done in the past. Often, the stories are huge exaggerations. Always check. This is the obvious use of verification.

A less obvious and therefore more important use is to get external verification on the value of their ideas. Often Narcissistic Legends present a good idea in such an obnoxious way that it's easy to discount it. Paranoid vampires do the same.

Virtually all really great ideas sound threatening or impertinent when you first hear them. Sometimes you need an outside opinion to keep your own ego from getting in the way of a real creative breakthrough.

3. DO WHAT THEY DON'T

Whatever the task, do the hard part first. In dealing with Narcissistic Legends, the hard part is demanding what you want from them clearly and up front. This is particularly difficult, and important, if you see yourself as a giver. With Narcissists, unless you're willing to take, you will be taken.

If you do have the capacity to give, you have a tremendous opportunity that is forever denied to Narcissists. You can be a part of the group, a regular person who plays by the same rules as everyone else. Rejoice in being part of something larger than yourself. Narcissists are condemned to live in a world where nothing can be bigger than their own egos.

4. PAY ATTENTION TO ACTIONS, NOT WORDS

If you have to deal with Narcissists, the word to remember is *accountability*. Build it into whatever relationship you have from the beginning. It will be far more difficult to tack on the notion later. Narcissistic Legends are famous for taking on projects that they never finish because they never get down to doing the difficult parts. They may look like they're working hard, but they're really hardly working, at least at the things that pay off. If Legends are doing something for you or with you, specify tasks and set time limits and dollar amounts. Inspect deliverables carefully to make sure you're getting what you expected. Narcissistic Legends sometimes mistake cutting corners for art.

5. IDENTIFY HYPNOTIC STRATEGY

Narcissists want you to think they're special.

If, beneath a Legend's bull and bluster, you think you see a sad, frightened person who would be oh so grateful if somebody really cared, watch out!

Be even more careful if you see someone who needs to be made an example of because of his or her insensitivity. The example will be you. Narcissists have the frightening capacity to turn into underdogs as soon as you attack them.

6. PICK YOUR BATTLES

If you think you can teach a Narcissist to care about what other people feel, it's probably best to sit in a dark, quiet room until the delusion goes away. Narcissistic Legends don't understand empathy, and they're never going to understand by listening to what you tell them.

With well-chosen words and well-constructed contingencies, you may be able to get them to change annoying Narcissistic behaviors, but not the narcissism underneath.

7. LET CONTINGENCIES DO THE WORK

When you hear Narcissistic Legends talking big, ask yourself why, if they're so smart, they aren't rich. This isn't a rhetorical question. The answers you come up with will be essential in helping you deal effectively with these vampires.

The reason Narcissistic Legends don't succeed is that they can't make themselves do things they don't want to do. You need to know what these things are. Make sure your dealings with Legends are structured so that these vampires get the biggest rewards for actually doing the difficult stuff rather than just talking about it.

8. CHOOSE YOUR WORDS AS CAREFULLY AS YOU PICK YOUR BATTLES

The words you have to use most carefully around Narcissistic Legends are any that sound even a little like criticism. No matter how constructive it is, to Narcissistic vampires, the tiniest criticism feels like the fiery sting of a crucifix. They'll scream, snarl, and rationalize until dawn, but unless the criticism is delivered exceedingly well, they will not learn anything.

To deal with Narcissistic Legends at home or at work, you have to learn to criticize effectively, because they make a lot of mistakes that they will never recognize on their own.

Criticism is a tool that is easy to use badly with vampires. Or anyone. Unless you're very careful, you can do more harm than good. Here are some ideas about how to maximize the positive effects and minimize the damage.

Give More Praise than Criticism.   If you want to use criticism well, especially with Narcissistic vampires, the first step is to use praise more often. Narcissists need tons of praise, and to get anywhere, you'll have to give it. Just make sure you give it for the right things. Catch them being good and reward them.

Don't Be Spontaneous.   Criticism given spontaneously is usually in the form of an emotional explosion—a way of expressing hurt or anger rather than a planned intervention to help the other person improve. There is a place for emotional expression of course, but not as a method for getting other people to change their behavior.

Know Your Goal.   What do you want the vampire to do as a result of what you say? You don't have to spell out what vampires did wrong to ask them to do it right next time. Sometimes a simple request is the best criticism.

Ask Permission. Before you criticize, ask: "Are you open to some feedback?" If the vampire says yes, then you have at least a rudimentary agreement to listen.

Criticize the Behavior, Not the Person. We all know this rule, but we break it every day. Focus on the words you choose. If you begin any statement with the words *you are* and the next word is not *wonderful,* whatever you say will be perceived as a personal attack, no matter what you intend. Be more effective by asking for what you want or saying what you feel.

Instead of saying, "You are insensitive," a better approach is to say, "When you answered before I finished talking, I felt put down. Is that what you intended?" Or simply ask the vampire to wait until you finish talking before answering. Remember, the word *interrupt* carries an accusation within it. For best results, use neutral language.

Give the Vampire an Out. Allow a socially acceptable reason for making a mistake before you say what the mistake was. Begin your criticism with "I know you're busy" or some other statement that implies the vampire was trying to do a good job.

Rehearse. Practice criticizing Narcissists as you would an important speech. Listen to yourself and imagine how you would feel if someone said that to you. Then multiply by 10.

Give the Vampire Time to Think. If the vampire responds immediately, it will most likely be with an attempt to explain why he or she is right and you are wrong. Saying "I don't expect you to answer immediately—we'll talk about it tomorrow" is a way to discourage knee-jerk defensiveness. Remember to say it and walk away immediately.

Criticism is an important tool for changing vampire behavior. As with any other tool, if criticism is to work it must be used with attention, skill, and forethought.

9. IGNORE TANTRUMS

Most of the vampires we've met so far use temper tantrums to get their way. Narcissists practice tantrums as if they were a martial art. They hold black belts in both the endless lecture and the shoulder of ice. Despite their obvious skill, Narcissistic Legends throw tantrums that are relatively easy to tune out. Anger is a form of theater, and Legends are terrible actors. They don't pay enough attention to their audience to draw people into the performance. Remember, they can't sell much of anything.

They are creative, however. Narcissists have developed a form of manipulative emotional explosion all their own. Call it a guilt tantrum. When things go really badly, and these vampires sense that they are in major trouble, they may erupt into a torrent of self-blame. To the unwary, it may look as if these self-absorbed children of the night are finally catching on to what everyone has been trying to tell them for years. No way. The feelings are temporary, and if you scratch their newfound self-knowledge even slightly you'll find self-pity just below the surface. And incredibly transparent guilt trips.

> *"I don't blame you for wanting to leave." Tyler's voice cracks and his eyes fill with tears. "Who would want to live with a failure?"*
>
> *"You're not a failure," Rachel says. She's crying too. "You're just—"*
>
> *Tyler holds up his hand. "Don't deny it. We both know I'm a pretty sorry human being."*

Stick to your guns. It hurts, but in the end, it's kinder to everyone.

10. KNOW YOUR OWN LIMITS

Narcissists require an enormous amount of praise, attention, and other supplies. As with pigeons in the park, when you run out of popcorn, they fly away. Sometimes it's best to let them.

Even with good intentions and good technique, sometimes there's nothing you can say or do to match the lure of Narcissistic Legends' grandiose internal fantasies. If the going gets too rough, they can create an alternate reality for themselves and retreat into it forever.

> *By day, Tyler is a ne'er-do-well who can't seem to hold a job living alone in a grubby apartment. By night, as Trollmeister, he stalks the Internet, a bold warrior defeating all comers in fantasy games. He's a legend among a small, select cadre of gamers. Nobody knows his real name or where he's from. Only that he's the best.*

11 Vampire Superstars

**You've got to love these guys!
Worship them, actually.**

Narcissistic Superstars play the lead in their own life story, which, to them, is indistinguishable from the history of civilization. These vampires believe at the depths of their souls that they are the most important people on earth. If you understand and accept this one central fact, Superstars cease to be a danger and become merely an annoyance. If the fact that they believe themselves to be the crown of creation offends you and makes you want to point out to them that they're not so great as they think they are, get away quickly, because they will destroy you.

Unfortunately, there are few places you can get away to, because wherever you go, there will likely be a Narcissistic Superstar in a position of authority over you. So, what's it to be? Do you fight them, run from them, or learn how to deal with them?

Everything we've learned until now about Narcissistic vampires is also true of Superstars, except that, unlike Legends in their own minds, they know how to work and they know how to sell. These vampires are willing and able to do what it takes to turn their grandiose dreams into reality. Almost. Superstars' dreams are always beyond their grasp. Whatever they are and whatever they have is never enough. They always want more.

Narcissistic Superstars' abilities, coupled with their tremendous hunger, may bring them success, but never satisfaction. They build empires, lead nations, create great works of art, and amass huge sums of money for one purpose only: to prove how great they are. Superstars may boast incessantly about what they have and what they've done, but once they have it or have done it, whatever it is loses value in their eyes. They always need more.

Whether it's money, honors, status symbols, or sexual conquests, Superstars always want something. They get what they want too. Every one of them has a trophy collection. Adding to it is the sole purpose of Narcissists' existence; there is no higher goal.

The most dangerous place you can be is between a Narcissistic Superstar and the next trophy.

With surgical precision, Vampire Antonio unpacks the boxes of photographic equipment spread across the dining room table.

Oriana stands in the doorway, shaking her head. "Another camera?"

Antonio holds up what looks like a large black box. "This isn't a camera; it's a Hasselblad!" He removes a lens from a leather case and reverently connects it to the camera body. "See this? It's the finest lens made. The resolution is incredible. Here, look."

He holds the camera out to Oriana, who dutifully looks through the eyepiece. "Very nice," she says. "But it doesn't seem that much different from all your other cameras."

Antonio tenses up. "Here we go again," he says. "Let's hear the spending-too-much-money-on-cameras lecture. I know it's coming."

"I didn't say—"

Antonio puts the camera down. "What's the matter? You don't think I work hard enough?" He begins ticking off points on his fingertips. "Twelve years of round-the-clock training, 60 or 70 hours of surgery cases a week, plus the time I spend on publications. You'd think the least I could expect out of my life is to use some of the money I earn to give myself a little pleasure. It's not as if you and the kids are doing without anything. I mean, that is your Mercedes in the driveway, isn't it?"

Oriana stands there quietly, waiting for Antonio to finish.

DEALING WITH SUPERSTARS' INSATIABLE NEEDS

Superstars love expensive toys. They have to have the best, because it shows that they *are* the best. An unrelenting drive to achieve and acquire is the center of their personality. There is no point in asking Narcissistic Superstars why they need to have so much and do so much. They don't know, any more than a flower knows why it turns toward the sun.

Don't waste your time trying to figure it out. Use it. For all their talent, intelligence, and temporal power, vampire Superstars are pathetically easy to manipulate. Here's how.

First, Kiss Up. There is no way around it. If you want to maintain any sort of relationship with Narcissistic Superstars, you have to admire them, their achievements, and their toys incessantly. Typically, it won't take much effort on your part to kiss up to Superstars. They'll be more than happy to come up with reasons to congratulate themselves. All you have to do is listen and look interested.

Know Your Needs. It's important to know what you want for yourself as clearly as Superstars know what they want for themselves. Superstars *always* know what they want, and they're always trying to figure out how to get it. If your own needs are unclear to you, or you wait for these vampires to give you what you deserve, you'll never get anything.

Tie Your Needs In with Theirs. Superstars are going to get what they want whether you're a part of it or not. Make yourself a part of it. To get even slightly reasonable treatment from vampire Superstars, you'll have to play all the angles, just as they do.

Oriana doesn't want her own camera, but there are many things she does want from Antonio. At the top of the list is for him to spend more time with her and the family, which is an almost universal desire among people close to Superstars. To get what she wants, Oriana will have to somehow tie it into Antonio's desire to do great deeds and own great things. Here's an example of how she might go about it:

> *"Can I hold it?" Oriana asks. Antonio hands the Hasselblad to her, and she cradles it gently. "So tell me," she says. "What does this camera do that makes it so special?"*
>
> *Antonio beams. "What **doesn't** it do is more like it. This is the most advanced camera made anywhere in the world today. Let's start with the lens mount . . ."*
>
> *Oriana listens patiently and enthusiastically throughout Antonio's lengthy presentation. Finally, she senses an opening. "This may be a dumb question, but can that camera take pictures of things that are moving, even though they're far away? Like maybe a sports event?"*

> *"This camera can catch the beads of sweat on a quarterback's nose at a hundred yards."*
>
> *"Wow! You mean it can really pick up sports action, and even the expressions on the players' faces?"*
>
> *"Absolutely! Why do you ask? Do you have some particular sport you want a picture of?"*
>
> *"Well, the other day at Ramon's soccer game I was looking at the boys. I started thinking about what a wonderful photo essay somebody could do on third-grade soccer. It was so cute how they were playing like grown-ups in the game, then playing in the mud puddles when they were on the sidelines. If somebody could catch those contrasts . . . Of course, it would take a really good photographer and really excellent equipment to get the kinds of one-in-a-million shots I'm thinking of."*
>
> *Antonio pats his new camera. "This is the baby that can do it, right here."*

Is Oriana being manipulative? You bet. With Superstars, there's no way around manipulation either. Vampires understand that most human interactions have a manipulative component, but that some techniques work better than others. Telling Antonio how sad Ramon is that his dad doesn't come to his soccer games is also a manipulative strategy, but it's one that won't work on Superstars. They never feel guilty about being too busy to meet anybody else's needs. If you can't get over the fact that Oriana has to stoop to trickery to get Antonio to do things a normal father would be happy to do, you probably shouldn't marry a Narcissistic Superstar. Or work for one. In order for Narcissistic Superstars to act like normal human beings, they generally have to be manipulated into it.

Manipulating Narcissistic Superstars is a growth industry. Retailers set lavish vampire traps, where they sell common items like food, clothing, and automobiles for about five times what they're worth. Whether the items in question are Rolls-Royces or fountain pens, the ambience is remarkably similar. The store is more tastefully decorated than anyone's home, the service is obsequious, with just enough hauteur for the vampires to believe that they're winning the help over with their charm and intelligence—and, of course, the prices are astronomical. If you have to ask what it costs, you can't afford it.

The bottom line is this: With Narcissistic Superstars everything is always a transaction. If you want to get anything for yourself, you have to be as much like one of these stores as possible. Look good, suck up, and price yourself way above the market. Always remember that the more something costs, the more vampire Superstars will want it.

SPECIAL PEOPLE EXPECT SPECIAL TREATMENT

Narcissistic Superstars absolutely refuse to live by the rules of ordinary mortals, or their compensation packages.

> *At the law firm meeting, Vampire T. Buford Whiting, senior partner, arises.*
>
> *"I have always said that it is the rainmakers who are the lifeblood of this firm. Without those of us who have established the reputation of this firm through years of intimate contact with the business community, our client base would be little more than wills, divorces, and personal injuries. It is our reputation that has made us prosperous, and therefore I think it is only proper that the people who have created our reputation should prosper. To that end, I move that the compensation for case referral should be raised at least five percentage points."*
>
> *Several of the younger lawyers get up to argue that raising the referral percentage means that the firm will be paying almost twice as much for playing golf with businesspeople as it does for actually doing legal work.*
>
> *In his rebuttal, Buford describes their position as childish naivete about how law firms are actually run.*
>
> *The motion passes.*

Narcissistic Superstars always consider whatever they do to be the most valuable part of the process. They are also sophisticated enough to have all the votes they need *before* they bring up a motion.

Superstars' flagrant disregard of the rules of fairness can enrage the people who work with them, but the anger generally plays right into the Superstars' hands, at least in the short run. To the builders of the system, who are mostly Superstars themselves, impertinent upstarts who get angry about how it operates are simply demonstrating that they aren't smart enough to use it. Like Buford, most Superstars see political savvy as the most important trait an individual can possess. Over the long run, these vampires' value systems tend to distort the organizations they work in to the point that internal politics becomes more important than the product or service the company sells.

In Buford's firm, talented young attorneys who would rather work on knotty legal problems than play golf with big shots are penalized financially. If they don't like it, they can leave. There are plenty of hungry young lawyers to take their place. The downside of this strategy shows up only gradually. The firm loses a few big lawsuits, and even then people like Buford soothe egos and explain that the real issue is the poor caliber of judges these days, and that the ruling will surely be overturned on appeal. Regardless of the quality of the legal services it provides, Buford's firm is successful at its real purpose: attracting and maintaining clients. And making lots of money.

Superstar endeavors have a way of drifting away from being driven by product or service toward being driven by politics. These vampires don't always do the best job, but they do give the best ego massages. If their clients are also Superstars, that's what matters most.

WHO CARES WHAT THE LITTLE PEOPLE THINK!

Narcissistic Superstars seldom become beloved leaders. The reason is that they don't understand their followers well enough to inspire trust and loyalty. In the world of Superstars, other people come in two distinct types: those who have something the vampires want, and those who are beneath notice. Superstars can seldom resist the temptation to point out to little people just how little they are.

> *It's the day of judgment at RYCO. Bonuses are being handed out. On this day each year you find out your actual dollar-and-cent value to the owner, Vampire Charlie Ryan. At RYCO there is no other value.*
>
> *Blake's hand trembles as he opens the envelope. He gasps when he sees the number, thinking at first that payroll has left off a zero. Nobody gets $1000! It's worse than no bonus at all.*
>
> *Cautiously, Blake approaches Sonya, his boss. "Do you think there could be some kind of, uh, you know . . ."*
>
> *"There's no mistake," Sonya says. "I'm sorry, Blake."*
>
> *"But I was the top performer in the whole division."*
>
> *"I know you were."*

"Then, why?"

Sonya lets out a long sigh. "It was the picnic; you didn't show up."

"But my wife was sick. I mean, how important is a picnic compared with—"

"It's important to Charlie Ryan, Blake. Really important."

Superstar vampires always seem to forget that someday the people who are beneath notice may have something to offer. Narcissists' paths through life are always marked by scorched earth and burned bridges.

Narcissists get away with utter disregard for other people's feelings because they can. If these vampires want to build a business then drive off their best talent for lack of reverence or political skill, there's no way to stop them. They have the money and power to do what they want, and they certainly don't give a damn what others think about it.

Among numerous authors on the way of Narcissists, Christopher Lasch is by far the most eloquent.* He believes that narcissism is becoming an epidemic, especially in the worlds of business and politics. Lasch may be correct, but that still leaves us with the question of what to do about it. Narcissists certainly won't change because some expert tells them it's bad to be Narcissistic.

No amount of negative press will change Narcissistic Superstars. They always have glee clubs of self-interested supporters to sing their praises. Narcissists prefer sucking up to reasoned criticism every time.

People tend to love Superstars or hate them. There's no in between, and there's very little predicting who will feel what. Some people forgive any amount of Narcissistic behavior because of the vampire's talents and success; other people become outraged at even small amounts of entitlement. Remember that the next time you want to grumble about your Narcissistic boss.

SUPERSTAR HYPNOSIS

Superstars create an alternate universe in which they are special, and your success and happiness is contingent upon indulging their every whim. If you

---

*Christopher Lasch, *The Culture of Narcissism: American Life in an Age of Diminishing Expectations.* New York: W. W. Norton, 1991.

work for them, their power over you may be sufficient to turn their alternate universe into the one you have to live in. To make things more confusing, these managerial vampires often create systems that they themselves don't understand, because they don't design them. Everything is jury-rigged by employees to compensate for deficiencies in the manager's personality. There is only one rule in such systems: Humor the boss. Superstar vampires like to spout off about teamwork, empowerment, and flattening the organization, blissfully unaware that when they're around all real work stops because job number one is entertaining the boss. The comic strip *Dilbert* is a far better guide to this kind of organizational structure than any management text.

SUPERSTAR SEX

Superstars are famous for making fools of themselves over sex. People marvel at how such bright people can act like such complete idiots when their pants are off. Why do they do it?

Sex is just one of the many forms of adulation that Narcissistic Superstars expect from other people. Superstars are major-league seducers and world-class adulterers, but absolute rookies when it comes to love. Often they don't see sex as related to love, at least when they do it.

It's not so much the sex that Narcissists like; it's the keeping score. Antisocials pursue sex because it's fun. If a relationship gets too difficult, they tend to move on because there are other fish in the sea. Not Superstars; as a matter of principle, they want every fish, in every ocean, all the time. Sex for Narcissistic vampires is more important as a token of obeisance than because it feels good or is a form of human closeness. The problem is that the people they get the sex from don't always feel that way.

Superstars are most stupid about using their power as a kind of foreplay. They can delude themselves into thinking that office romances are perquisites of their jobs.

Scene 1: Foreplay

"I gave you the job because you were the most qualified," the vampire manager says. "What more can I tell you?"

"It's not what you say I'm worried about. It's what other people say. They might not think I have enough experience."

"Take my word for it, none of them think that. In their hearts they know you've got what it takes—up here, where it really counts."

"But I just got my MBA last year."

"That's what I mean. We need those new ideas to shake things up a little. Light a fire under the department. Believe me, it needs it."

"You really think I'm qualified?"

"Absolutely!"

Scene 2: Six Weeks After the Affair Begins

"Do you mind telling me how you arrived at this quote on the Austin contract?" the vampire manager asks.

"What's wrong with it? I asked the techs to estimate the amount of time the job would take, then I added in 40 percent for overhead."

"That much, huh? What about management support? Or are you bidding your time at 25 cents an hour these days?"

"But I thought you said it was important that we get this contract. The folks at Austin are on a tight budget, and—"

"Everybody's on a tight budget. Did it ever occur to you that they might just be saying that to scare you into lowballing? Look, how about the next time you write up a quote, come in and schmooze with me about it before you send it out? We'll come up with a number everybody can live with."

"The other managers don't have to run their bids by you."

"Come on, baby, don't take it that way. I'm just trying to help. This business is full of sharks, and I don't want to see you get eaten alive."

Scene 3: A Week Later

"What's this I hear about you complaining to Franklin that I'm micromanaging you?"

"I didn't complain to him. I just asked his advice."

"You asked an executive vice president for advice on how to deal with me? How could you do a thing like that? Why didn't you talk to me about it first?"

"I did, a couple of times. But you didn't seem to take it seriously."

"What do you mean? I just asked you to—"

"Submit all my bids for approval before I send them out."

"But I was just trying to help you learn the ropes."

"You said I was qualified to do this job. Sometimes it seems like you've changed your mind."

"Baby, you've got to understand, this is business. We can't let our personal issues get in the way."

They already have.

There are, of course, all sorts of legal and political implications to this little story, but if you focus only on those, you end up making judgments about who's right and who's wrong and how much in damages the case is worth. There are enough people doing that already.

When Narcissists want something from people, they actually see them as great and wonderful. That's why their hypnosis is so effective. Once Superstars get what they want, their perceptions return to what, for them, is normal—seeing ordinary people as inadequate. The problem is that the people they seduce may still be laboring under the delusion that they are as special as the Superstars said they were.

Everyone is affected adversely by Superstars' peccadillos: the people they seduce, the coworkers who feel they were passed over for promotion, and all the other folks standing on the sidelines watching this soap opera proceed to its unhappy conclusion so they can get on with their jobs. And that's even before the lawyers arrive.

THE PLOT TO CHANGE SUPERSTARS' STYLE

Superstars are usually powerful people. The most effective way to change them as human beings is to change the way they use their power. As you might guess, this task requires some pretty potent hypnosis.

The strategy that has the best chance of changing Superstars' selfish view of power is to create an alternative universe in which paying attention to other people is directly related to the fulfillment of these vampires' grandiose dreams.

Narcissistic Superstars are as vain about their management skills as they are about everything else. They'd like to inspire the fall-on-my-sword-for-you sort of loyalty that they believe to be the mark of great leadership. Actually, they're far more likely to make people want to stab them, or merely go away and work somewhere else. Superstars seldom admit it, but their failure to inspire loyalty hurts their managerial egos. Also, high turnover rates can cause an embarrassing blight on their bottom lines.

Narcissistic Superstars seldom acknowledge problems, but they can jump on a more effective idea when they see one. Their strength is their ability to turn raw ambition into reality; all they need is someone to show them how.

The need is filled by people who make their livings by manipulating Superstars. The best management consultants and business writers are often closet idealists whose mission is to get successful Narcissists to become more responsible human beings.

The Druckers, Coveys, and Senges of the world do their magic by tying success to the simple human strategies that the rest of us learned in kindergarten—listening, sharing, taking turns, and telling things as they actually are—and by reassuring Narcissists that the techniques have worked well for people who are even more successful than they are. Manipulative? You bet, but it's manipulation that works.

If Narcissistic managers learn to pay attention to the needs of other people, it can change their lives. Not only do their bottom lines improve, but they get more authentic respect from the people who work with them. Their newfound insight also opens the door to the empty room in their hearts.

Remember the three requirements for mental health that I outlined in Chapter 2—perception of control, pursuit of challenge, and feeling connected to something larger than yourself? Narcissistic Superstars make top scores in two out of three. They stand proudly at the helm of their own lives, captains of their fate. They love challenge, the tougher the better. Their great deficiency is that they live in a miniature universe no larger than their own desires.

Good consultants make the Superstar's universe bigger. Imagine the mind-expanding rush you'd feel if you had been alone all your life and suddenly found yourself to be a part of humanity.

Management gurus use their hypnotic skills to entice Narcissists into joining the team and working together, which is no small task. It's not that Superstars haven't heard of teamwork; it's just that they're more apt to consider it a public relations ploy rather than an actual way of running their businesses or living their lives.

SUPERSTAR DEPRESSION AND ANGER

Despite the best efforts of consultants, therapists, and significant others, many Superstar vampires never seem to grasp the idea of connecting to something larger than themselves. It is this lack that ultimately makes their lives unsatisfying. Yet these vampires invariably believe that their lack of satisfaction results from other people criticizing them unfairly or just not making enough effort to please them.

Antonio has that pinch-browed look on his face when he comes through the door. Oriana knows that things have gone badly at the clinic. She also knows that within the next few minutes Antonio is going to find something—anything—on which to vent his frustrations.

> *Oriana looks around the living room, hoping that the kids remembered to take their backpacks upstairs. Marta's shoes are in the hallway. Oriana swoops down and whisks them out of sight before Antonio notices. "How was your day?" she ventures.*
>
> *Antonio doesn't answer. A bad sign.*
>
> *Oriana thinks about positive things to bring up. "Ramon got three goals at soccer practice."*
>
> *Antonio grunts, and continues flipping through the mail. "Did you pick up my tweed jacket at the cleaners?" he asks.*
>
> *Oriana feels an electric tingle along her spine. "I meant to," she says, "but I didn't have time."*

Vampire Superstars tend to experience two different kinds of anger that may be indistinguishable to the outside observer.

In the world of Superstars, incompetence is the gravest crime. Their standards for themselves are high, and even higher for the little people around them whose job it is to keep everything running smoothly so that the Superstars can do their jobs. Needless to say, Superstars get angry quite often, especially if other people's mistakes cause even slight inconvenience. These vampires' favorite tantrum is the condescending lecture on standards of minimal competence. Such lectures seldom have the desired effect of inspiring people to work harder and be more careful. Often Superstars feel, correctly, that the little people around them are *purposely* ignoring their requests and instructions. This usually leads to more tantrums.

The other kind of anger that Superstars experience is at themselves when they don't win. Their spirits can drop like a stone at the slightest evidence that they've made a mistake. Superstars are their own severest critics, but when they begin criticizing themselves, they always seem to find things to criticize about other people as well. Being angry at everybody else tends to divert Superstars from their disappointment in themselves. It's hard to say whether Superstars get angry because they're depressed or get depressed because they're angry, but it's absolutely certain that when Narcissistic vampires get depressed, *everyone* gets drained.

If you're close to a Superstar, rather than cringing in fear at his or her irritability or retaliating, it's more helpful to try to find out what the real problem is and discuss it.

> *"Tonio, what do you say we get beyond the grumpiness and talk about what's really going on?" Oriana says.*

"What do you mean?" Antonio replies.

Oriana puts her hands on her hips. "You tell me. All I know is that you don't get this upset unless something really big is bothering you. Has something happened at the clinic?"

"I guess I am upset," Antonio says. His lower lip quivers almost imperceptibly as he pushes it into a fatalistic smile. "I mean, it's not that big a deal, but they, uh, put me on probation for yelling at a nurse in the OR."

Passive-aggressive behavior enrages Superstars, yet they draw it like a magnet. It makes sense. The way they whack people over the head with blunt criticisms, who could blame *anybody* for retaliating? Superstars, that's who.

Narcissistic Superstars and Passive-Aggressive Histrionics are a match made in hell. Each can cause the other to escalate into spasms of self-destruction. If you ever have to deal with Superstar anger, the most important thing to remember is not to respond the way a Passive-Aggressive Histrionic would.

Understate Superstars' transgressions rather than exaggerating them, even slightly. Annoying as they are, Narcissists aren't sadistic like Antisocial Bullies; they don't enjoy inflicting pain for its own sake. Superstars are just a bunch of insensitive babies throwing very creative tantrums. Call them irritable, call them obnoxious, call them SOBs, but don't call them abusers. Abuse is a crime. If you use that word, all you'll get from Superstars is defensiveness. If you impugn their reputations, they'll be more interested in proving you wrong than in hearing what you have to say.

Histrionics tend to use the word *abuse* for anything that causes them discomfort, and that usage has moved into the vernacular. As a rule, the only time it's appropriate to use the term *abuse* is when you've consulted an attorney, or if you're going on a daytime talk show.

Even though Superstars' anger is different from that of Antisocial Bullies, the same strategies will work. If you have to deal with an angry Superstar, you might review the approaches suggested for Bullies in Chapter 7. Your goal, as always, is to get vampires to stop picking on you, not to have them acknowledge how much it hurts to be picked on.

In addition to the strategies outlined for Bullies, there's one more thing to remember about Superstar anger.

Superstars, because of their competence, achievement, and general arrogance, are often more respected than liked. People who love these vampires, in a misguided attempt to humanize them, will sometimes share stories of funny little mistakes that Superstars have made. Don't even think of doing this! Superstars' mistakes are not little, and they are absolutely *not* funny.

THE 10 ELEMENTS OF VAMPIRE FIGHTING STRATEGY: HOW TO STOP BEING TREATED LIKE A GROUPIE
When you deal with Superstars, lose the backstage pass.

1. KNOW THEM, KNOW THEIR HISTORY, AND KNOW YOUR GOAL

Narcissistic Superstars draw you in because of their talents, abilities, and power. They are often special people, and you feel special being around them. You're not. For Narcissists, other people are sources of supplies, rather than real, full-blown human beings. Only Superstars are three-dimensional.

One of the easiest ways to spot Narcissistic vampires is to look around when you need help at an inconvenient time. They're the ones who aren't there.

Superstars' histories are often impressive lists of achievements. Don't be too impressed to find out how they've treated other people while they were doing their great deeds. Whatever happened to those other people is what will happen to you.

There will always be two kinds of people in Superstars' past. The people above them will always think they were wonderful, but if you really want to know what these vampires were like, you have to talk to their peers and the bit players in their lives. There is no greatness without narcissism, and narcissism is caustic to human relationships. The question you want answered about Superstars' past is not whether they were Narcissistic, but how well they kept it contained.

Superstars run many businesses, perhaps yours. If you work for them, they expect to be treated in a particular way, and you'd better know how. Watch the people who are successful and do what they do.

Your goal with Superstars is to get the best return on your effort. This is true whether you are involved in a personal or business relationship with them. I know this sounds mercenary, but it is the approach that works best. Narcissists of all types are famous for unbalanced relationships in which the other person does all the giving. It's harder to get caught if you keep an eye on the bottom line from the beginning. Superstars will not give you anything because you deserve it. In their world they are the only ones who deserve anything. They will, however, give a great deal to get something they want. It makes sense, then, to always know what they want and to make Superstars pay for it by giving you what you want.

If you want Superstars' attention, you'll have to sell yourself and your ideas. Whatever you're selling should be presented in the same way as a Rolls Royce—as a top-of-the-line item that Narcissists *might* not be able to afford. They usually find a way to pay for high-status luxuries. As long as you're one of those, you'll do fine. With Superstars, there's no point in being a bargain.

2. GET OUTSIDE VERIFICATION

With Superstars, it's a bigger problem trying to *give* outside verification than to get it. Behind their backs, everybody agrees that Superstars make mistakes. Nobody wants to tell them to their faces, because Superstars have strong propensities both to ignore information that suggests they're less than wonderful and to kill messengers who bring them bad news.

If you do have bad news to give a Superstar, make sure there are facts and figures to back it up, or opinions from people with status *much* higher than the vampire's own.

As to getting outside verification, Superstar vampires are famous for paying off their debts with vague promises and lots of ego massages. The massages feel very good, so it may be helpful to check with other people to make sure you're getting substance rather than ambience.

3. DO WHAT THEY DON'T

Value the little people and listen to them. Also, help them understand what they have to do to be big people. This is especially important at work, where the temptation will be strong to emulate Superstars, rather than learning from their mistakes.

For all their talents, Superstars are terrible at being team players or coaches of effective teams. In Superstar organizations, the word *teamwork* gets batted around like a softball at the company picnic, but the real emphasis is on individual incentives for top players. The star system, of course, cancels out any motivation to work as a team.

Every person in a position of authority has to make his or her own decision about whether to reward team play or give all the goodies to the rising Superstars. Choose carefully.

4. PAY ATTENTION TO ACTIONS, NOT WORDS

Superstars can talk the talk. They've read the management best-sellers, and they know all the buzzwords, but they're the guys who invented not walking the walk.

5. IDENTIFY HYPNOTIC STRATEGY

The signs to watch out for are the combination of seeing the person as special and experiencing instant rapport. Narcissistic Superstars create an alternate reality in which they are the greatest, and you will be the greatest too if you just give them what they want. In their world, all you're supposed to want in return is the pleasure of their company. They work hard to make you see them as special enough to be exempt from the rules that apply to other people.

In Superstar-run organizations, confusion is the order of the day. Do you believe the flowery speeches and gilt-framed mission statements, or what you see with your own lying eyes? These vampires are famous for trying to hypnotize people into believing that what's best for Superstars is what's best for business.

6. PICK YOUR BATTLES

The most important battle to win is the one for Superstars' respect. You won't get respect because you deserve it, or because of your own talents and achievements. No matter what these vampires say, they will always believe that they are better than you. The only way to win respect from Superstars is by driving a hard bargain. If you hang around with these vampires, you have to show them that you're capable of playing in their league. If you don't constantly demonstrate that you're as tough as they are, they'll just take whatever they want from you and never give anything back at all.

With Superstars, there are some battles you don't want to win. Actually, these are battles you can *appear* to win but in fact lose. To get you off their case, Superstars may tell you what you want to hear even though they don't actually feel it. The price for this kind of false deference is their respect.

Superstars never feel wrong, they never feel gratitude, they don't believe other people are entitled to the same rights and privileges as they are, and they seldom see other people's actions as worthy of spontaneous praise. If you demand any of these indulgences, Superstars will speak whatever words you want to hear and never again give you anything more than lip service. Superstars will formally acknowledge your worthiness at the price of genuine regard. In public, they will say whatever you deem to be politically correct, and laugh in private at your presumptuousness. If they praise you, either they're trying to sneak up on your Narcissistic side or they're indicating that you are one of the little people who needs occasional doses of praise to keep going, much as a car has to be filled with gas.

Be very careful what you ask of Superstars. They're famous for taking the best of what people have and giving back only hollow words, worth less than nothing. It's always up to you to know the difference between inconsequential trinkets and tokens of real respect.

7. LET CONTINGENCIES DO THE WORK

The most meaningful contingency with Superstars is the transaction. To keep from being sucked dry by these vampires, you must always think of yourself as a commodity, because they do. To survive with Superstars, you have to know what they want from you and what you want in return. Then you have to negotiate to get the best price you can. Superstars have absolutely no sense of fairness. If they want something, however, they will generally pay the price, provided it is demanded up front. Don't extend credit.

To negotiate a good price, you have to know what Superstars value. At the top of the list is whatever will make them look good. This can be anything from an impressive bottom line and employees who can do a bang-up job without much supervision, to trophy wives and fancy cars. Narcissistic supplies come in all shapes and sizes.

Next on these vampires' wish list is adoration. With Superstars you just can't suck up too much. If you're selling an idea to Superstars, do it quickly. Always cut to the chase, and tell them what's in it for them if they give you what you want. Forget about snow jobs; these vampires are not easily fooled. Always do your homework. You can bet Superstars have done theirs.

The chance to make money is always a good bargaining chip. Sex might be worth something, if you're attractive and play hard to get. Superstar vampires also like challenges, and interesting company that stimulates their minds. They love a good argument, but you probably won't be able to convince them of anything they don't already believe. It's fine to try, so long as you don't resort to moralism to make your point. Superstars fall asleep during sermons.

Superstars *expect* loyalty, so they're usually not willing to pay much for it. They will, however, spend quite a bit of money and effort to get back at somebody they think has betrayed them.

What Superstar vampires don't value at all is being fair to others, or being seen as nice. They pride themselves on not suffering fools gladly, and they destroy those who try to embarrass them.

What these vampires hate most is whining, unless they're doing it. They absolutely do not care about the trials and tribulations of your life. They may take them on as a problem to solve, but they will never just listen quietly and sympathize.

No matter what they pretend to be, on the inside, Superstars are tough and cynical. If you can't be as tough as they are, stay away from them. They'll eat you alive.

8. CHOOSE YOUR WORDS AS CAREFULLY AS YOU PICK YOUR BATTLES

Superstars are even more sensitive to disapproval than Legends. It might be a good idea to review the section on how to criticize Narcissists in Chapter 10.

The words you should pay most attention to are the ones in your sales pitches. If you think that dealing effectively with Superstars is a lot like door-to-door sales, you're doing it right. Your most important products are yourself and your ideas.

Many people have a hard time promoting themselves because they think it's conceited. They're not about to act like, well, those stuck-up populars in middle school. Unfortunately, stuck-up populars are exactly what you have to sound like.

If you have a problem with that, ask yourself why you think what those populars did was bad. Did someone teach you that shyness was next to godliness? Or did you make up the idea yourself as you sat tight-throated in class, knowing the answer but not daring to speak? The first step in promoting yourself is realizing that a little public relations isn't a bad thing, only difficult.

Next, you need to remember what it was that those populars actually *did*. They didn't boast about themselves, or put other people down (at least in public). They were smoother than that. Here are some self-promotion techniques that you may have missed in middle school. They work just as well today.

Don't Be Afraid to Ask for What You Want. *"I'd really like a part in the school play."* Forget about working so hard and doing such a good job that people come to you with opportunities. In the real world, people get very little that they don't ask for.

Be Enthusiastic. *"Of course I can play quarterback!"* Keep your doubts to yourself. Never discuss mixed feelings with someone who is considering you for a challenging task.

Suck Up. *"I was really impressed with how the debating club performed in the finals last year. Your coaching really paid off."* The most impressive thing you can say to people is that you are impressed with them. If you want others to look favorably on you, give them a list of their achievements, not yours.

Tell Stories That Accentuate Your Strengths. *"When I was campaigning for captain of the cheerleading squad . . ."* List your achievements by telling stories about what happened and what you learned doing responsible, high-status tasks in the past.

Practice. None of this stuff comes naturally or spontaneously. It's play acting, and it has to be rehearsed. Those vampire-in-training populars knew that, and you should too.

9. IGNORE TANTRUMS

Superstars regularly throw tantrums when other people make life difficult for them. They demand competence and severely punish tiny mistakes. It helps to get outside verification to decide whether the vampires actually have a point or are merely trying to manipulate you. If they're trying to manipulate you, stand up to them directly, or lodge a formal complaint. If you try to get back at them in sneaky ways, you'll be the one who gets hurt. Don't call what these vampires do *abuse* or *harassment* until you've checked with your attorney.

If you manage Superstars, *don't* ignore their tantrums. They destroy morale, and people *do* check with their attorneys.

Superstars throw another kind of tantrum that is quieter, but far more destructive. They use their power to frighten people into letting them have everything their own way. Over time they make their worlds over in their own image.

Business is the Superstars' world; everywhere, it bears their marks. In the darkness beneath their towering shadows there can be no dreams greater than personal glory and this quarter's bottom line.

The numbers say business is prospering, yet in cubicles and on production floors times are always hard and the lives of little people are cheap.

Careers are bought and sold in vast bazaars where little people must shout their own praises to passing strangers. It is harder than ever to see the big picture, much less where any of us fit into it.

Unvarnished truth is rarer than a spotted owl, and ethics are simply a function of how you slice and dice the data. Bold vision statements have turned into bland wallpaper, and ground-breaking programs decay into the nameless dust of cost control.

Work groups of unclear authority wander the flattened terrain, hoping they don't make any big mistakes. In some quarters, human sacrifices are still offered to angry gods, and always, hungry lawyers snap and snarl just beyond the light.

In the gray pinstriped hearts of Superstars, unasked questions stir, then roll over and go back to sleep. Words that used to inspire hang above, thin as clouds, pumped with hot air and sucked dry of content. Our prophets are spin doctors, and the still, small voices are drowned out by the thunder of conflicting press releases.

We try our best to do our jobs, but often feel overwhelmed and lost. How do we find our way in a world of vampires? The answers are in our hearts, where they've been all along, like directions written on a scrap of paper and stuffed into a jumbled drawer.

We must control what we can. Fate and vampires deal the cards, but we must play our own hands. We must face our fears, turn them into challenges, and pursue them. Most of all, we have to remember that we are connected to something larger than ourselves. No matter how deep the darkness, if we travel together, we won't get lost.

10. KNOW YOUR OWN LIMITS

If you want to be successful with Superstars, you have to compete in their league and play by their rules. If you do, however, there is a very real danger that you will become like them. With their bites, Superstars create more new vampires than do all the other vampire types combined. Don't enter their world unless you know how to get out. Many have been lost.

THERAPY FOR NARCISSISTIC VAMPIRES

What should you do if you see signs of Narcissistic behavior in yourself or someone you care about? This section is a thumbnail sketch of the sorts of self-help and professional therapeutic approaches that might be beneficial. Always remember that attempting psychotherapy on someone you know will make you both sicker.

THE GOAL

Most of all, Narcissists have to develop a sense of connection to the rest of humanity. Until Narcissistic vampires learn empathy, they are condemned to walk the night in search of one victim after another. Unfortunately, learning empathy takes years. The immediate goal for Narcissists is to act, in public and in private, *as if* they value other people's needs, thoughts, and feelings. With sufficient effort at pretending, Narcissists may eventually discover that their tiny souls can grow to match the size of their egos.

PROFESSIONAL HELP

Narcissists do better with old, rather frumpy therapists who are not impressed with them. These are, of course, not the sorts of therapists that Narcissists would typically select for themselves. They want young, well-dressed yuppies, or eminent and important experts in the field. One of the first therapeutic lessons Narcissists have to learn is that getting what they want may not be what's best for them.

SELF-HELP

Listen!   If you're a Narcissist, the most important thing you can do for yourself is to try to understand and value other people. It's especially helpful to listen quietly when people are criticizing you. Don't answer immediately; take at least 24 hours to consider your response. During that time, think about all the ways the criticisms could be right.

Avoid Talking About Yourself.   You can listen to other people only if you're not trying to convince them of how great you are. If you must mention yourself, talk about your mistakes.

Be a Follower. In as many endeavors as possible, let other people lead and just do what they tell you.

Spend Time with People Who Are Different from You. Join an organization that is made up of good people who are different from you—and participate. If you're a liberal, join Rotary; if you're conservative, join a bowling league in the inner city. The goal of this exercise is to learn that being a good human being is independent of politics and social standing.

Do Charity Work. Charity work does not mean fund raising at fancy affairs! I'm talking about actual get-your-hands-dirty, menial work. Pick up trash, build houses, or serve soup. Wash your hands before doing that last one.

Most of all, *never miss an opportunity to do an anonymous good deed.*

WHAT WILL HURT

Narcissists will be further damaged by just about any situation in which they are treated as different from ordinary people.

4 Too Much of a Good Thing

The Obsessive-Compulsive Types

A pale, attractive woman steps out of the darkness. "Are you a hemophiliac or an intravenous drug user, or do you engage in unprotected sex with multiple partners?"

"No," you say, wondering what this is all about.

"Do you frequently eat ethnic food that has been seasoned with garlic?" She sniffs the air. "No, I guess not. Do you know your blood type? I'm AB intolerant, but occasionally I splurge. I have to take pills though, or I get terrible gas."

Suddenly, you realize what this overly cautious woman intends to do. You turn and dash off into the night.

"Wait," she calls. "I have only one or two more questions."

Can you imagine a vampire who drains you by working hard, being conscientious, and always doing the right thing? I'm sure you can, if an Obsessive-Compulsive vampire has ever caught you making an insignificant mistake or going out to play before all the work was done. Obsessive-Compulsive vampires are the living embodiment of too much of a good thing. In their world, no mistake is insignificant, and all the work is never done.

These vampires have characteristics of **Obsessive-Compulsive personality disorder.** Again the name is confusing because it's also the name of a neurotic condition characterized by ritual repetitions, such as hand washing and door locking. Obsessive-compulsive *disorder* probably involves some disruption in brain chemistry and is often treated with medication. Obsessive-compulsive *personality* is a pattern of thoughts and actions that typically doesn't respond to drugs. To make things more confusing, obsessive-compulsive *disorder* usually occurs in people with obsessive-compulsive *personalities.* As you can already see, dealing effectively with these vampires means keeping your details straight.

The engine that runs both the disorder and the personality is fear. Obsessive-Compulsive vampires are deathly afraid of doing anything wrong. To them, the smallest crack in their perfect facade leaves them open and vulnerable to all the seeping horrors of the universe.

Obsessive-Compulsive vampires see their existence as a battle against the forces of chaos. Their weapons are hard work, adherence to rules, scrupulous attention to detail, and the capacity to delay gratification into the next life if need be.

Without Obsessive-Compulsives to do the unpleasant and painstaking tasks that make the world go, nations would fall, businesses would grind to a halt, and households would collapse into utter confusion. At least, that's what these vampires think, and it may be true. We *do* need them. We trust in their honesty, we depend on their ability, and we rely on their tireless effort. You could almost believe that *we're* the ones who drain *them.* There is, however, more to the story.

Obsessive-Compulsive vampires want to create a secure world by making everybody Obsessive-Compulsive. Only then can they be safe from themselves.

Here's their secret: Inside every Obsessive-Compulsive is an Antisocial trying to claw its way out. These overly conscientious vampires distract themselves from the scrabblings and scrapings of the unacceptable creature within by keeping their hearts in the right place and their noses to the grindstone. The internal battle is too terrifying for them to face, so they force their gaze outward. At you. As long as Obsessive-Compulsive vampires are safely protecting you from your base impulses, they never have to look at their own.

WHAT IT'S LIKE TO BE OBSESSIVE-COMPULSIVE

Imagine your entire future riding on a single critical action—an examination, a presentation, a sports event, or perhaps a job interview. You can't stop thinking about it. You go over every detail to make sure it's perfect, punctuating your thoughts with jolts of adrenaline when you envision making a mistake. One part of Obsessive-Compulsive consciousness is this sort of incessant anxiety over even the smallest of performances.

For the other part, picture yourself walking into your office with your mind already filled to overflowing, then seeing your in-basket stacked to the ceiling and lines of people in the hall bringing in more work. Next, imagine looking around the office and noticing that everybody else is talking, laughing, and generally goofing off. This is the Obsessive-Compulsive's consciousness—always rehearsing something, terrified of mistakes, overwhelmed by trivial tasks, and resentful of other people's lack of attention to detail. Can you imagine how terribly lonely you'd feel being the only competent person on the planet?

All the incessant work and mental activity is designed to keep Obsessive-Compulsives from thinking about that frightening creature inside them. It's not as if these vampires would be serial killers if they let themselves go. The monster inside is little more than a rebellious teenager, so long walled off from the rest of the personality that it has taken on the aspect of an alien menace. Obsessive-Compulsives, like Histrionics, attempt to get rid of the unacceptable in themselves rather than learning how to live with it. Histrionics can just ignore what they don't like. Obsessive-Compulsives have to bury it in piles of work, or drive it off with a flaming sword.

HOW MUCH IS TOO MUCH?

There is no success without compulsion. Since you're reading a book on improving your interpersonal skills instead of watching TV, you probably know this. Being a little Obsessive-Compulsive leads to an accomplished and virtuous life. Being too Obsessive-Compulsive leads to defeating yourself and draining other people. How much is too much?

As we saw in the case of Narcissistic Legends, one of the elements of socialization is learning how to make yourself do things you don't want to do because they need to be done. Obviously, that has to stop somewhere, but where? There must be a point at which a person works too hard or is too good.

Unfortunately, the answer can't be expressed as some sort of optimum good-to-evil or work-to-play ratio. The difference between normal conscientiousness and Obsessive-Compulsive vampire behavior lies not in how much work people do, but in the strategy they use to keep themselves working when they'd rather play. Obsessive-Compulsive vampires use psychological violence—jolts of fear, pangs of guilt, and sharp, icy threats of punishment. And that's just on themselves.

PUNISHMENT, WHERE GOOD AND EVIL MEET

Obsessive-Compulsive vampires believe punishment is synonymous with justice. Punishment is the only strategy that Obsessive-Compulsives know for controlling their own behavior or that of other people. It is also the only one they want to know.

Punishment has two distinct purposes. First, it's a way to keep people from doing bad things. In that respect, it's not particularly efficient. Any psychologist will tell you that rewarding people for positive behavior is far more likely to get them to do what you want.

It is the second use of punishment that makes it so popular with Obsessive-Compulsive vampires. Punishment is a clever device that allows good people to do bad things without seeing themselves as evil.

Obsessive-Compulsives have the same kinds of innate violent tendencies as everybody else, but they deplore them as uncivilized, dangerous, and definitely outside the fence. Unless, of course, they're doing violence to somebody *bad*. The secret reason that Obsessive-Compulsives keep themselves from sin is so they can be first in line when it's time to throw stones.

Obsessive-Compulsives use punishment in all its forms, from condescending lectures and poor performance ratings to witch burning. They always see it as for the person's own good. No matter how and how often they use punishment, Obsessive-Compulsives never grasp its true nature, or understand that it just doesn't work. The only predictable effect of punishment is that it creates more need to punish.

Obsessive-Compulsive vampires coined the phrase "This hurts me more than it does you," and they believe it absolutely. There is no clearer window through which to see the murky confusion of their souls.

Obsessive-Compulsives are always trying to establish order. The problem is that the human mind is basically disorderly. Along with noble impulses, our thoughts are full of mixed feelings and uncivilized urges. These hapless vampires must hide from this reality behind enormous piles of work. From there, they can safely throw stones.

THE OBSESSIVE-COMPULSIVE VAMPIRE CHECKLIST: VICE MASQUERADING AS VIRTUE

True or false: Score one point for each *true* answer.

1.	This person is a workaholic.	T	F
2.	This person has a hard time relaxing.	T	F
3.	This person believes there's a right way and a wrong way to do everything.	T	F
4.	This person can usually find something wrong with other people's way of doing anything.	T	F
5.	This person takes an inordinately long time to make up his or her mind, even about small matters.	T	F
6.	Once this person has made up his or her mind, it's almost impossible to change it.	T	F
7.	This person seldom gives a simple yes or no answer.	T	F
8.	This person's attention to detail may be annoying, but it has saved people from making dangerous or costly mistakes.	T	F
9.	This person has a very clear moral code.	T	F
10.	This person never seems to throw anything away.	T	F
11.	This person runs his or her life according to the adage "if you want something right, do it yourself."	T	F
12.	This person can spend almost as much time organizing a task as doing it.	T	F
13.	This person always looks neat and well organized.	T	F
14.	In meetings, this person will often suggest delaying action until more information can be obtained.	T	F
15.	This person balances his or her checkbook to the penny.	T	F
16.	This person is controlling.	T	F
17.	This person does not see himself or herself as controlling, only right.	T	F

18. When asked to give input on something written, this person   T   F
will always correct the grammar and spelling, and sometimes
make no comment on the overall idea.
19. This person expresses anger by asking hostile questions that   T   F
he or she sees as simple requests for information.
20. This person becomes irritated or upset if asked to deviate   T   F
from his or her routine.
21. This person often feels overwhelmed by all the work he or   T   F
she has to do.
22. Though this person never says it directly, it's clear that he   T   F
or she takes pride in working harder than everybody else.
23. This person takes as much pride in a perfect attendance   T   F
record as he or she does in any other achievement.
24. This person has a hard time finishing tasks.   T   F
25. This person will go through any amount of personal   T   F
difficulty to make good on a promise, and expects you to do
the same.

Scoring: Five or more true answers qualifies the person as an Obsessive-Compulsive Emotional Vampire, though not necessarily for a diagnosis of obsessive-compulsive personality disorder. If the person scores higher than 10, don't get too close or you'll get zapped.

WHAT THE QUESTIONS MEASURE

The specific behaviors covered on the checklist relate to several underlying personality characteristics that define an Obsessive-Compulsive Emotional Vampire.

Love of Work

Forget about simple carnality. The great passion in the lives of Obsessive-Compulsive vampires is work. It is their pride, their joy, their obsession, their drug, the alpha and omega of their existence. It is their gift, and the cross they have to bear. When Obsessive-Compulsives are working, they feel good about themselves and safe. If you want to feel safe, you'd better be working too.

Reliability

You can trust Obsessive-Compulsive vampires. They keep their promises, and they're honest to a fault. Their word is as good as a legal contract, and often as labyrinthine and confusing. In their world the law is all letter and no spirit.

Rigidity

Black-white, right-wrong, good-bad—Obsessive-Compulsives invented the dichotomy, which, like the straight line, does not exist in nature. Obsessive-Compulsives also invented the straight line. Though these vampires love complexity, they have a hard time with ambiguity, especially moral ambiguity. They struggle all their lives to impose order on a capricious universe.

Preoccupation with Details

Obsessive-Compulsive vampires are famous for not seeing forests because of all the trees. They dash frantically from one detail to the next, never quite grasping that all the little details fit together into some sort of big picture.

Perfectionism

Perfectionism is a vice that masquerades as a virtue. It can lead to excellence, but it usually doesn't. Doing everything correctly can become the top priority, eclipsing the importance of the task or the feelings of other people. The wake of Obsessive-Compulsive vampires is an orderly row of insignificant tasks done to perfection, and significant people leaving in frustration because they don't measure up.

Emotional Constriction

Most Obsessive-Compulsives suffer from emotional constipation. Freud thought this was caused by strict toilet training. He called them *anal-retentives,* because not going potty on demand was how they gained control of their overly demanding universe.

For anal-retentives, holding back is a creative act. Emotional control is their major art form. They take pride in it the way any artist would. Obsessive-Compulsive vampires all seem to come from the same planet as

Star Trek's Mr. Spock, a place where irritation at illogical thinking is the only feeling allowed.

Indecisiveness

Obsessive-Compulsives try to keep their options open long after the windows of opportunity have shut. Their basic life strategy is minimizing loss rather than maximizing gain. This strategy is reflected in every conscious decision these vampires make, or rather fail to make.

One of the most common manifestations of Obsessive-Compulsive indecisiveness is the amount of stuff that these vampires accumulate, because they can never bring themselves to throw anything away. Often these vampires require more space to store useless items than they do to live or work in.

Unacknowledged Hostility

Obsessive-Compulsives secretly resent people who are not as hardworking and upstanding as they are. That turns out to be most everyone. The resentment is hidden only from them; everybody else knows about it all too well.

THE OBSESSIVE-COMPULSIVE DILEMMA

Say what you will about Obsessive-Compulsive vampires being difficult and draining. You have to admit that they put their money where their mouth is. Without their hard work and stern example, we all probably would go over the edge.

12 Vampire Perfectionists and Puritans

Can the undead be anal-retentive?

Under the skin, the two major subtypes of Obsessive-Compulsive vampires are similar enough that the same general strategies work for both of them. Perfectionists and Puritans are obsessed with control. They're most draining when they try to lower their own anxieties by managing your life. Perfectionists attempt to control your actions, what you do, and especially how you do it; Puritans try to control your soul.

At first, these vampires don't appear in the least dangerous. They're intelligent, responsible, and hardworking, if a bit uptight. They seem mild-mannered, surely not the sort of people who would lose their tempers or make a scene. They draw you in with their competence and reliability. You may even look up to them. Only later, when you make a mistake, or try to get them to do something *your* way or, perish the thought, give you a little praise, do you come to realize how vicious these vampires can be.

Perfectionists and Puritans drain you by withholding approval, giving in its place petty criticisms and unsolicited comments about the error of your ways. No matter how hard you work, how good you are, or how carefully you try to follow the rules, it won't be enough. The first time you make a mistake, Obsessive-Compulsive vampires will imply that you are lazy, immoral, or at the very least careless. They don't lose their tempers. Their words seem to come from a place of rectitude and moral authority, but they sting like fire and carry the scent of brimstone. Obsessive-Compulsive vampires are not above using the powers of hell to achieve what they consider to be heavenly goals.

WHY DO THEY ALWAYS SEEM ANGRY?

Though they never admit it, Perfectionists and Puritans are angry much of the time. They carry around a good deal of free-floating resentment that they can easily attach to anyone who doesn't follow the same rules about work and morality that they do, which is virtually everyone. These vampires always feel overwhelmed, underappreciated, and disappointed at the laxity of others. They're famous for sighing, shaking their heads, and muttering under their breath as they work themselves up for their next lecture. To hear them tell it, no one even *tries* to help them.

Inside, Obsessive-Compulsive vampires want to rebel just as much as other people want to rebel against them. They never leave the straight and narrow path, however, because their own cruel consciences keep prodding them along and holding their feet to the fire. The pain they cause for you is nothing compared with what they inflict on themselves.

To make matters worse, these vampires are unaware of their anger, their urge to rebel, or any other untoward thoughts they may be having. In their minds everything unacceptable is buried under stacks of rule books and piles of work.

Perfectionists and Puritans are angry because they're good people who are somehow stuck in a bad world.

OBSESSIVE-COMPULSIVE HYPNOSIS

Beware of confusion! Obsessive-Compulsive vampires purposely fog their minds with minutiae to obscure the objectives of their own actions. If you don't watch out, they'll do the same to you. Obsessive-Compulsives create an alternate reality in which even the simplest tasks are fraught with hundreds of confusing and esoteric details that must be kept under tight control lest everything fall apart. What they're really trying to keep under control are their own aggressive impulses.

As we have seen throughout our study of vampires, unacceptable impulses forced out of awareness always come back in darker and more dangerous form. Obsessive-Compulsive vampires could be the poster children for this process. The last thing these children of the night would consider doing consciously is taking hostile action in their own self-interest. Their aggressive impulses are relegated to the top of their unconscious agenda, where they're pursued with a vengeance.

Perfectionists and Puritans try to hypnotize you into believing that their anger is praiseworthy, since it is in the service of goodness and light. Don't be fooled; behind all the moralizing and responsibility, under the piles of rules, and beneath the rationalizations, Obsessive-Compulsive vampires are bullies. As long as you remember that, they can't sneak up out of the fog and bite you.

PRODUCT VERSUS PROCESS

To deal effectively with Obsessive-Compulsives, you have to know what they're doing even when they don't. This statement, like everything else relating to these complex and confusing vampires, has meanings on several different levels. To keep the levels straight, let's consider the notions of product and process.

Product is *what* you're trying to do. Process is *how* you do it. The two are separate—a point you need to remember, because Obsessive-Compulsives won't.

Think of all actions as having a product or goal. At work the products, in addition to what gets sold, include improving quality, reducing costs, writing marketing plans, and making specific decisions. At home the products may be getting the dishes washed, keeping the house clean enough for unexpected company, and raising moral and responsible children.

Obsessive-Compulsives habitually confuse process with product. To them, *how* something is done can become more important than whether it gets done at all. It always helps to use well-constructed questions to keep these anal-retentive vampires focused on the product rather than lost in the forests of process, which in their view surround everything. Questions like "What's our overall goal here?" and "What would you like me to do?" are extremely useful in dealing with Obsessive-Compulsive vampires.

Product-clarifying questions can help you keep tasks in focus. Obsessive-Compulsives tend to think that there is only one way to achieve any goal. The more clearly the endpoint is defined, the more likely these vampires are to allow a number of ways of getting there. If you are unfortunate enough to work for an Obsessive-Compulsive boss, you'll make your life more bearable by contracting for specific deliverables on specific dates. When the boss starts checking to see *how* you're going about your task, you can gently point out that the product will be on the boss's desk by the due date. If the boss quibbles about process (and any Obsessive-Compulsive will), you can go back to the original contract and say that *what* you're sup-posed to do is in it, but *how* is not. Does this mean the boss is changing the terms of the agreement? By taking this approach, you make the *how* a sub-ject for negotiation rather than a foregone, but unstated, conclusion.

Needless to say, this strategy will work only if you put out deliverables that are on time and up to previously agreed-upon specifications.

If you can get Obsessive-Compulsives to specify in advance what prod-uct you're supposed to be working on, they're less likely to change the goal later on. Unlike other vampires, Obsessive-Compulsives have a strong sense of fairness. Their own internal logic dictates that if there are rules, they have to play by them. Your best bet is to do everything you can to get the rules on the books before the game starts.

By the way, the technique of asking questions to clarify the product works almost as well on Obsessive-Compulsive vampires who only *think* they're your boss.

DEMANDING PRIORITIES

For Obsessive-Compulsives, product is a moving target. When you ask, "What do you want me to do?" their list grows longer and longer the more they think about it. In their minds, as soon as a product is specified, it begins to turn back into process. You can actually see it happening. Before your eyes, overall goals morph into smaller and smaller tasks of ever-decreasing relevance.

At that point you need to ask your second question: "What's the top priority?" For Obsessive-Compulsive vampires, being in control is always the main goal. The easiest way for them to maintain control is to make prod-ucts and priorities vague, and keep all discussion fixed endlessly on process. By asking what specifically they want you to do, and in what order they want it done, you may be able to gain some control over your own destiny.

This brings us to a consideration of *your* hidden goals. If your top prior-ity is demonstrating to these vampires that they can't tell you what to do, you are apt to make more than your share of mistakes. Unfortunately, Obsessive-Compulsives are often right. If you want to deal with them effec-tively, you have to put aside any tendencies toward rebellion for its own sake, and learn from them when they know more than you.

The other goal you may be trying to achieve in your interactions with Obsessive-Compulsive vampires is winning their approval. Give it up. Before

Obsessive-Compulsives can give a compliment, they have to figure out all the possible ways you might have messed up, and then make sure you didn't do any of them. By the time they've assembled enough information to justify praise, you'll probably have forgotten what it was you did in the first place.

If there are Obsessive-Compulsives in your life, you have to learn to evaluate your own performance and praise yourself for your achievements. They never will, even when they love you.

PERFECTIONISTS

Perfectionism is a vice that masquerades as a virtue. For people who only want everything to be right, Perfectionistic vampires can cause an incredible number of things to go wrong.

Sunday at 6:32 p.m. Kevin startles the cat by jumping up and shouting "Yes!" far more loudly than he'd intended. Finished at last! Vampire Sarah and the kids have been at her mom's all weekend, and he's spent the entire time taking care of a whole to-do list of little jobs that have been piling up for months. He's also managed to clean the house from top to bottom. Sarah always says she wants him to take some initiative about chores, and this time he has. As Kevin drives to the airport to meet her 7:30 plane, he thinks about how pleased she'll be.

At 8:47 p.m. Kevin pulls into the driveway with his family. He's anticipating the surprised expression on Sarah's face when she sees the house. Before he even turns off the ignition, Sarah looks at the curb and shakes her head. "Tomorrow is garbage day. Will you put the cans and recycling out while I get something for the boys to eat? They're starving."

"Sure," Kevin says. Damn it, he thinks. She would have to notice the one thing I forgot.

As soon as he carries the suitcases into the entryway, Kevin hurries into the kitchen to take out the garbage.

Sarah is leaning over the sink scraping at a plate with her fingernail. "Kevin," she says, "I've asked you to rinse the dishes off before you put them in the dishwasher. Once the food gets caked on, you know it's almost impossible to get off."

Instead of saying anything, Kevin shuffles into the family room and turns on the TV.

Perfectionists, bless their neurotic little hearts, don't have a clue about what a pain they are to everybody around them. It's not that they don't care what the people close to them feel; it's just that they get so distracted by little details in the process of living that they miss the overall product. If Kevin also loses sight of the big picture, he will make the situation worse for himself, and for Sarah.

Kevin needs to realize that Sarah's withholding of praise, no matter how much it hurts his feelings, isn't in itself an attack. It's an oversight that he can correct if he stays focused on the product he wants to achieve. If he blows up, withdraws, or refrains from helping around the house in the future, Sarah *will* attack because there will be good reason to dump some of her free-floating resentment onto him.

To understand how Kevin can avoid further disaster, we have to go back to the beginning and see how he got into this unfortunate situation.

For his hard work, Kevin expected a spontaneous expression of delight from Sarah. This is unrealistic to say the least. Perfectionists never do anything spontaneously, except perhaps notice mistakes. To Obsessive-Compulsives, the notion of a pleasant surprise is an oxymoron. Spontaneity means a loss of control, which is usually too threatening to consider. If Kevin thinks back, he'll probably remember that most of his attempts to surprise Sarah have not come to good ends.

Kevin should also realize that to a Perfectionist, few jobs are done well enough to warrant unsolicited praise. He *can* get Sarah to acknowledge his efforts and his intent to please her, but he will have to ask for what he wants directly. Instead of sulking in the family room—a response that Sarah will interpret, correctly, as typical male withdrawal—Kevin needs to tell her that his feelings are hurt by her lack of attention to his labors. She will understand this because she's felt the same way most of her life. They can both agree that it hurts to be overworked and underappreciated, and that they ought to do something so neither of them has to go through this sort of thing again. The stage is set for a deal.

Kevin can offer to take care of more jobs around the house if Sarah will agree to specify the product—washed dishes, a vacuumed rug, a mowed lawn, or whatever—and let him be in charge of the process.

I'm not naive enough to believe that Sarah can stick to this agreement, but the important thing for Kevin is to establish it as a rule on the books. Perfectionists usually play by the rules, whether they like them or not. By clarifying product and process, Kevin can turn a difficult and painful situation with a Perfectionist into a template for further productive discussion. As a solution, it beats TV.

HOW THE IMPERFECT CAN DEAL WITH PERFECTIONISTS

If you have to live or work with a Perfectionist, here are some ideas that may lead to productive discussions instead of heated arguments and cold shoulders.

Ask for What You Want Directly. Saying, "You always tell me what I do wrong, never what I do right," won't get you anywhere, even if it's true. Instead ask, "What did you like about what I did?" Consider three criticisms or less to be an A+.

If Your Feelings Are Hurt, Say So. Don't try to make your point indirectly by rebelling, withdrawing, "accidentally" making mistakes, or griping to friends, family, and coworkers. Passive-aggressive behavior just makes Perfectionists feel more justified in their anger. There's no point in throwing gas on the fire.

Don't Criticize Perfectionism. Perfectionists may *say* that their perfectionism is a problem, but they don't really believe it. Secretly, they're very proud of how hard they work and what they accomplish. Also, if you're pointing the finger at their faults, they'll feel justified in attacking yours. Their overriding fault is being too good. Do you really want to compete with that?

Negotiate for Product. This is the ideal to strive for, rather than a real goal. Not meddling in the process is the one thing Perfectionists can't do perfectly. Nevertheless, the more clearly you can specify in advance the product you're responsible for, the easier your job will be.

Demand Priorities. With Perfectionists, tasks have a way of mounting up. You always have the right to ask which should be done first. Exercise it. It will help you, and it will encourage Perfectionists to maintain perspective. The primary task of management is to set priorities for those managed. Always make sure that the people who try to manage you are doing their job.

Show Some Appreciation. You can be sure that however hard they are on you, Perfectionists are twice as hard on themselves. Face it, they're better than we are. They have to be.

PURITANS

Puritans are moral perfectionists. They try to make the world safe for truth, justice, and love, using censorship, punishment, and cruelty. They never realize that they're the primary instigators of the forces of evil that they labor so hard to combat. If there's a Puritan in your life, you know it's far easier to be a saint than it is to live with one.

> *Karma marches into Rebecca's office wearing more ribbons on her chest than a Bulgarian general. Red for AIDS, pink for breast cancer, yellow for the holocaust, black for something Rebecca can't remember at the moment.*
>
> *"What's up, Karma?" Rebecca asks.*
>
> *"It's this memo," Karma says, holding up a sheet of bright red paper and laying it down on Rebecca's desk with a thump.*
>
> *Rebecca recognizes the memo; she sent it out yesterday with the bonus checks to thank people in the department for their hard work over the year, and to wish them a happy holiday season. She pulls it closer and reads it again. "I don't see what the problem is," Rebecca says, as she hands the memo back to Karma.*
>
> *"That **is** the problem. You don't **see** that this memo, with its direct references to a Christian observance, could be offensive to some people who don't choose to celebrate the same holidays as the dominant culture."*
>
> *"But there's nothing in here about Christmas," Rebecca says. "I purposely didn't mention any specific holiday. I thought the memo could refer to Christmas, Hanukkah, or Kwanzaa."*
>
> *"What about Rahim, who's a Muslim? Muslims don't have a so-called holiday season at this time of year. Or did you ever think about Kelly, who's a Jehovah's Witness? She doesn't believe in celebrating **any** holidays."*
>
> *"I didn't know that Rahim and Kelly were upset. They didn't say anything—"*
>
> *Karma folds her arms and glares. "Frankly, Rebecca, I expected a little more cultural sensitivity from you, of all people. Being*

African-American, you must know what it's like to have people ignore your heritage."

Puritans are a mass of contradictions. They'll make your life hell attempting to get you to heaven. They see no logical flaw in making people suffer to end suffering, or publicly ridiculing some people to spare the feelings of others. Puritans try to bully everyone into being as fair and kind as they are. No matter how much they secretly enjoy making you suffer, Puritans always see their actions as totally selfless. If they are annoying or punitive, it's for your own good, or for the good of humanity.

Before we consign these heartless vampires to the pit, we ought to make an effort to understand them. It's possible that a little knowledge might help us make them a little less annoying.

WHY ARE PURITANS SO MEAN?

Puritans think that the world is unkind to moral people, so they feel justified in returning the favor. Actually, the world is more ambiguous than unkind, but Puritans seldom appreciate this subtle distinction. The problem lies in the typical Obsessive-Compulsive confusion of process and product.

People with rigid black-and-white moral codes spend their lives following rather arbitrary rules because they expect concrete rewards for keeping the rules and punishment for breaking them. Puritans don't understand that virtue is its own reward. They keep expecting some higher power to step in to praise the saints and punish the sinners. Puritans invented the idea of heaven and hell for this purpose, but for many of them, the afterlife isn't soon enough to settle the score. They feel they have to step in and do God's work, at least when it comes to punishing sinners.

What Puritans are really looking for are a few earthly rewards. The problem is that here in the real world, rewards go to people who know how to get them, not necessarily to people who deserve them. Puritans scrupulously follow a process that they expect will lead to glory and riches, but all it gets them is stars in their crown.

Following rules *can* reward people with a feeling of connection with something larger than themselves—namely, the rest of humanity. Unfortunately, Puritans, in their quest for bottom-line settling up of moral accounts, often miss out on the greatest reward life has to offer. No wonder they're resentful.

DEALING WITH PURITANS WITHOUT GETTING BURNED

There are two basic ways to deal with Puritans: You can humor them and laugh behind their backs, or you can show them how to get the earthly rewards they really want. The first is easier, and far more commonly practiced.

If you want to try the second, you need to point out, gently, that it's their reliance on punishment and censorship that's causing the problems. Gentleness is necessary because Puritans model their external strategies on what they do inside their own heads. If you're too emphatic, they'll point out proudly that such tactics have made *them* what they are. This may leave you in a rather embarrassing position.

Punishment is a terrible strategy for improving other people's behavior. Its main effect is making people want to avoid the punisher, or to retaliate. Censorship doesn't work either. It just makes people more curious about what they're not allowed to see. The Puritans' process for dealing with sin generally causes it to increase rather than decrease. This happens inside the Puritans as well, but trying to explain *that* to them might just get you burned at the stake.

Instead, try to explain the process for getting earthly rewards. Love goes to people who are nice, respect goes to people who give respect, and riches go to people who know how to seize an opportunity.

Take Karma in our example. In addition to justice for the downtrodden, she probably wants influential people like Rebecca to respect her, listen to her ideas, and see her as a good employee, worthy of responsible work and possibly promotions. Karma is making just the opposite impression.

What can Rebecca tell her? About the memo, nothing. Rebecca should thank her, and let the issue drop as quickly as possible. Rebecca needs to see the incident as an indication that Karma feels unappreciated, and that Karma is probably a bellwether for other moral and high-principled people in the office who aren't willing to be as obnoxious.

In most business settings, people who work hard and play by the rules are disappointed by their lack of success. At least part of the reason for this is censorship, which seems to be the strategy everyone thinks of when Puritans are involved. Nobody tells Obsessive-Compulsives what they really need to do to get ahead because the truth is a little embarrassing. Karma and her hardworking cohorts spend their days plugging away at the tasks *they* believe should make a difference and getting more and more resentful when their efforts don't pay off. Rebecca needs to disabuse them of the notion that hard work, in and of itself, will be rewarded and let them know how to really get the goodies.

She could start by explaining that doing a good job and succeeding are totally different concepts. Doing a good job means competently managing the people below you in the organizational hierarchy. Success comes from managing the people above you. The skills involved are usually very different, so it's not a good idea to mistake one for the other.

For example, the following activities are all part of doing a good job, but will probably not have anything to do with whether you advance in the corporate hierarchy:

1. *Working directly with customers.* In most companies customer service is an important corporate goal, but it is not accomplished by important corporate people. Selling is a possible exception. If you want to get ahead and you have to deal with customers, it is much better to be close to the people who buy your product than to the people who use it.

2. *Serving on work groups at your level or below.* Task forces and committees solve problems, organize work, and get things done. They don't yield much in the way of glory to their participants.

3. *Training.* Training is an absolute necessity, but the corporate world believes the old adage: "If you can, do. If you can't, teach."

4. *Coming up with high-cost ways to improve quality or morale.* If you're the owner or CEO, you can think big and be praised for it. If you're anybody else, it will be taken as evidence that you don't understand what business is all about.

The following activities may have little to do with doing a good job, but they *will* lead to corporate advancement:

1. *Bringing in new business.* It doesn't have to be much business or even good business. In the corporate world, it is always the rainmakers who are on top of the heap. Compared with bringing in new business, winning the Nobel Prize is small potatoes.

2. *Cutting costs.* Cost cutting is a divinely ordained task of management. Do it often and conspicuously to show that you are leadership material. At meetings, always be the one who asks if it can be done cheaper. There's one important exception: Never talk about cost cutting and executive salaries in the same breath.

3. *Doing anything with people of higher rank.* This is especially true if you are the person in front of the room with an overhead projector and killer graphics. If not, be the one who asks if it can be done cheaper.

4. *Taking management's side on controversial issues.* Doing a good job often involves cooperation and compromise. Getting ahead involves looking after your own interests. It may be sad, but it's true. Promotions are not awarded by popular vote.

5. *Generating paper.* Most anything that goes out with your name on it (other than memos criticizing management) will enhance your reputation. Reports, policies and procedures manuals, goal statements, mission statements, quality improvement plans, and pieces about corporate values are all good choices. Avoid documents explaining government regulations, because they will cause people to mistake you for the government.

6. *Socializing.* The biggest rewards always go to the people who are out shaking hands, not the ones sitting in their offices producing product.

In the corporate world, the real secrets of success are often censored because Puritans like Karma might be outraged if they knew them. Outrage is likely, but it's what Puritans do after the fuming and fussing dies down that's really important. Most Puritans don't want to be martyrs for their principles. What they really want are the same things everybody else does. If you tell it to them like it is instead of patronizing them, they may respond. At first, they'll be offended. They'll undoubtedly want to lecture you on morality, but if you stick to your guns and don't apologize for telling the truth, they may come to respect you. Then, they may even listen.

Have a little faith in Perfectionists and Puritans and all the rest of the Obsessive-Compulsives. Remember, we need them as much as they need us.

THE 10 ELEMENTS OF VAMPIRE FIGHTING STRATEGY: WHAT TO DO WHEN THE GOOD GUYS ARE AFTER YOU

Convince Obsessive-Compulsives that you're not really one of the bad guys.

1. KNOW THEM, KNOW THEIR HISTORY, AND KNOW YOUR GOAL

It's easy to recognize Perfectionists. They'll walk right up to you and identify themselves. Then they'll probably tell you what's wrong with whatever you're doing. Puritans are also easy to spot; they seldom go long periods of time without getting offended at something. Both of these vampire types try to control whatever situation they're in, down to the tiniest details. Especially the tiniest details. These vampires contain their anxieties about bigger issues through overconcern with the small. If you let them, they'll manage their own anxieties by delegating them to you.

It's easy to play right into their hands. If you go along with their demands, they'll just pile on more. If you rebel or get angry at their pettiness, they'll try to put you under even tighter control, because it's clear that you're the one with the problem.

Your goal should be negotiation, not recrimination. Every task has an end product—whatever it is that needs to be done. A task also has a process—the actual behaviors through which the end product is achieved. Negotiate to deliver a very specific product at a very specific time. If you hand over the goods, there is less motivation to quibble about how you got them. Not that Obsessive-Compulsive vampires won't try. Treat attempts to control the process as requests to change the end product, which means reopening the whole negotiation. If the end product isn't affected, why change the process? Needless to say, you have to have some history of delivering the goods for a strategy like this to work.

Bottom line: If you do what you say you'll do when you say you'll do it, these overcontrolling vampires will go and drain somebody less reliable.

2. GET OUTSIDE VERIFICATION

Obsessive-Compulsives vampires tend to structure their lives to minimize failure rather than maximizing success. As a result, they will be quick to tell you what's wrong with any new idea. Don't let these vampires be your only source of information as to what's possible. They are the ones who told Leonardo Da Vinci his flying machine would never get off the ground.

If you work with Obsessive-Compulsive vampires, you can make them less draining and more focused by getting clarification of goals and priorities from above—the higher above, the better. Take advantage of the fact that the Obsessive-Compulsive code of conduct often precludes arguing with authority figures.

At home, you'll never win an argument with an Obsessive-Compulsive vampire on the strength of your ideas alone. For Perfectionists, the documented opinion of an eminent expert might open up the discussion. For Puritans, a few biblical quotes may help. They tend to forget the ones about mercy and forgiveness.

3. DO WHAT THEY DON'T

Look at the big picture, paying attention to details as they fit into the overall pattern. Know what you want, and realize that there's always more than one way to get it. Have a sense of humor about yourself. Most important, use punishment only as a last resort.

4. PAY ATTENTION TO ACTIONS, NOT WORDS

Obsessive-Compulsive vampires want you to pay attention to how hard they work, how much they do, and how well they do it. Don't be distracted by the quantity or even the quality of their work. Pay attention to how relevant what they do is in achieving the overall goal.

5. IDENTIFY HYPNOTIC STRATEGY

Obsessive-Compulsives' favorite hypnotic technique is scaring the hell out of you with an old-fashioned hellfire-and-brimstone sermon. Perfectionists run on about the terrible problems that will result if you don't do everything exactly as they say. Puritans tell you that if you don't believe exactly as they do, you'll burn in a lake of fire. Both vampire types secretly enjoy inflicting pain because they've hypnotized themselves into believing it's for your own good.

These vampires are not heartless. Sometimes you can break the spell by telling them that they're *unintentionally* hurting your feelings. If you try to convince them that they're hurting you on purpose, believe me, you'll fry.

6. PICK YOUR BATTLES

Forget trying to talk Obsessive-Compulsives out of being controlling. Even seasoned therapists have trouble with that. (Between you and me, at least part of the difficulty lies in the fact that it's always hardest to cure people who have the same neuroses that you do.)

Never expect Obsessive-Compulsive vampires to see anything selfish or purposely hurtful in their own actions. They are experts both in self-deception and in the letter of the law. If certain actions have made it past an Obsessive-Compulsive's internal censors, it means they've been thoroughly rationalized and are, in the vampire's mind at least, completely legal, moral, and altruistic.

As we've seen already, the battles you're most likely to win involve having Perfectionists and Puritans specify products and priorities and negotiating some latitude in how to achieve them.

7. LET CONTINGENCIES DO THE WORK

Always understand that Obsessive-Compulsive vampires are sincerely trying to be good people and do a good job. The problem is that they're pretty naive about how human beings operate. They let their beliefs about how things should be blind them to the way things really are. Consequently, these vampires are sometimes dead wrong about what process leads to what product.

You might be able to help them make better choices by explaining the contingencies that are actually operating. Gently remind them that rewards go for results rather than good intentions. Tell them that it's human nature to want to see what you're not supposed to see and do what you're not supposed to do. Deferentially suggest that the more you criticize people for messing up, the angrier you make them—and the more incentive you give them to mess up even more as a way of getting you back.

Most of all, let these vampires know what contingencies they have to follow to get what they want from you. This is especially important if they're your employees. Tell them the unwritten rules, because they'll never figure them out on their own. Even though Obsessive-Compulsive vampires practice censorship to avoid embarrassment, you shouldn't.

Finally, respect the fact that Obsessive-Compulsives structure their lives to minimize losses rather than to maximize gains. In order for these vampires to risk doing anything differently, the benefits have to be very clear and very large.

8. CHOOSE YOUR WORDS AS CAREFULLY AS YOU PICK YOUR BATTLES

Perfectionists and Puritans are never wrong. If you criticize these vampires, they're likely to respond with a list of incidents in which you did something worse—complete with time, date, and witnesses.

One of their favorite defenses is explaining how whatever they did was the result of your miscommunication about what you wanted. They will, of course, twist your words unmercifully. Unless you have a tape recording, don't bother trying to explain what you actually said.

When Obsessive-Compulsives criticize you, don't try to use their own strategies on them. They're better at them than you are. Instead, ask questions that invite them to focus on the product that they are trying to create. "Why are you telling me this?" is a good beginning, followed by "What would you like me to do?"

In any difficult situation involving an Obsessive-Compulsive vampire, it's always more effective to ask questions than to make statements that can be disputed. If you let vampires start questioning you, it will turn into a cross-examination followed by a swift conviction.

9. IGNORE TANTRUMS

Obsessive-Compulsive tantrums are nothing if not subtle. These vampires express their feelings of overwork and underappreciation with sighs and disdainful snorts at the less industrious. They'll swear it's just a sinus problem. Don't waste your time trying to get them to take responsibility for non-verbal editorial comments. You'll need all your energy for their major tantrums, which usually take the form of long and exhausting guilt trips.

Always remember that though their words may sting like scorpions, they're still only words. In the end, the only weapons these vampires have are verbal attacks on your perception of yourself as a moral and effective person. *If you know who you are, they can't hurt you. If you need their approval to maintain your self-esteem, you're dead.*

10. KNOW YOUR OWN LIMITS

It's better to know your own limitations. Perfectionists and Puritans always have something to teach you about the areas in which you don't measure up. Their lessons are hard, but valuable. Obsessive-Compulsives are the world's toughest audience. If you can convince them, you're probably right. If you feel the need to hide something from them, it's probably wrong. They can help you be a better person, but you alone have to decide how good you want to be.

THERAPY FOR OBSESSIVE-COMPULSIVE VAMPIRES

What should you do if you see signs of Obsessive-Compulsive behavior in yourself or someone you care about? This section is a thumbnail sketch of the sorts of self-help and professional therapeutic approaches that might be beneficial. Always remember that attempting psychotherapy on someone you know will make you both sicker.

THE GOAL

The goal of all treatment for Obsessive-Compulsives is to help them move away from fear of bad consequences as the prime mover in their lives and the lives of people around them. Obsessive-Compulsives need to focus on the big stuff and not sweat the small, and not make other people sweat at all. The big stuff for them is their relationships, which they can unwittingly destroy by trying to make those close to them into better people.

PROFESSIONAL HELP

Essentially, anything that will hurt a Histrionic will help an Obsessive-Compulsive, and vice versa. Obsessive-Compulsives can profit from techniques that focus on expressing feelings and generally being positive. New Age approaches, art and dance therapy, and random exploration of emotions may damage other vampires, but they can help Obsessive-Compulsives. A useful rule of thumb is: If the Obsessive-Compulsive vampire thinks the approach is scary or stupid, it will probably do some good.

Avoid approaches that analyze thoughts in great detail, or that require a lot of written work. Obsessive-Compulsives love these, but seldom change as a result of such techniques.

SELF-HELP

If you recognize Obsessive-Compulsive tendencies in yourself, the following exercises will be very difficult for you, but they will make a difference.

Always Know Your Top Priority.   Not for the moment, but for your whole life. Think about what you'd like to have carved on your tombstone and work toward that. The other details will take care of themselves.

Judge Not, Lest Ye Be Judged.   Pay attention to the negative judgments you make about people and things. Every time you catch yourself thinking that something is bad, quickly, in your mind, list two good things about it. If you can't come up with two, ask somebody to explain the good parts to you.

Goof Off.   Spend a little time every day just sitting and doing nothing. Computer solitaire was invented for this purpose. Learn some sort of relaxation technique and practice it every day, especially on the days you think you're too busy.

Specify Products and Don't Meddle in Process.   Define the final product you want from other people as clearly as possible, then step back and let them do their best. Performance never improves when you stand over someone's shoulder. Let people learn from their mistakes rather than your lectures.

Criticize Only on Thursdays.   The rest of the week, use praising people for what they do right as your only device for behavioral control. If you save all your criticisms for one day of the week, you may be surprised at how few will be needed by the time Thursday rolls around. Remember, the Thursday rule applies to your own actions as well.

Publicly Acknowledge at Least One Mistake per Day.   Maybe you could acknowledge two on Thursdays.

WHAT WILL HURT

Obsessive-Compulsives love psychoanalysis and other process-oriented approaches. They can be in them for years, trying to comprehend the underlying reasons for everything they do, and never changing anything. They can do pretty much the same thing with highly structured behavioral and cognitive techniques, because they do all the exercises perfectly but forget to learn anything from them.

5 Seeing Things That Others Can't

The Paranoid Types

The vampire throws down the paperback in anger. "It's a conspiracy, I tell you. In every single story it's the same thing—evil vampires attacking the poor little defenseless human women. So later, when the big macho guys come with the stakes to kill us while we sleep, you think they're heroes instead of cold-blooded murderers. Give me a break! Even the Nazis get better press than we do."

He opens his laptop and stares pensively at the screen, his face bathed in greenish light. "I think it's about time that somebody opened a Web site to tell it like it really is." His fingers begin to fly over the keys.

Another confusing name. To most people, *paranoid* means delusions of persecution. The word really describes an exquisitely simple way of perceiving a complex world. Paranoids can't tolerate ambiguity. In their minds, nothing is accidental or random; everything means something, and everything relates to everything else. This sort of thinking can lead to genius or to psychosis, depending on how it's used.

There's no question that Paranoid vampires see things that other people can't. But do the things they see actually exist? *That's* the question.

These vampires have tendencies toward **Paranoid personality disorder,** which, like the vampires themselves, is often misunderstood, even by the people who treat it. The word *paranoia,* which means "thinking beside oneself," has been used to describe virtually all forms of craziness, especially those involving false beliefs. The problem with the concept, as any Paranoid will tell you, is that it's not all that simple to determine which beliefs are false and which are true.

Paranoia is easier to understand if you look at the patterns of thinking that lead to false beliefs, rather than at the beliefs themselves. Paranoids are blessed and cursed with the ability to perceive very tiny cues. Unlike Obsessive-Compulsives, who become unfocused and overwhelmed by life's small details, Paranoids drive themselves crazy by trying to organize details into a coherent and unambiguous whole.

Paranoid vampires' perceptive ability and compulsion to organize may have their roots at the neurological level. Wherever they come from, these behaviors create tremendous problems in relating to human beings. When Paranoids look at other people, they see too much for their own good. And everybody else's.

Paranoids long for a simple world in which people can be trusted to mean what they say, particularly when those people are talking about the Paranoids in their midst. Instead, Paranoid vampires see the human condition in all its ambiguous detail. People exist on many different levels at the same time. No human thought is singular and no feeling pure. Many of the conflicts that people experience are observable in slight hesitations, small changes in expression, slips of the tongue, and the like. Most people ignore these tiny cues, but Paranoids try to sort them into either-or categories— love or hate, yes or no, truth or falsehood. Sometimes, in their search for simple answers, Paranoids can see through all forms of subterfuge to the heart of a matter. Just as easily, they can rip that heart out and tear it to pieces—especially when it belongs to someone close to them whose only crime is being human.

Paranoid vampires draw you in with their perceptiveness; they see the confusing and uncertain details of life so clearly. Later, they drain you with endless probing of the uncertainty they perceive in you.

What Paranoids never see is their own role in creating the ambiguity that so terrifies them. Their distrust invites duplicity. Their suspiciousness keeps people from telling them the whole truth. Their incessant doubts drive away the people who say they'll always be there. Paranoids can feel like they're at the center of a vast conspiracy to rob them of the certainty they so fervently desire. Naturally, they become even more guarded and suspicious.

What these vampires really fear is the uncertainty at the center of their own souls. They desperately want to be close, but are terrified at the ambiguity that comes with closeness. They try to drive the desire for intimacy out of their hearts. In place of love, Paranoid vampires search in vain for purity and truth.

PARANOID PURITY

Paranoid vampires try to remove the ambiguity from their lives by organizing everything around a small number of black-and-white principles. Truth, loyalty, courage, honor, and the like are not abstractions in the minds of Paranoids. They are living, breathing presences that these vampires live by, and will kill or die for if called upon to do so. At least that's the way the Paranoids themselves imagine it. The reality is, of course, more complex. Paranoids are just as likely as anybody else to justify their self-serving actions according to high-sounding principles. More likely, actually. The most dangerous thing about Paranoids is their utter certainty of their own virtue.

Even Obsessive-Compulsive Puritans are aware enough of their own failings to grudgingly forgive others their trespasses—if they acknowledge the error of their ways. Paranoids seldom forgive. Puritans try to punish only the sin; Paranoids happily consign sinners to the flames.

Aside from their questionable approach to morality, Paranoids are capable of extreme purity of thought. Many discoveries of the organizing principles that bind the universe together are the products of Paranoid thinking. So is every crackpot theory you've ever heard of.

Paranoid vampires vacillate between extreme naivete and utter cynicism. Their goal is to achieve a happy world (or family, or business) in which everyone follows the same simple and rigid rules as they do. When people go along, Paranoids are happy, loving, and giving. If by some chance other people want to think for themselves, Paranoid vampires take it as a personal insult. They feel disappointed and hurt when people try to leave their little paradises. When Paranoids get hurt, they hurt others.

Of all the vampire types, Paranoids are the most determined and conscious hypnotists. They invented cults, and the brainwashing that keeps them running. Whenever Paranoids put together any sort of organization, be it a cult, a family, a business, a political party, or a religious movement, they use their persuasive power to create unambiguous alternate realities in which all rewards are dependent on belief and loyalty. Obsessive-Compulsives tell you to work hard if you want to get into heaven. Paranoids say all you have to do is believe in them. If you stop believing, there will be hell to pay.

WHAT IT'S LIKE TO BE PARANOID

Imagine a date with the man or woman of your dreams. You talk of nothing in particular, yet you desperately search your companion's every word for clues to what he or she *really* thinks about you. Your heart soars at tiny signs of acceptance, and falls to the pit of your stomach at the slightest hint of rejection. This is business as usual for Paranoid vampires, who analyze every conversation with the same degree of scrutiny. Awash in a flood of ambiguity, they grasp at straws, often clutching them so tightly as to make them break up and drift away.

To the vampires, many of the straws turn out to be anvils. Paranoid existence is one perceived betrayal after another. Their suffering is exquisite, the sorrowful and pretentious center from which their entire universe radiates. Being Paranoid hurts.

Some of them give up and withdraw completely into a world of delusion. Those with better social skills can attract friends and lovers, on whom they rest the entire burden of keeping them safe and sane.

Even thinking about Paranoids is exhausting; imagine what it's like being one. That, strangely enough, is one of their saving graces. Paranoids long to make sense of themselves and to be understood by others. That totally selfish quest can bring suffering to the rest of humanity, or generous gifts in the form of art, philosophy, and religion. Paranoia and narcissism are the world's two main sources of creativity.

The internal struggle of Paranoids is the subject of much of the world's great literature. Science fiction is a particularly pure example. How many times have you read about regular-seeming folks who discover mysterious powers in themselves that place them at the center of a cosmic battle? They win, of course, with a little help from a few loyal and loving friends. The force that draws people to Paranoids is the same urge for simplicity that attracts them to *Star Wars*. Needless to say, that force also has a dark side.

THE NARCISSIST-PARANOID DILEMMA

Paranoids and Narcissists are sworn enemies because the psychological aberration that makes people want to lead is strongest in these two personality types. Their battle plays out everywhere—from faraway universes, through most of the revolutions in human history, to the executive council of the PTA. Always, it's idealists against realists, or, as the vampires would have it, good against evil, with each side claiming to be good. The dilemma for the rest of us is discovering which is which, and deciding whom to follow.

With Narcissists, you get power and wealth going to a privileged few. With Paranoids, you get persecution of people who don't live by the same stringent rules that they do. Either way, a lot of little people get squashed. Perhaps the best we can hope for is that there will always be enough minions of both sides of darkness to hold each other in check, so that the rest of us can live in the relative peace at the eye of the storm.

THE PARANOID EMOTIONAL VAMPIRE CHECKLIST: NEXT STOP, THE TWILIGHT ZONE

True or false: Score one point for each *true* answer.

1. This person is overly suspicious.	T	F
2. This person has very few close friends.	T	F
3. This person can make a big deal out of nothing.	T	F
4. This person tends to see many situations as struggles between good and evil.	T	F
5. This person never seems to let go of a hurt or mistreatment.	T	F
6. This person seldom takes what he or she is told at face value.	T	F
7. This person cuts people out of his or her life for tiny slights.	T	F
8. This person is able to detect deception in one or two parts per billion, and sometimes sees it when it isn't there at all.	T	F
9. This person demands absolute loyalty in thought and deed.	T	F
10. This person is fiercely protective of his or her family (or one or two close friends).	T	F
11. This person sees connections among things that most people would consider unrelated.	T	F

12. This person sees little mistakes, such as lack of punctuality   T   F
or forgetting instructions, as indications of disloyalty or
disrespect.
13. This person tells people what others only say behind their   T   F
backs.
14. This person may have a good sense of humor, but cannot   T   F
seem to laugh at himself or herself.
15. What will make this person angry seems completely   T   F
unpredictable.
16. This person sees himself or herself as a victim of multiple   T   F
discriminations.
17. This person believes that trust is something to be earned.   T   F
18. This person is known to take ill-considered actions "on   T   F
principle."
19. This person often talks about suing people to redress wrongs.   T   F
20. This person questions people to determine their loyalty and   T   F
fidelity.
21. This person collects little details that seem to prove his or   T   F
her pet theories.
22. This person believes in the literal interpretation of the Bible   T   F
or other religious text.
23. This person believes in UFOs, astrology, psychic phenomena,   T   F
or other concepts that most people consider to be on the
fringe of credibility.
24. This person openly advocates cruel and unusual punishment   T   F
for certain classes of people. A typical comment might
begin, "They should take all the bigots and . . ."
25. Though I won't always admit it, this person is sometimes   T   F
embarrassingly correct in his or her assessment of me.

Scoring: Five or more true answers qualifies the person as a Paranoid Emotional Vampire, though not necessarily for a diagnosis of paranoid personality disorder. With twelve or more true answers, watch out for imperial storm
troopers.

WHAT THE QUESTIONS MEASURE

The specific behaviors covered on the checklist relate to several underlying
personality characteristics that define a Paranoid Emotional Vampire.

Perceptiveness

Paranoid vampires see things that others can't. They may even see more than you want them to. They're always looking below the surface for hidden meanings and deeper realities. Sometimes they discover great insights, but more often they find reasons to doubt the people whom they should be able to trust. In the world of Paranoids, the line between perceptiveness and suspicion is thin as a spider web, and sharper than a razor blade.

Intolerance of Ambiguity

Paranoids need answers, even when there are none. They love to explain how complex situations boil down to a few black-and-white concepts. For Paranoids, everything is simple and clear. The only reason everyone doesn't know what they do is that someone, somewhere is conspiring to cover up the truth. Paranoids love nothing more than a good conspiracy theory.

Paranoid vampires' oversimplification of the world can also lead to great courage and dedication. They are fierce defenders of themselves, their principles, and the few people and things they consider closest to them. Paranoids have been known to give their lives for what they believe in. They've also been known to take lives.

Unpredictability

Paranoid vampires can shower you with affection one minute and with ice water the next. Their moods are dependent on momentary perceptions of the honesty and faithfulness of the people around them. If Paranoid vampires sense treachery, they attack so fast that you won't know what hit you. Or why.

They can back off just as quickly. Many of their attacks are tests of loyalty. If you pass, they calm down immediately. If you don't, brace yourself to argue all night.

Unlike most other vampire types, Paranoids have the ability to say that they're wrong. They accept criticism and can make changes in a limited way for a short period of time. Often they will shift slightly to get some sort of concession from you. If you don't live up to your end of the so-called bargain, the Paranoid vampire will add one more perfidy to your list of betrayals.

Bombast

Paranoids long to be understood. Their idea of intimacy is to spend six or seven hours sharing their theories of life, or explaining how your actions have hurt them.

Jealousy

Paranoid vampires don't understand the concept of trust. They never seem to realize that trust is supposed to be in their own minds, rather than in the actions of other people. Consequently, if you're close to one of these vampires, you'll have to re-earn his or her trust every hour on the hour. This is especially true if your relationship is sexual. A Paranoid vampire's idea of foreplay is 20 minutes of questioning about exactly what you were thinking the last time you made love.

Ideas of Reference

In their search for truth, Paranoids connect everything with everything else, then take it all personally. To poor, virtuous Paranoids, the universe is a conspiracy designed to make them miserable.

If you associate with Paranoid vampires, it won't be possible for you to say or do anything that does not relate to them.

Vindictiveness

Paranoid vampires believe that revenge is the cure for what ails them. They never seem to see that it is also the cause. It's not that Paranoids never forgive; they just do it at the same rate as glaciers melt.

HOW TO PROTECT YOURSELF FROM PARANOID VAMPIRES

Paranoid vampires live in a simple alternate universe in which everything is wonderful as long as everyone is faithful to them in word and deed. The certainty of their world can be very attractive from the outside, but once you go in, it's hard to get out, and even harder to pass the ever-increasing tests of loyalty. To be safe, first and foremost, know what you're getting into.

If you're already inside the world of a Paranoid vampire, there are two things to remember:

1. *Don't hide anything.* The vampire will find it.
2. *Be loyal, but never accept the burden of proving your loyalty.* Once you pick it up, you'll never be able to put it down.

13 Vampire Visionaries and Green-Eyed Monsters

Inspiration always involves blowing things out of proportion.

Paranoids fall into two subtypes: Visionaries and Green-Eyed Monsters. Again, the strategies for dealing with these subtypes are similar enough to be included in one chapter. Although the things they say and do may be very different, Paranoids themselves are remarkably similar. For you, they can create two very distinct sorts of problems. The first arises if you pay too much attention to them; the second, if you don't pay enough. Either way, Paranoids can be very draining.

To protect yourself, you need to know which ideas arise from Paranoids' unique way of looking at the world, and which are just characteristic representations of their own internal conflicts, or yours. The discrimination is difficult; it will require all the wisdom you've gained studying the other vampire types, and more. To be safe from Paranoid vampires you must know them well, but you must know yourself even better.

THE PARANOID QUEST

Paranoid vampires are always searching for their Holy Grail, the one simple idea that explains everything. These vampires hate ambiguity so much that they refuse to believe it exists. Whether they're confused about the movements of the stars, the fluctuations of the stock market, or why other people just aren't as caring as they would like them to be, Paranoid vampires believe that the answers are out there, and they're willing to do what it takes to find them.

Paranoids are always looking for clues. They'll peer into microscopes, sift through volumes of forgotten lore, or cross-examine their loved ones as to exactly where they went, when, and with whom.

Paranoid vampires' greatest weakness is that they are much more willing to believe in conspiracy than ambiguity. They can draw you in with elegant theories that are often more convincing than mere facts. Paranoid vampires can drain you by demanding that if you care about them you must believe in their dubious hidden truths. That, however, is nothing compared with what they'll do to you if they suspect that you're the one who's hiding the truth from them.

PARANOID HYPNOSIS

Paranoid vampires have delusions, but they can also delude. They hypnotize with their dogged determination to make you believe in the hidden realities they've discovered. They get to you by relentlessly hammering away at your resistances. Sometimes, however, Paranoids' craziest ideas sound eerily sane, as if they cut through all the garbage to a shining nugget of truth that somehow you've known was there all along. Those are the ideas to watch out for. People who tell us what we want to hear always have more power than people who tell us the truth. Use your own feelings to guide you. The more you want to believe, the more skeptical you should be.

One of the most reliable warning signs of Paranoid hypnosis is that the vampire will discourage you from getting outside opinions. In Paranoid vampires' simple world, the very idea that another person's opinion might carry more weight than theirs is tantamount to treason. Don't let their hurt feelings prevent you from checking out their ideas with someone you trust. Always remember the rule about not letting a vampire be your only source of information.

Unlike Used Car Salesmen, Paranoids actually believe what they tell you. Don't let the force of their conviction persuade you to ignore the facts. As we've seen many times, the most effective hypnotists are those who have hypnotized themselves.

VISIONARIES

At this point, you might be wondering why you should have to worry about Paranoid vampires at all. Maybe you should just stay away from them.

It's not that simple. You may try to stay away from Paranoids, but they won't stay away from you. Maybe the Paranoids themselves will keep away, but not their ideas. You'll hear them everywhere—by the water cooler, over the back fence, and, most of all, on the Internet. A good portion of the new ideas you hear every day are products of Paranoid thinking. Some of them are crazy—just old Paranoid standbys dressed up in different outfits. Some Paranoid ideas are really novel, useful, and profitable. The trick is knowing the difference.

> *Vampire Waylon takes a pull on his second beer and laughs, snorting a bit through his nose. "Whoa," he says. "I can't remember the last time I had two in a row. It's been a great week."*
>
> *Gary raises his own beer in a toast. "It's about time somebody had a good week," he says. "What happened?"*
>
> *Waylon looks around to see if anyone is eavesdropping. "Well, for years I've been working on this formula to predict changes in the stock market. And, I can't believe it, the damn thing finally seems to be paying off."*
>
> *"Really?" Gary says, taking a sip of beer.*
>
> *"Yeah," Waylon says. "You know how they talk about expansion and contraction cycles that correspond to Fibonacci numbers? Well, everybody knows they're great for estimating overall market trends, but, until now, nobody's been able to apply the number to the movements of a single stock. At least not well enough to make solid predictions, anyway. The thing they haven't gotten is this." Waylon grabs a cocktail napkin and writes down a long equation, then turns it around so Gary can read it.*
>
> *Gary has no idea what a Fibonacci number is. He taps at the scribblings on the napkin with his finger. "Are you telling me you can predict the stock market with this?"*
>
> *"No, this is just the algorithm. I've used it to generate a mathematical model and then written a program to crunch the numbers and make the actual predictions."*
>
> *"And it works?"*

"Let's put it this way," Waylon says. "A month ago I invested $1000. I put it in three stocks that the model predicted were going to go up, and every one of them did. In two weeks I had just about tripled my initial investment. Then, I put it all into a stock that the model said was just about to go through the roof, and this afternoon it started taking off."

Gary wonders if Waylon should be showing his equation to Scully and Mulder on the X-Files, but decides to keep his mouth shut. Instead, he asks if Waylon will tell him the name of the stock.

Waylon thinks about it for a minute or so while he takes another pull on his beer, then he writes a name on the napkin, cupping his hand around it so no one else can sneak a peek. FibreCom.

Two days later, Gary sees a headline in the business section:

> COMMUNICATIONS STOCKS SOAR
> *FibreCom leads the pack with 15-point gain.*

Mulder, I think you should see this, he thinks to himself.

Before you laugh and say Gary should just go home and forget about Waylon's crazy ideas, remember that people like Bill Gates and Steve Jobs probably had a few weird barroom conversations when their radical visions were little more than crackpot schemes. What if you had been there and they'd offered you the chance to buy in? How would you feel today if you'd laughed?

On the other hand, how would you feel if you'd decided to invest your life savings in something that later turned out to be a delusion?

HOW TO RECOGNIZE CRAZY IDEAS

With the advent of the Internet, Paranoid ideas travel almost as fast as off-color jokes. Every day chat rooms and in-baskets overflow with health fads, investment schemes, rumors about people, and warnings of impending doom. Some are the insights of true Visionaries; and some are just the rantings of fools. The good news is that crazy ideas, whether dangerous or merely silly, tend to follow predictable patterns. To know what's sane, you must first disregard what is definitely crazy. This isn't easy, because sometimes your own needs can get in the way. Here are some ways of sifting through the daily pile of new ideas.

Know the History of the Idea.   From time immemorial, the same attractive but incorrect ideas have resurfaced from the depths of the Paranoid unconscious and reached out to grasp the unwary. Some well-known delusions include perpetual motion, turning base metals into gold, astrology and other psychic phenomena, ancient predictions of current events, secret drugs that cure cancer, and effortless ways to lose weight. These ideas have a great deal of power because people would like to believe them. Unfortunately, they are seldom true. It's not that these ideas can never be true; it's just that in the past they've been proved false on many occasions. If they are to be true now, there has to be some very convincing new reasoning that gets around the ancient fallacies.

Be especially wary of ideas presented as secret or forbidden knowledge, or of any theory that explains everything.

Understand How the Idea Works.   Just because an idea is complex and difficult to understand doesn't mean it's good. Remember that confusion is one of the warning signs of hypnosis. The first step in evaluating an idea is to understand it. In order to test Waylon's theory about using Fibonacci numbers to predict the stock market, Gary needs to know what the numbers are. This task will take time and effort, but it is essential. A good rule of thumb is never to throw money at something you don't fully comprehend. The important part to understand about any idea is the mechanism, *how* it's supposed to work. Most crazy ideas are weakest at this point.

Fibonacci numbers are sequences in which each term is the sum of the two immediately preceding. Many natural processes seem to correspond to this progression, which is quite interesting, but not definitive. To evaluate Waylon's idea, Gary needs to know *how* the relationship between Fibonacci numbers and the stock market operates, not just that there seems to be a connection.

Get Outside Verification.   The angrier a Paranoid becomes when you suggest a second opinion, the more you need one. A good rule of thumb for evaluating a new idea is: If you can get two Obsessive-Compulsives to accept it, you probably should also.

Understand the Motivation.   Always ask yourself who would gain what if you were to buy into the idea. Look at financial considerations, of course, but remember that, more than money, Paranoids want disciples to validate their theories.

The most important motivation to understand is your own. The world is full of tempting Paranoid ideas that we wish were true, but aren't. Miracle diets, mysterious cures, and offers of salvation through belief alone prey on our fervent hope that health and happiness can be achieved without effort.

If an idea taps into your own secret fantasies, you're more likely to believe it without question. Paranoid Visionaries know this, because they have the same fantasies. They'll be happy to confirm that anybody who has more than you do got it by unfair means, or that only a select few people really know what's going on in the world, and you're one of them.

Visionaries can also come up with ideas we wish weren't true but are. Doomsaying economists try to persuade us to save more. Annoying doctors tell us that our bad habits can kill us. Futurists have been saying for years that we need to become technology-literate more quickly. Environmentalists keep hammering away at the simple, though much disputed, truth that we all need to make personal sacrifices to protect the planet. Many of us are inclined to doubt these Paranoid ideas, not because they lack supporting evidence, but because belief would require us to make unpleasant changes in our lives.

Put the Idea to the Test. The best way to evaluate an idea is to make predictions based upon it and see if the predictions come true on a regular basis. This is the principle behind the scientific method. Waylon's Fibonacci number theory is unusual among Paranoid ideas in that it actually generates predictions that can be checked. If Gary wants to know how valid the idea is, he needs to know some of Waylon's predictions in advance to keep a box score on his hit rate. One prediction doesn't mean anything. A list of accurate picks from the past isn't enough to prove the theory either, because Gary won't be able to tell how many bad picks were in with the good. If Waylon should want to charge for predictions, Gary should regard the transaction like any other form of gambling, and not spend any more than he can afford to lose.

Before you buy into ideas, check them out to see how well they work. This is what scientific studies are all about. You don't have to do the research yourself, but you do have to know it. Scientists are as slow as anybody else in accepting ideas that make them change the way they think, but they *are* persuaded by evidence. Even though we've all heard of ideas rejected by science that later turned out to be true, the fact is, there aren't that many.

The craziest Paranoid ideas are usually untestable. They're better at explaining the past than predicting the future, and their acceptance depends more on the needs of believers than on the objective merits of the belief. Just because an idea sounds good doesn't mean it is good.

If creativity means looking at things differently, Paranoid Visionaries are certainly the most creative of the vampires. Some of what they create exists only in their own minds, but sometimes their ideas can let you in on the ground floor of a new way of looking at the universe. You have to decide.

PARANOIDS AND RELIGION

It would take a whole book to examine the relationship between Paranoids and religion. Religion is their greatest invention, the shining triumph at the end of the Paranoid quest. Without Paranoids' faith in hidden truth, none of us would know God. Religion is also the black hole that sucks the Paranoid soul into cruelty unimaginable to the rest of humanity. With Paranoids in the world, there's no need for Satan.

GREEN-EYED MONSTERS

Next to religious fanaticism, jealousy is the most dangerous Paranoid idea. It's also the most universal. Who among us has never suspected that people don't love us as much as we love them? Most of us tolerate the ambiguity, but Green-Eyed Monsters cannot. Loyalty is everything to them, so important that they can't simply accept it on faith. They poke it, prod it, and all too often question it to death.

> *The last stragglers from rush hour make for slow going downtown. Still, there's plenty of time for a leisurely dinner and a movie. Linda leans against the door and relaxes, grateful that Vampire Jake is doing the driving. He always drives when they go out. When they first started dating, Linda wondered whether she should offer to drive half the time, to be politically correct and all. Now she's glad she didn't. It's such a luxury being driven around. It makes her feel taken*

care of. Jake is such a nice man. A little stiff, maybe, but always kind and considerate.

At a long intersection he turns toward her and smiles. "So, how was your day off?"

Linda thinks back on her hectic day—getting her hair done, grocery shopping, dropping off the dry cleaning, and grabbing a quick lunch with her sister. "Oh, the usual," she says, trying in vain to find something interesting enough to talk about. "You know, errands. Stuff like that. Nothing special."

"I figured you had a really busy day."

"I guess I did. But how did you know that?"

"Well, I called a couple of times and you weren't there."

"You did? There weren't any messages on the answering machine."

Jake shrugs. "I didn't leave any. It wasn't anything important. I just thought I'd call you back later."

"Oh."

"You were gone quite a while."

"Yeah, first one place, then another. You know how it is. I always seem to be busier on my days off than when I'm at work. It's nice to finally have a chance to sit down."

"So, where did you go?"

"Let's see," Linda says, surprised that Jake would have any interest in the dumb details of her day. "Haircut. Grocery store. Cleaners. Lunch. Cash machine. And I bought some new panty hose." She pulls her skirt up an inch or so above her knee. "Like them?"

"Yeah, they're great," Jake says. "Where did you go for lunch?"

"The Bagel Shop over on Forty-fifth. It's right next to Annie's office, and she only gets a half hour break, and—"

"So you had lunch with your sister?"

"Yes." Linda's voice comes out as a nervous giggle. "Jake." She laughs again, this time at the preposterousness of the idea that just popped into her head. "It sounds like you're checking up on me."

Jake laughs too. "No," he says. "Nothing like that. I'm just interested, that's all."

This is how Paranoid jealousy begins, with small, almost innocent questions. At first the prospective victims might even be flattered that someone cares enough about them enough to worry that they might be seeing someone else. The feeling of being flattered disappears quickly when the innocent little questions become a regular part of the relationship, and the victim realizes that there will never be enough answers.

Many Green-Eyed Monsters, like Jake, play to their victims' fantasies of being swept off their feet and taken care of. In relationships, these vampires endear themselves by protecting people, giving them gifts, and doing little things for them without being asked. All they expect for these services is absolute loyalty and complete devotion that must be proved and re-proved forever. Often, people like Linda accept the care without knowing its terrible price.

Paranoid vampires are always on the lookout for the tiniest hint of perfidy in word, deed, or thought. Inevitably, these vampires find what they're looking for, not because it's actually there in any objective sense, but because they continually focus on smaller and smaller details. No regular human can live up to a Paranoid vampire's standards for purity of mind.

One reason Paranoid jealousy is such a problem is that people usually handle it in exactly the wrong way, by trying to appease and reassure. This approach teaches the Green-Eyed Monster that jealous questions are appropriate in the relationship, and will be rewarded with answers. The Lindas of the world would do better to respond to the first jealous questions with something like this:

> *"Jake, I may be overreacting here, but it sounds like you're checking up on me, and that's kind of frightening. Let me tell you this once and forever: I'm a one-man woman. As long as we're dating, you can be sure that I'm not seeing anybody else. You don't need to check up, and I won't allow it. Either you trust me to be faithful or we need to end things right here."*

Unfortunately, people like Linda who have fantasies about being taken care of are seldom willing to risk a whole relationship by making such an assertive demand at the beginning. A time will come when she'll wish she had.

Here are some ideas for dealing with the Green-Eyed Monsters in your own life. Like many of the approaches for protecting yourself from Emotional Vampires, these strategies rely on doing the opposite of what you feel. Think carefully before deciding that they won't work in your life. Jealous Paranoids can be very dangerous.

Answer the Big Question, Not the Little Ones. The big question is: *Are you faithful to me?* Answer that one truthfully, then refuse to submit to further cross-examination.

The most dangerous thing about jealousy is that the more you do to make it better, the worse it gets. Answers about little details will only lead to more suspicion and questions. The only way to win the jealousy game is not to play. Jealousy has to be the Green-Eyed Monster's problem, or there will never be an end to it.

Never Agree to Tests of Love. There is no way to prove affection. Only a vampire would suggest that giving up your autonomy has anything to do with love. If someone you care for suggests that you can prove your love by taking a certain action, ask that person to prove his or her love by trusting you. This may help you explain that trust lives in the other person's mind, not in your behavior.

Being Paranoid means having problems with trust. Your actions cannot fix those problems. Paranoid vampires will offer up the painful betrayals of their past as reasons for you to reassure them now by doing their will and answering their questions. Take their pain seriously, but don't believe for a minute that anything you can do will heal it.

Never Try to Deceive a Paranoid. If a Paranoid vampire catches you in even the tiniest of white lies, it will provide justification for all further questions. Don't think that concealing anything will spare anyone's feelings or get you out of an argument. Paranoids have no compunctions about going through your drawers or checking your cell phone bill or the odometer of your car. Whatever evidence they find, however slight, will mean they were correct in making the search.

Green-Eyed Monsters will also search through your words and actions to find out exactly what you think of them. If your interest has begun to wane, there's no point in trying to hide it. They'll know. It may be less painful for all concerned to end the relationship at that point, or to find a really good couples therapist. If you ever doubt that you'll be able to answer the big question correctly, it's definitely time to leave. Paranoids believe in eternal punishment, even for fantasies of infidelity.

If the Relationship Ends, Avoid the Person. When you leave, or even when they throw you out, Paranoid vampires will usually want you back.

Typically this has more to do with vengeance than love. They will scrutinize your words and actions for the slightest sign that you've changed your mind. Don't be polite! Hopeful Paranoids will always mistake civility for rekindled love. If you're ending a relationship with a Paranoid vampire, don't discuss it. Just go. Once you've gone, don't accept phone calls or visits. If you're divorcing one, let your lawyer do the talking.

THE 10 ELEMENTS OF VAMPIRE FIGHTING STRATEGY: HOW TO GIVE PARANOIDS A GLIMPSE OF REALITY
Don't lecture, transcend.

1. KNOW THEM, KNOW THEIR HISTORY, AND KNOW YOUR GOAL

To Paranoids, nothing other than their own virtue is ever as it seems. They try to make the world fit the narrow bed of their beliefs, chopping and stretching reality to conform to their procrustean standards. Sometimes this process cuts away illusion and reveals the underlying structure of the universe. More often, it creates monstrous distortions. Your goal with Paranoid vampires is to know which is which.

2. GET OUTSIDE VERIFICATION

Paranoid ideas fester in darkness. They have to be dragged kicking and screaming into the light of day and verified according to consensual standards of reality. Paranoid vampires will, of course, regard this as the ultimate betrayal. Loyalty to them means keeping their secrets. Don't believe them if you value your sanity.

3. DO WHAT THEY DON'T

Look for complexity in everything that Paranoids say is simple. Real morality has to factor in human nature as something more than a miscalculation by God. It can never be as absolute as Paranoids would have you believe.

Look for simplicity in everything that Paranoids hold to be complex, like the reasons they're so cruel and unforgiving. They're just mad because everybody doesn't do everything their way.

Also, trust others until there's a reason not to, and always be open to second opinions.

One of the things Paranoid vampires want is to be understood. You can give them that without giving in to their pressure. Always listen, but never confuse listening with obedience.

4. PAY ATTENTION TO ACTIONS, NOT WORDS

Paranoids always see their own actions as completely virtuous. They often justify rage, rancor, and emotional abuse as conforming to a higher morality, applicable only to gods and Paranoids. Don't bother to ask them why they do anything. The answer will always be the same—because it was the Right thing to do. Once Paranoid vampires start rationalizing, anything is possible except them admitting that their motives were less than pure.

The fact is that Paranoids, like most vampires, behave like infants. They want the few people they trust to meet their needs immediately, and they punish those people severely for not coming through. Paranoids' reasons for doing so are elaborate, twisted, tortuous, intricately contrived, and ultimately irrelevant. Focus on what they actually do, not why they say they do it.

5. IDENTIFY HYPNOTIC STRATEGY

Paranoid vampires are always looking for simple answers to complex questions. Their hypnotic strategy involves convincing you that they've found the Word. Paranoids create an alternate reality in which you are expected to restructure your life according to their simple, rigid rules. If you don't conform, Paranoid vampires take it as personal rejection. If you don't stop them, they will actively hypnotize you with persuasive lectures and endless questions about what you think and do. The Paranoid bind is simple: "If you don't think what I want you to think, it's because you hate me." To Paranoid vampires, independent thinking is treason.

To deepen the trance, Paranoids try to isolate you from other sources of information so that everything you hear, and hopefully believe, comes from them. If you think Paranoid hypnosis smacks of brainwashing, you're absolutely correct. Paranoid vampires invented cults and the techniques to keep people believing in them. Paranoids use the same techniques in attenuated form to maintain their personal relationships. The more you allow them to isolate you, the worse it gets.

To protect yourself, you have to refuse to cooperate at the beginning. Put Paranoid vampires in your own hypnotic bind: "If you love me, you'll accept my right to believe whatever I want so long as it doesn't hurt you directly."

Get Paranoid vampires to make specific promises about what they will and will not do. The positive side of their rigid moral code is that they feel bound to keep their word. Here are some helpful promises to extract at the beginning of a relationship: a specified weekly amount of time that you are to be apart, no restrictions on your choice of associates, belief in fidelity without questioning the details of where you go and what you do, and the right to end arguments by invoking a time-out procedure.

At the beginning of a relationship, Paranoids will often make such promises quite readily. Later they will feel obligated to live by them. The best part about this strategy is that the less Paranoid the vampires act, the less Paranoid they feel. Needless to say, the whole structure will fall to pieces if they ever catch you in even the tiniest lie.

6. PICK YOUR BATTLES

The battle you can never win with Paranoid vampires is proving that you are trustworthy. You could die for them, I suppose, but even then they'd probably still have their doubts. There will always be tiny scraps of conflicting information that Paranoid vampires want you to explain. Don't start down this path, because it has no end. Paranoids have trouble tolerating the normal ambiguity of human relationships. This is not a handicap to be accommodated, but a deficiency that the Paranoids themselves must correct. Demand that they do so. Fight for the idea that trust is in their mind, not in your behavior. It's a difficult battle, but it's one you can win.

7. LET CONTINGENCIES DO THE WORK

With Paranoid Visionaries, the important contingency for any idea is: Does it work or not? It is not disloyal to ask.

With Green-Eyed Monsters, use your attention as a reward for trust, not for jealousy.

The kinds of "If you do this, I'll do that" contingencies that work on other infantile vampires also work on unruly Paranoids. For example, you might say, "If you ask me any more questions about where I was and what I was doing, I'm going into the other room so we can both cool down." Often, the most effective argument against Paranoid thinking is silence from behind a closed door. As I've said before in describing this sort of time-out technique, its value is completely negated if you take a parting shot before leaving.

The important contingency with Paranoids is to disrupt their tirades rather than reward the behavior by listening or fighting back. Paranoids love to argue; they can do it for hours without tiring or learning anything. The best way to stop them is not to let them start.

By the way, if you try the time-out strategy, even with full agreement, you'll probably still need to leave the premises or at least lock the door. Paranoid vampires consider it your duty and privilege to hear every bit of what they have to say. They'll try to convince you that not wanting to be yelled at is a kind of betrayal. Don't stay to argue the point. If they won't let you leave, recognize that as a form of violence—one that will most likely escalate over time.

8. CHOOSE YOUR WORDS AS CAREFULLY AS YOU PICK YOUR BATTLES

First and foremost, never ask why. Paranoids can explain anything, and will persist until you accept what they say out of sheer exhaustion.

Paranoids are sensitive to criticism, but unlike many other vampires they will listen to it, and sometimes learn. They would really like to be admirable people in your eyes and in their own. To criticize a Paranoid vampire effectively, take your cue from the very best of sermons. Ignore the hellfire-and-brimstone kind beloved by Obsessive-Compulsives, and pay attention to the kind that remind humans of the divinity within their own souls.

Most Paranoids have a small number of very important concepts by which they try to live their lives. Honor, loyalty, honesty, and love are real enough for Paranoids to kill or die for. In the darkness of the Paranoid mind, however, these grand concepts can quickly shrivel into vindictive pettiness. The most effective criticisms redefine the Paranoid's core concepts to include trust, mercy, and open-mindedness. Needless to say, this task requires tapping into your own Buddha-nature. It can't be done when you're angry.

For the less saintly, it is also effective to ask Paranoid vampires how their core concepts relate to the present situation. A question like "What is the honorable thing to do here?" or "Doesn't love require you to forgive?" or "Does loyalty mean never disagreeing?" can open doors in the Paranoid mind. If this sort of question doesn't work, you may be dealing with a different kind of vampire.

9. IGNORE TANTRUMS

Tears, lectures, sermons, rambling rationalizations, jealous questions, displaying anguish as if it were a work of art—once Paranoid tantrums begin, they usually go on all night. If you give in, they'll go on for the rest of your life. As we have seen throughout this chapter, the best time to stop Paranoid tantrums is before they start.

10. KNOW YOUR OWN LIMITS

Paranoids are in many ways the most difficult and dangerous of the Emotional Vampires. They will protect you, cherish you, and possibly illuminate your life. All they ask in return is absolute loyalty. No discounts; with Paranoids, it's all or nothing. For some people, it's the most wonderful deal of their lives. For others, it leads to nothing but exhaustion and endless suffering. Only you can decide whether you have what it takes to be close to a Paranoid vampire. One thing is certain, however. Before you attempt to understand Paranoid vampires, you must first know yourself.

THERAPY FOR PARANOID VAMPIRES

What should you do if you see signs of Paranoid behavior in yourself or someone you care about? This section is a thumbnail sketch of the sorts of self-help and professional therapeutic approaches that might be beneficial. Always remember that attempting psychotherapy on someone you know will make you both sicker.

THE GOAL

The goal for Paranoids is to learn how to tolerate ambiguity, especially ambiguity in others' feelings toward them. A second, related goal is to forgive perceived betrayals. It usually takes a well-trained professional to help Paranoids achieve these goals.

PROFESSIONAL HELP

Paranoids require experienced professionals who have been in the therapy business long enough that they won't be intimidated or overwhelmed. The kind of therapy is almost irrelevant, because developing a trusting relationship is the most important part of treatment. Often, to maintain control over the process, Paranoids choose therapists who are less experienced, or who are not trained as therapists at all. Good examples are primary care physicians or clergy. Paranoids try to hypnotize inexperienced therapists into accepting their alternate reality. Sometimes they succeed, but more often they just get kicked out of treatment. Either way, the Paranoids get worse.

SELF-HELP

If you recognize Paranoid tendencies in yourself, the following exercises will be very difficult for you, but they will make a difference.

Check Reality. The most important thing you can do for yourself is understand that some of the things you see or suspect are not actually there. You need a trusted confidant with whom to discuss your perceptions. The person should be strong enough to tell you when he or she thinks you're wrong. The confidant should *never* be a family member or someone with whom you are romantically involved.

Recognize That What Other People Do Has Little to Do with You. A common Paranoid tendency is to believe that if the people around you were appropriately loyal and respectful, they would automatically do everything the way you want them to. This borders on the delusional. Most of the time other people are not thinking of you at all. This is not disloyal, it is normal. Allow the people close to you to have parts of their lives that have nothing to do with you, and don't feel threatened by it.

Forgive and Forget. Paranoid memories tend to turn slights and oversights into betrayals and humiliations. As you run small transgressions over in your mind, they get bigger and more painful. If you catch yourself doing this, stop! You are creating anguish for everyone, yourself most of all. Let them all go. Forgive and forget. If you can't, maybe you ought to talk to a therapist.

WHAT WILL HURT

Paranoids often choose therapists on the basis of similarities of political or religious beliefs rather than training and experience. If Paranoids go to therapy to discuss politics or religion rather than their own behavior, it generally leads to increased suffering for everyone.

The greatest suffering, however, comes when Paranoids begin to see justification in their politics or religion for hurting people who do not believe with the same fervor as they do. There is no effective way to deal with these vampires. When you meet zealots on the road of life, run!

Sunrise at Carfax Abbey

Far off, a bell tolls the dawn. Vampires withdraw to the shadows, leaving you and Professor Van Helsing to greet the first tentative rays of the sun.

Van Helsing smiles. "We are safe now," he says. "For one more day at least." You walk with him, away from the abbey.

Both of you know that there will always be another night.

Congratulate yourself. You've faced the vampires and come away unscathed. So far.

Emotional Vampires can be the most difficult and draining creatures on earth. But, as you now know, their powers come from weakness, not strength. Vampire personalities are distorted by simple, immature needs that make the children of the night both attractive and dangerous. If you know the need, you know the vampire.

Antisocial vampires are addicted to excitement. They draw you in with devilish charm and the promise of thrills in the dark. You'll be drained if you expect them to remember their promises in the morning.

Histrionic vampires live for attention. They beguile you with their stunning performances, but when the curtain falls, they fall apart. Between shows you'll have to put them back together.

Narcissistic vampires think they're God's gift to the world. They'll tell you you're as special as they are, but as soon as they get what they want, they'll hardly remember your name. Until the next time they need something.

Obsessive-Compulsive vampires seem too good to be true. They strive for perfection by working hard, playing by the rules, and attempting to control everything within a 10-mile radius. That includes you.

Paranoid vampires prowl the night, searching for answers that are simple and true. Their certainty is so reassuring. Until they start having questions about you.

It's misleading to think that Emotional Vampires are sick. Personality disorders are caused not by microbes or lesions in vital organs, but by the misguided and sometimes predatory choices of the sufferers. There's a danger in perception of illness as well. Civilized people make accommodations for the sick, and accommodation is the last thing that vampires need. To deal effectively with the children of the night, you must know them for what they are. You must also know yourself.

Here is what you must always remember.

You, Not the Vampires, Are in Control. Vampires try to convince you that there are no options other than submitting to their will. This is never true. *When you're dealing with vampires, there is always another choice, even if it's only walking away.*

Strength Comes from Connection. Vampires are isolated by their insatiable needs. The only way they can drain you is by isolating you as well. They use hypnosis to pull you away from people you trust, and convince you that the rules you believe in no longer apply.

Don't listen! Throw back the curtain and let the sunlight in.

Your power against vampires comes from your relationship with the rest of humanity, and anything else larger than yourself. *When you're dealing with vampires, trust your oldest friends, and hold tightly to your values. Secrets can hurt you; the things you're most embarrassed to discuss are the things you most need to share.*

Safety Means Facing Your Fears. Vampires use fear and confusion to control you. If you ever find yourself running scared, stop and turn around. The path to safety always goes *through* fear rather than away from it. *When you're dealing with vampires, the choice that seems most frightening is usually the right one.*

Crosses and garlic won't save you from Emotional Vampires. Your best defenses are knowledge, maturity, and good judgment. You now have the knowledge; the maturity and judgment you must supply for yourself.

Index

Accountability:
Narcissistic Legends and, 150
(*See also* Consequences; Contingencies)
Achievements of Narcissistic vampires, 135
Actions versus words as vampire fighting strategy:
for Bullies, 81–82
for Daredevils, 48–49
for Hams, 94
for Narcissistic Legends, 150
for Narcissistic Superstars, 170
for Obsessive-Compulsive vampires, 200
for Paranoid vampires, 226
for Passive-Aggressive vampires, 120
for Used Car Salesmen, 65
Aggression:
Bullies and, 69–70
(*See also* Anger; Hostility)
Alternate reality created by hypnotists, 25
Ambiguity, Paranoid vampires' dislike of, 209, 213, 215–216
Anal retentives, 185–186
Anger:
Bullies and, 69, 73–74
in Narcissistic Superstars, 165–168
(*See also* Aggression; Hostility)
Antisocial vampires, 4–5, 33–85
Bully manifestation of (*see* Bullies)
characteristics of, 33–39

Antisocial vampires (*Cont.*):
Daredevil manifestation of (*see* Daredevils)
seduction and, 29–30
similarity to adolescents, 39
therapy for, 84–85
Used Car Salesman manifestation of (*see* Used Car Salesmen)
Appearance, Histrionics' concern with, 93
Appreciation, showing to Obsessive-Compulsive vampires, 194
Approval, Histrionics' need for, 87, 89, 92, 109, 118, 172
Attention:
Histrionics' love of, 87, 92
paying to Passive-Aggressive vampires, 121–122
Attitudes, essential for mental health, 11–12
Authority:
Used Car Salesmen's use of, 61, 66
(*See also* Power)

Battles, picking (*see* Picking your battles as vampire fighting strategy)
Behavior, past, knowledge of (*see* Knowledge as vampire fighting strategy)
Bombast of Paranoid vampires, 213
Boredom:
learning to endure, 84–85
of Narcissistic vampires, 136
Bullies, 69–85
aggressive instinct and, 69–70
coping with, 71–73

Bullies (*Cont.*):
doing the unexpected and, 72–77
as hypnotists, 71
strategy for fighting, 77–83

Challenge, pursuit of, 12
Charity work for Narcissistic vampires, 177
Charm of Antisocial vampires, 39
Checklists:
for Antisocial vampires, 37–38
for Histrionic vampires, 90–91
for Narcissistic vampires, 133–134
for Obsessive-Compulsive vampires, 183–184
for Paranoid vampires, 211–212
Choosing your words as vampire fighting strategy:
for Bullies, 83
for Daredevils, 50–51
for Hams, 106–107
for Narcissistic Legends, 151–152
for Narcissistic Superstars, 172–173
for Obsessive-Compulsive vampires, 202
for Paranoid vampires, 228–229
for Passive-Aggressive vampires, 123–124
for Used Car Salesmen, 67
Cialdini, Robert B., 55
Competitiveness of Narcissistic vampires, 136
Compulsion, amount of, 181–182
Conformity, Used Car Salesmen's use of, 58–59, 66
Confusion as danger sign of hypnosis, 29, 99
Connection, feeling of, 11–12
Consequences:
considering, 85
Used Car Salesmen's use of, 61–62, 66
Consistency:
with Passive-Aggressive vampires, 123
Used Car Salesmen's use of, 59–61, 66
Contingencies as vampire fighting strategy:
for Bullies, 82–83
for Daredevils, 50
for Hams, 105–106

Contingencies as vampire fighting strategy (*Cont.*):
for Narcissistic Legends, 145–146, 147–148, 150–151
for Narcissistic Superstars, 171–172
for Obsessive-Compulsive vampires, 201–202
for Paranoid vampires, 227–228
for Passive-Aggressive vampires, 121–123
for Used Car Salesmen, 66–67
Control:
by hypnotists, 25
perception of, 11
Creativity of Narcissistic Legends, 146–147
Criticism:
avoiding taking personally, with Bullies, 80–81
giving to Bullies, 81
giving to Narcissistic Legends, 151–152
learning from, with Bullies, 81
Narcissistic vampires' inability to accept, 137
by Obsessive-Compulsive vampires, 205
of perfectionism, 193

Daredevils, 41–51
grooming process conducted by, 44–47
as hypnotists, 42–44
physiology of excitement and, 41–42
strategy for fighting, 47–51
Deception:
of self, by Histrionic vampires, 111
by Used Car Salesmen (*see* Used Car Salesmen)
Dependency of Histrionic vampires, 92–93
Depression in Narcissistic Superstars, 165–168
Details, Obsessive-Compulsive vampires' preoccupation with, 185
Deviation from standard procedures, as danger sign of hypnosis, 27–28, 98
Dishonesty, recognizing, 62–63
Distorted perceptions as danger sign of hypnosis, 28, 98

Doing what they don't as vampire fighting strategy:
for Bullies, 79–81
for Daredevils, 48
for Hams, 104
for Narcissistic Legends, 149–150
for Narcissistic Superstars, 169–170
for Obsessive-Compulsive vampires, 200
for Paranoid vampires, 225–226
for Passive-Aggressive vampires, 119–120
for Used Car Salesmen, 64

Emotional constriction of Obsessive-Compulsive vampires, 185–186
Emotionality of Histrionic vampires, 92
Empathy, 12
lack of, of Narcissistic vampires, 136–137
Entitlement felt by vampires, 18
Narcissistic, 135–136
Evil, immaturity versus, 13–14
Exaggeration, avoiding, 82
Excitement, physiology of, 41–42
Explanations, avoiding with Bullies, 80

Fairness:
Narcissistic Superstars' disregard for rules of, 159–160
sense of, 12
False choices created by hypnotists, 25–26
Feedback for Passive-Aggressive vampires, 121–122
Fight or flight response, 70
Forgiveness by Paranoid vampires, 230
Fun, Daredevils and, 48

Gender of Histrionic vampires, 88
Giving by Passive-Aggressive vampires, 113–114
Goals, knowledge of (*see* Knowledge as vampire fighting strategy)
Grandiosity of Narcissistic vampires, 135
Gratification, vampires' unwillingness to delay, 18
Gratitude, Narcissistic Legends' lack of, 144
Grooming process, conducted by Daredevils, 44–47

Hams, 95–107
as hypnotists, 97–99
illness and, 100
motivation and, 100–103
role to protect oneself against, 99
strategy for fighting, 103–107
History, knowledge of (*see* Knowledge as vampire fighting strategy)
Histrionic vampires, 5–6, 87–127
characteristics of, 89–94
gender of, 88
Hams (*see* Hams)
Passive-Aggressive (*see* Passive-Aggressive vampires)
protecting oneself against, 94
therapy for, 126–127
Honesty, 62
(*See also* Dishonesty)
Hostility:
of Obsessive-Compulsive vampires, 186
(*See also* Aggression; Anger)
Hurt feelings, admitting to Obsessive-Compulsive vampires, 193
Hypnosis, 23–32
by Bullies, 71
coping with, 30–32
danger signs of, 27–29
by Daredevils, 42–44
by Hams, 97–99
by Narcissistic Legends, 143–146
by Narcissistic Superstars, 161–162
by Paranoid vampires, 216
by Passive-Aggressive vampires, 115
recognizing, 26–27
seduction and, 29–30
strategies used for, 24–26
by Used Car Salesmen, 55–62

Ideas, Paranoid, recognizing, 218–221
Identification of hypnotic subjects, 24
Identifying hypnotic strategies as vampire fighting strategy:
for Bullies, 82
for Daredevils, 49
for Hams, 104–105
for Narcissistic Legends, 150
for Narcissistic Superstars, 170

Identifying hypnotic strategies as vampire fighting strategy (*Cont.*):
for Obsessive-Compulsive vampires, 200–201
for Paranoid vampires, 226–227
for Passive-Aggressive vampires, 120
for Used Car Salesmen, 65–66
Ignoring tantrums as vampire fighting strategy:
for Bullies, 83
for Daredevils, 50–51
for Hams, 107
for Narcissistic Legends, 152–153
for Narcissistic Superstars, 173–175
for Obsessive-Compulsive vampires, 202
for Paranoid vampires, 229
for Passive-Aggressive vampires, 124
for Used Car Salesmen, 67
Illness:
of Histrionic vampires, 93–94, 100
Passive-Aggressive vampires and, 114–115
Immaturity:
evil versus, 13–14
vampire's ability to create in others, 20
Impulsiveness of Antisocial vampires, 39
Incompetence, Narcissistic Superstars' lack of tolerance for, 166
Inconsideration of Narcissistic vampires, 130, 132
Indecisiveness of Obsessive-Compulsive vampires, 186
Insight:
Histrionics' lack of, 93
vampires' lack of, 20
Intelligence of Narcissistic vampires, 134–135
Irrelevancies, ignoring with Passive-Aggressive vampires, 121–122
Isolation by hypnotists, 24–25

Jealousy of Paranoid vampires, 214, 221–225
Job interviews, vampires' success in, 27
Judgments, Obsessive-Compulsive vampires and, 205

Knowing your own limits as vampire fighting strategy:
for Bullies, 83
for Daredevils, 51
for Hams, 107
for Narcissistic Legends, 153
for Narcissistic Superstars, 175
for Obsessive-Compulsive vampires, 203
for Paranoid vampires, 229
for Passive-Aggressive vampires, 125
for Used Car Salesmen, 68
Knowledge as vampire fighting strategy:
for Bullies, 77–78
for Daredevils, 47–48
for Hams, 103–104
for Narcissistic Legends, 148–149
for Narcissistic Superstars, 168–169
for Obsessive-Compulsive vampires, 199–200
for Paranoid vampires, 225
for Passive-Aggressive vampires, 117–118
for Used Car Salesmen, 63–64

Lasch, Christopher, 161
Laws, obeying, 85
Liking, Used Car Salesmen's use of, 55–56, 65
Limits, knowing (*see* Knowing your own limits as vampire fighting strategy)
Losing, Narcissistic Superstars' lack of tolerance for, 166–167
Lying:
recognizing, 62–63
by Used Car Salesmen (*see* Used Car Salesmen)

Maturity:
attitudes and, 11–12
lack of, evil versus, 13–14
Mental health, attitudes essential for, 11–12
Milgram, Stanley, 61
Misdirection, hypnosis and, 24
Mistakes, acknowledgment of, by Obsessive-Compulsive vampires, 205
Moral perfectionism (*see* Puritans)

Motivation:
  Histrionic vampires and, 100–103
  recognizing crazy ideas and, 219–220

Narcissistic Legends, 139–153
  characteristics preventing success in,
    142–143
  creativity of, 146–147
  as hypnotists, 143–146
  socializing, 147–148
  strategy for fighting, 148–153
Narcissistic Superstars, 155–177
  depression and anger in, 165–168
  disregard for rules of fairness, 159–160
  as hypnotists, 161–162
  insatiable needs of, 156–159
  lack of understanding of others,
    160–161
  sex and, 162–164
  strategy for fighting, 168–175
  use of power by, changing, 164–165
Narcissistic supplies, 130
Narcissistic vampires, 6–7, 129–177
  characteristics of, 129–137
  Legends (*see* Narcissistic Legends)
  mixed feelings evoked by, 131–132
  Paranoid vampires and, 211
  self-esteem of, 132–133
  Superstars (*see* Narcissistic Superstars)
  therapy for, 176–177
Needs:
  of Antisocial vampires for stimulation,
    38–39
  of Daredevils for risk, 44
  of Histrionics for approval, 87, 89, 92,
    109, 118, 172
  of Narcissistic Superstars, insatiability
    of, 156–159
  of Narcissistic vampires for recogni-
    tion, 131

Objective information:
  for coping with hypnosis, 31
  lack of concern with, as danger sign of
    hypnosis, 29, 99
Obsessive-compulsive personality, 180
Obsessive-compulsive personality disor-
    der (*see* Obsessive-Compulsive
    vampires)

Obsessive-Compulsive vampires, 7–8,
    179–205
  anger in, 188
  antisocial tendency of, 180
  characteristics of, 179–186
  demanding priorities from, 190–191
  as hypnotists, 188–189
  Perfectionists (*see* Perfectionists)
  product versus process and, 189–190
  punishment and, 182–183
  Puritans (*see* Puritans)
  strategy for fighting, 199–203
  therapy for, 204–205
Outcomes:
  considering, with Bullies, 79
  (*See also* Consequences; Contingencies
    as vampire fighting strategy)
Outside verification as vampire fighting
    strategy:
  for Bullies, 78–79
  for Daredevils, 48
  for Hams, 104
  for Narcissistic Legends, 149
  for Narcissistic Superstars, 169
  for Obsessive-Compulsive vampires,
    200
  for Paranoid vampires, 225
  for Passive-Aggressive vampires, 119
  recognizing crazy ideas and, 219
  for Used Car Salesmen, 64

Paranoid vampires, 8–9, 207–231
  black-and-white principles of, 209–210
  characteristics of, 207–214
  dislike of ambiguity, 209, 215–216
  as hypnotists, 216
  inability to avoid, 217–218
  jealousy in, 221–225
  Narcissistic vampires and, 211
  protecting oneself from, 214
  recognition of crazy ideas and, 218–221
  religion and, 221
  strategy for fighting, 225–229
  therapy for, 230–231
  as visionaries, 217–218
Passive-Aggressive vampires, 109–127
  behavior in relationships, 115–116
  giving by, 113–114
  high self-esteem of, 116–117

Passive-Aggressive vampires (*Cont.*):
   as hypnotists, 115
   illness and, 114–115
   strategy for fighting, 117–125
Past behavior, knowledge of (*see* Knowledge as vampire fighting strategy)
Peer pressure, Daredevils and, 46
Perceptiveness of Paranoid vampires, 213
Perceptual distortions as danger sign of hypnosis, 28, 98
Perfectionism of Obsessive-Compulsive vampires, 185
Perfectionists, 187, 191–194
   anger of, 188
   dealing with, 193–194
   as hypnotists, 188–189
   moral (*see* Puritans)
   recognizing, 199
   (*See also* Obsessive-Compulsive vampires)
Permission, asking of Narcissistic Legends, 152
Personality, splitting of, by Passive-Aggressive vampires, 111
Personality disorder, obsessive-compulsive (*see* Obsessive-Compulsive vampires)
Personality disorders, 3–4
   antisocial (*see* Antisocial vampires)
   narcissistic (*See* Narcissistic Legends; Narcissistic Superstars; Narcissistic vampires)
Persuasion, basic patterns of, 65–66
Physical symptoms:
   of Histrionic vampires, 93–94, 100
   Passive-Aggressive vampires and, 114–115
Picking your battles as vampire fighting strategy:
   for Bullies, 82
   for Daredevils, 49–50
   for Hams, 105
   for Narcissistic Legends, 150
   for Narcissistic Superstars, 170–171
   for Obsessive-Compulsive vampires, 201
   for Paranoid vampires, 227
   for Passive-Aggressive vampires, 120–121
   for Used Car Salesmen, 66

Power:
   Narcissistic Superstars' use of, changing, 164–165
   secrets as source of, 20
   (*See also* Authority)
Praise, giving to Narcissistic Legends, 151
Priorities:
   demanding from Obsessive-Compulsive vampires, 190–191, 193
   setting, as self-help for Obsessive-Compulsive vampires, 205
Process, product versus, Obsessive-Compulsive vampires and, 189–190, 193, 205
Professional help:
   for Antisocial vampires, 84
   for Histrionic vampires, 126
   for Narcissistic vampires, 176
   for Obsessive-Compulsive vampires, 204
   for Paranoid vampires, 229
Promises, keeping, 85
Protection against vampires, 20–21
Punishment:
   avoiding with Passive-Aggressive vampires, 122–123
   Obsessive-Compulsive vampires and, 182–183
Puritans, 187, 194–198
   anger of, 188
   dealing with, 196–198
   as hypnotists, 188–189
   meanness of, 195
   recognizing, 199
   (*See also* Obsessive-Compulsive vampires)
Purity of thought of Paranoid vampires, 209–210

Rapport, quick development of, as danger sign of hypnosis, 28, 98
Reality:
   alternate, created by hypnotists, 25
   checking of, by Paranoid vampires, 229
Reciprocity, Used Car Salesmen's use of, 57–58, 65–66
Recognition, Narcissistic vampires' need for, 131

Reference, ideas of, of Paranoid vampires, 214
Rehearsal, Narcissistic Legends and, 152
Relationships, Passive-Aggressive vampires' behavior in, 115–116
Relaxation by Obsessive-Compulsive vampires, 205
Reliability of Obsessive-Compulsive vampires, 185
Religion, Paranoid vampires and, 221
Resentment of Obsessive-Compulsive vampires, 186
Respect of Narcissistic Superstars, gaining, 170
Responsibility, vampires' failure to accept, 18
Rigidity of Obsessive-Compulsive vampires, 185
Risk, Daredevils' need for, 44
Role playing:
    to protect oneself against Hams, 99
    by vampires, 19

Salespeople, Daredevils as, 48
Scarcity, Used Car Salesmen's use of, 59, 66
Secondary gain, Passive-Aggressive vampires and, 124
Secrets as source of power, 20
Seduction, hypnosis and, 29–30
Self-absorption of Narcissistic vampires, 130
Self-deception by Histrionic vampires, 111
Self-esteem:
    of Narcissistic Superstars, 155
    of Narcissistic vampires, 132–133
    of Passive-Aggressive vampires, 116–117
Self-help:
    for Antisocial vampires, 84–85
    for Histrionic vampires, 126–127
    for Narcissistic vampires, 176–177
    for Obsessive-Compulsive vampires, 204–205
    for Paranoid vampires, 229–230
Selfishness of vampires, 18
Sensitivity with Passive-Aggressive vampires, 123

Sex:
    Daredevils and, 46
    Narcissistic Superstars and, 162–164
Showing off by Narcissistic vampires, 130
Similarity, Used Car Salesmen's establishment of, 56, 65
Sociability of Histrionic vampires, 91
Socialization of Narcissistic Legends, 147–148
Socially acceptable responses, Used Car Salesmen's use of, 54–55
Sociopaths (see Antisocial vampires)
Special cases as danger sign of hypnosis, 28–29, 98
Spontaneity with Narcissistic Legends, 151
Stimulation, Antisocial vampires' high need for, 38–39
Substance abuse:
    by Bullies, 74
    by Daredevils, 49
Suggestibility of Histrionic vampires, 93

Talent of Narcissistic vampires, 134–135
Tantrums:
    ignoring (see Ignoring tantrums as vampire fighting strategy)
    thrown by vampires, 18–19
Therapy:
    for Antisocial vampires, 84–85
    for Histrionic vampires, 126–127
    for Narcissistic vampires, 176–177
    for Obsessive-Compulsive vampires, 204–205
    for Paranoid vampires, 229–230
Time to think:
    asking for, with Bullies, 79
    for Narcissistic Legends, 152
Twelve-step programs for Antisocial vampires, 84

Unexpected responses to fight Bullies, 72–77
Unpredictability of Paranoid vampires, 213
Used Car Salesmen, 53–68
    honesty and, 62
    as hypnotists, 55–62

Used Car Salesmen (*Cont.*):
  recognizing lies and, 62–63
  strategy for fighting, 63–68

Vampire fighting strategies, 168–175
  for Bullies, 77–83
  for Daredevils, 47–51
  for Hams, 103–107
  for Narcissistic Legends, 148–153
  for Narcissistic Superstars, 168–175
  for Obsessive-Compulsive vampires,
    199–203
  for Paranoid vampires, 225–229
  for Passive-Aggressive vampires,
    117–127
  for Used Car Salesmen, 63–68
Vampires:
  characteristics of, 19–20
  differences from other people, 17–19

Vampires (*Cont.*):
  people with characteristics of, 14
  protecting oneself from, 20–21
  reasons people become, 13
  seeing tendencies in oneself, 14–15
Vindictiveness of Paranoid vampires,
  214

Words (*see* Actions versus words as
  vampire fighting strategy; Choosing
  your words as vampire fighting
  strategy)
Work, Obsessive-Compulsive vampires'
  love of, 184

Yelling:
  avoiding, 85
  stopping Bullies from, 79–80

About the Author

Albert J. Bernstein, Ph.D., is the author of *Dinosaur Brains, Neanderthals at Work,* and *Sacred Bull.* A clinical psychologist, speaker, columnist, and business consultant, Dr. Bernstein is well known for teaching people to confront difficult and frightening situations with wit, wisdom, grace, and liberal doses of humor.